THE MIGHTY CAPTAIN MARVEL

DARK ORIGINS

MARGARET STOHL
WRITER

MICHELE BANDINI
ARTIST

ERICK ARCINIEGA
COLOR ARTIST

VC'S JOE CARAMAGNA
LETTERER

PHIL NOTO
COVER ART

SANA AMANAT
WITH MARK BASSO
& SARAH BRUNSTAD
EDITORS

COLLECTION EDITOR **JENNIFER GRÜNWALD** ASSISTANT EDITOR **CAITLIN O'CONNELL**
ASSOCIATE MANAGING EDITOR **KATERI WOODY** EDITOR, SPECIAL PROJECTS **MARK D. BEAZLEY**
VP PRODUCTION & SPECIAL PROJECTS **JEFF YOUNGQUIST** SVP PRINT, SALES & MARKETING **DAVID GABRIEL**
SPECIAL THANKS TO **ANTHONY GAMBINO**

EDITOR IN CHIEF **C.B. CEBULSKI** CHIEF CREATIVE OFFICER **JOE QUESADA**
PRESIDENT **DAN BUCKLEY** EXECUTIVE PRODUCER **ALAN FINE**

THE MIGHTY CAPTAIN MARVEL VOL. 3: DARK ORIGINS. Contains material originally published in magazine form as CAPTAIN MARVEL #125-129. First printing 2018. ISBN 978-1-302-90607-8. Published by MARVEL WORLDWIDE, INC., a subsidiary of MARVEL ENTERTAINMENT, LLC. OFFICE OF PUBLICATION: 135 West 50th Street, New York, NY 10020. Copyright © 2018 MARVEL No similarity between any of the names, characters, persons, and/or institutions in this magazine with those of any living or dead person or institution is intended, and any such similarity which may exist is purely coincidental. **Printed in Canada.** DAN BUCKLEY, President, Marvel Entertainment; JOHN NEE, Publisher; JOE QUESADA, Chief Creative Officer; TOM BREVOORT, SVP of Publishing; DAVID BOGART, SVP of Business Affairs & Operations, Publishing & Partnership; DAVID GABRIEL, SVP of Sales & Marketing, Publishing; JEFF YOUNGQUIST, VP of Production & Special Projects; DAN CARR, Executive Director of Publishing Technology; ALEX MORALES, Director of Publishing Operations; DAN EDINGTON, Managing Editor; SUSAN CRESPI, Production Manager; STAN LEE, Chairman Emeritus. For information regarding advertising in Marvel Comics or on Marvel.com, please contact Vit DeBellis, Custom Solutions & Integrated Advertising Manager, at vdebellis@marvel.com. For Marvel subscription inquiries, please call 888-511-5480. **Manufactured between 3/30/2018 and 5/1/2018 by SOLISCO PRINTERS, SCOTT, QC, CANADA.**

10 9 8 7 6 5 4 3 2 1

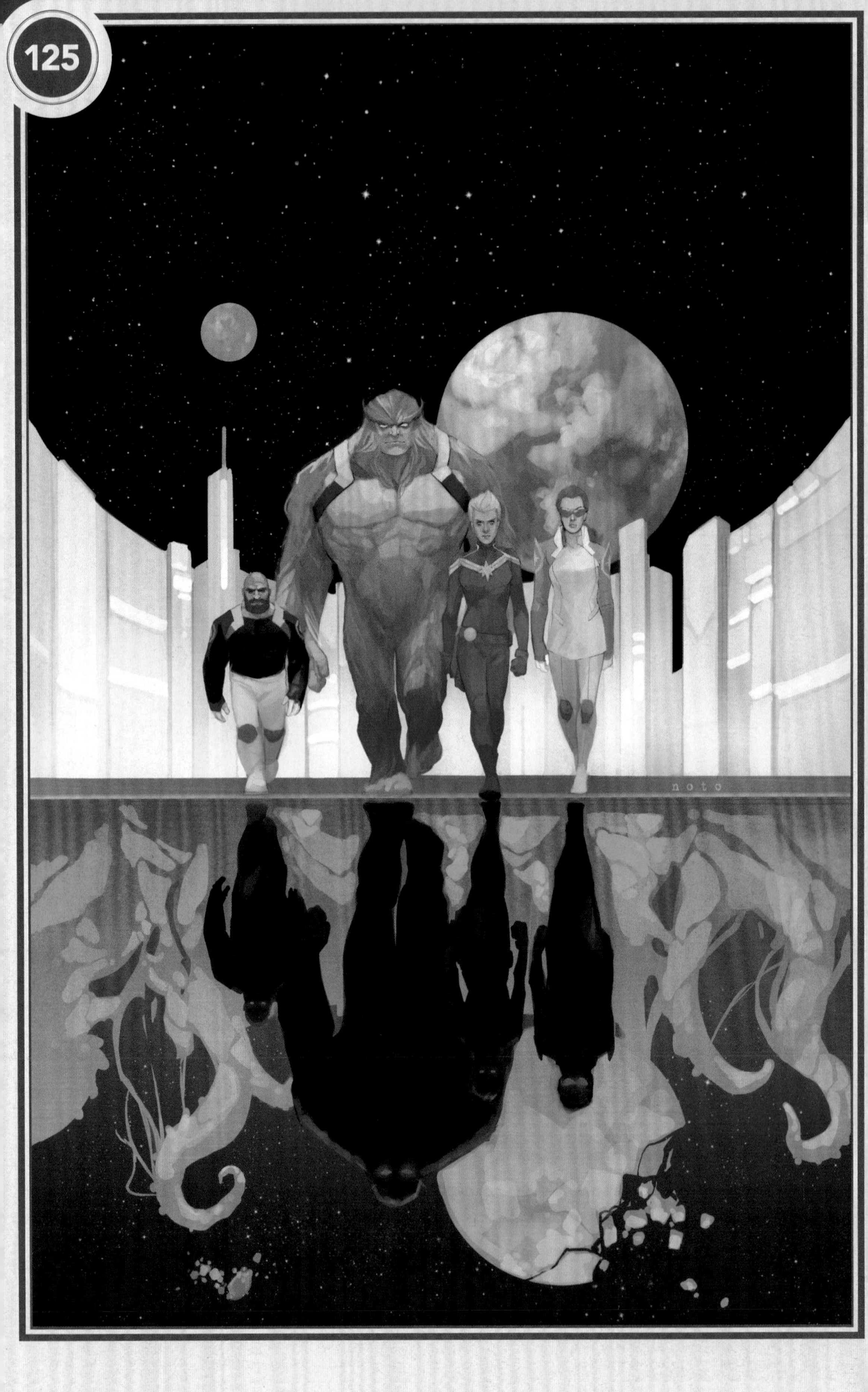
125
noto

NO CHALLENGE IS TOO GREAT FOR THE FORMER AIR FORCE PILOT TURNED SUPER HERO. CAROL DANVERS HAS COME A LONG WAY SINCE AN INCIDENT WITH ALIEN TECHNOLOGY LEFT HER WITH AMAZING POWERS. PART KREE, PART HUMAN, CAROL IS NOW THE MOST POWERFUL AND POPULAR SUPER HERO ON EARTH, AND FROM THE ALPHA FLIGHT SPACE STATION MILES ABOVE THE PLANET, SHE AND HER CREW DEFEND THE WORLD FROM INTERGALACTIC THREATS.

THE MIGHTY CAPTAIN MARVEL

DARK ORIGINS

THE ALPHA FLIGHT SPACE STATION IS NO MORE. SACRIFICED IN A FAILED EFFORT TO
BRING DOWN THE ENERGY SHIELD THAT KEPT CAROL AND THE OTHER SPACEBOUND
HEROES OFF OF EARTH WHILE ROGERS RAN THE U.S. AS AN AGENT OF HYDRA, ITS
DESTRUCTION MARKED THE END OF ALPHA FLIGHT AS SHE KNEW IT.

WITH THE WORLD CRISIS UNDER CONTROL, CAROL IS BACK DOWN ON EARTH,
BUT UNSURE OF HER NEXT STEP. BETWEEN THE LOSS OF THE SPACE STATION
AND THE LOSS OF HER KREE FRIEND BEAN TO PARTS UNKNOWN, CAROL IS IN
NEED OF A NEW BEGINNING.

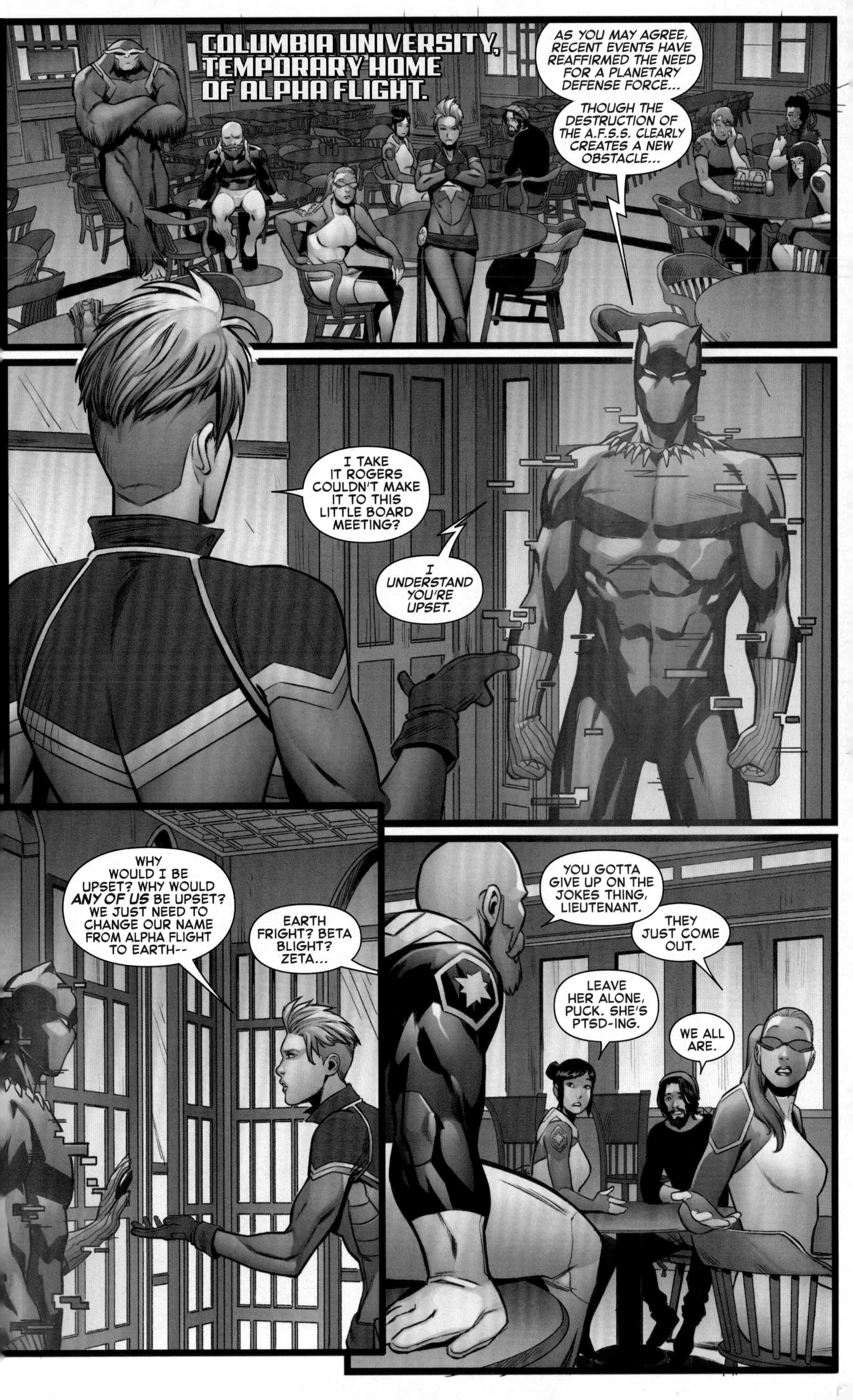
COLUMBIA UNIVERSITY, TEMPORARY HOME OF ALPHA FLIGHT.
AS YOU MAY AGREE, RECENT EVENTS HAVE REAFFIRMED THE NEED FOR A PLANETARY DEFENSE FORCE...
THOUGH THE DESTRUCTION OF THE A.F.S.S. CLEARLY CREATES A NEW OBSTACLE...
I TAKE IT ROGERS COULDN'T MAKE IT TO THIS LITTLE BOARD MEETING?
I UNDERSTAND YOU'RE UPSET.
WHY WOULD I BE UPSET? WHY WOULD ANY OF US BE UPSET? WE JUST NEED TO CHANGE OUR NAME FROM ALPHA FLIGHT TO EARTH--
EARTH FRIGHT? BETA BLIGHT? ZETA...
YOU GOTTA GIVE UP ON THE JOKES THING, LIEUTENANT.
THEY JUST COME OUT.
LEAVE HER ALONE, PUCK. SHE'S PTSD-ING.
WE ALL ARE.

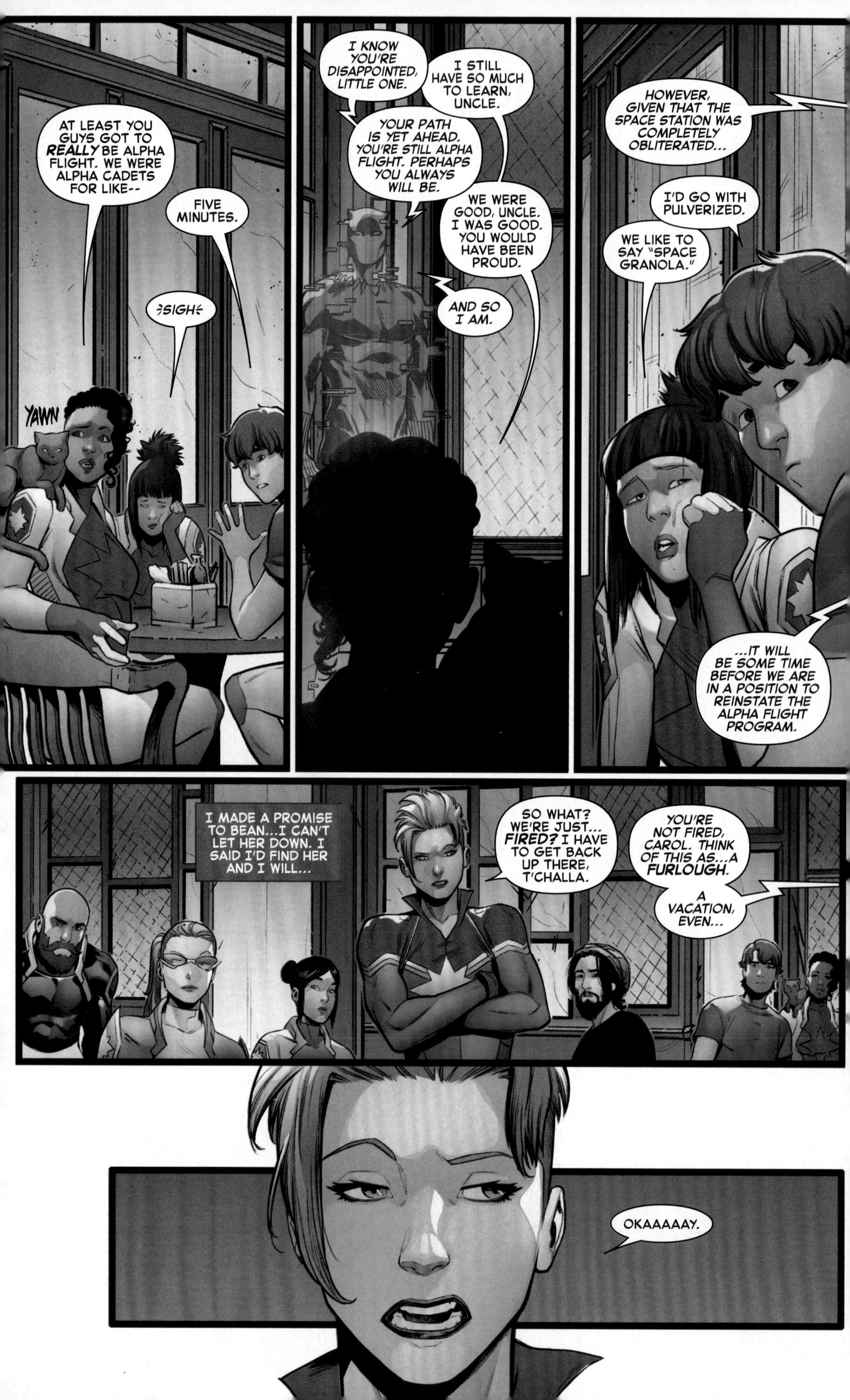
AT LEAST YOU GUYS GOT TO REALLY BE ALPHA FLIGHT. WE WERE ALPHA CADETS FOR LIKE--
FIVE MINUTES.
SIGH
YAWN
I KNOW YOU'RE DISAPPOINTED, LITTLE ONE.
I STILL HAVE SO MUCH TO LEARN, UNCLE.
YOUR PATH IS YET AHEAD. YOU'RE STILL ALPHA FLIGHT. PERHAPS YOU ALWAYS WILL BE.
WE WERE GOOD, UNCLE. I WAS GOOD. YOU WOULD HAVE BEEN PROUD.
AND SO I AM.
HOWEVER, GIVEN THAT THE SPACE STATION WAS COMPLETELY OBLITERATED...
I'D GO WITH PULVERIZED.
WE LIKE TO SAY "SPACE GRANOLA."
...IT WILL BE SOME TIME BEFORE WE ARE IN A POSITION TO REINSTATE THE ALPHA FLIGHT PROGRAM.
I MADE A PROMISE TO BEAN...I CAN'T LET HER DOWN. I SAID I'D FIND HER AND I WILL...
SO WHAT? WE'RE JUST... FIRED? I HAVE TO GET BACK UP THERE, T'CHALLA.
YOU'RE NOT FIRED, CAROL. THINK OF THIS AS...A FURLOUGH.
A VACATION, EVEN...
OKAAAAAY.

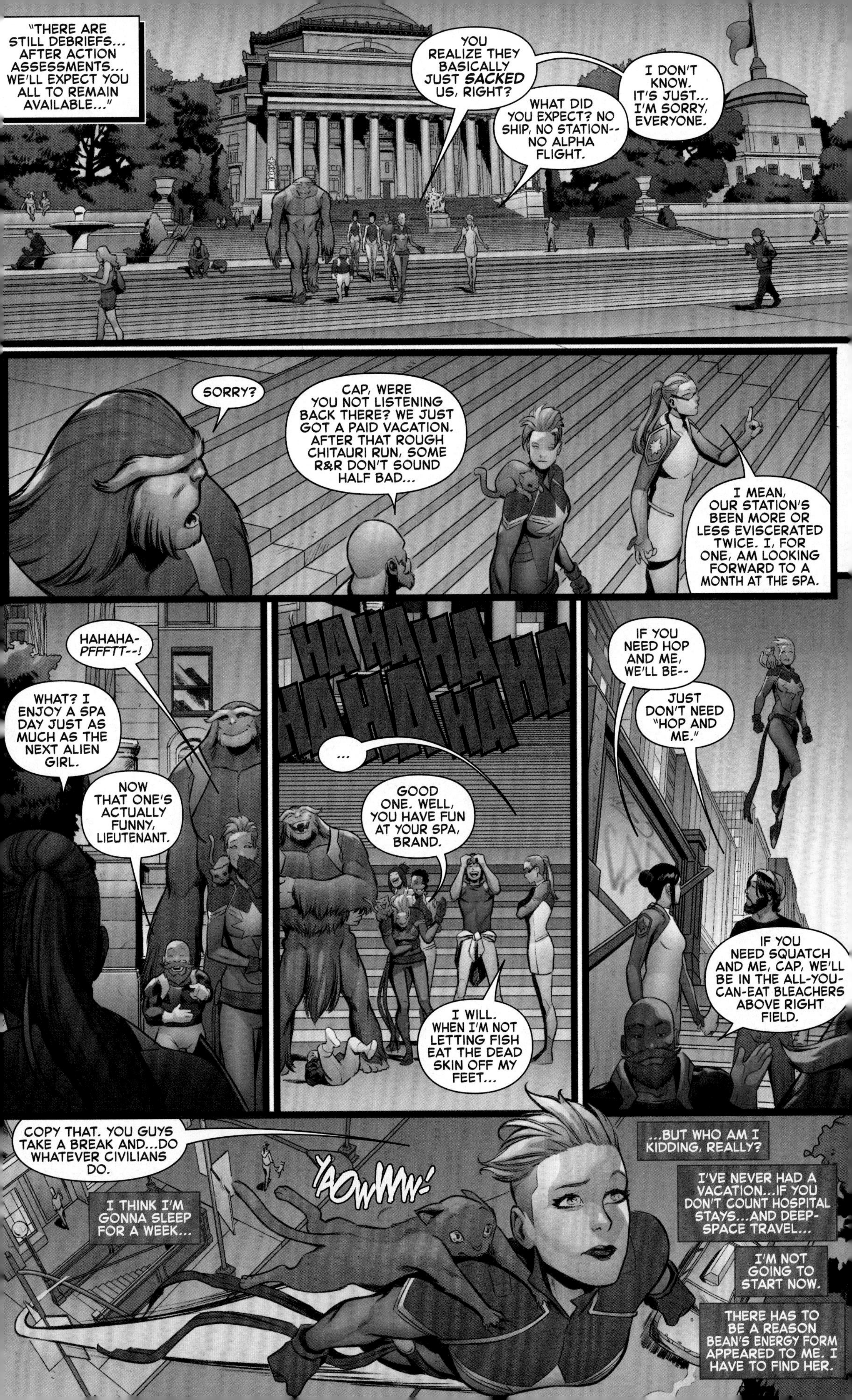

"THERE ARE STILL DEBRIEFS... AFTER ACTION ASSESSMENTS... WE'LL EXPECT YOU ALL TO REMAIN AVAILABLE..."
YOU REALIZE THEY BASICALLY JUST SACKED US, RIGHT?
WHAT DID YOU EXPECT? NO SHIP, NO STATION-- NO ALPHA FLIGHT.
I DON'T KNOW. IT'S JUST... I'M SORRY, EVERYONE.
SORRY?
CAP, WERE YOU NOT LISTENING BACK THERE? WE JUST GOT A PAID VACATION. AFTER THAT ROUGH CHITAURI RUN, SOME R&R DON'T SOUND HALF BAD...
I MEAN, OUR STATION'S BEEN MORE OR LESS EVISCERATED TWICE. I, FOR ONE, AM LOOKING FORWARD TO A MONTH AT THE SPA.
HAHAHA-PFFFTT--!
WHAT? I ENJOY A SPA DAY JUST AS MUCH AS THE NEXT ALIEN GIRL.
NOW THAT ONE'S ACTUALLY FUNNY, LIEUTENANT.
HAHAHAHAHAHAHAHA
...
GOOD ONE. WELL, YOU HAVE FUN AT YOUR SPA, BRAND.
I WILL. WHEN I'M NOT LETTING FISH EAT THE DEAD SKIN OFF MY FEET...
IF YOU NEED HOP AND ME, WE'LL BE--
JUST DON'T NEED "HOP AND ME."
IF YOU NEED SQUATCH AND ME, CAP, WE'LL BE IN THE ALL-YOU-CAN-EAT BLEACHERS ABOVE RIGHT FIELD.
COPY THAT. YOU GUYS TAKE A BREAK AND...DO WHATEVER CIVILIANS DO.
I THINK I'M GONNA SLEEP FOR A WEEK...
YAOWWW!
...BUT WHO AM I KIDDING, REALLY?
I'VE NEVER HAD A VACATION...IF YOU DON'T COUNT HOSPITAL STAYS...AND DEEP-SPACE TRAVEL...
I'M NOT GOING TO START NOW.
THERE HAS TO BE A REASON BEAN'S ENERGY FORM APPEARED TO ME. I HAVE TO FIND HER.

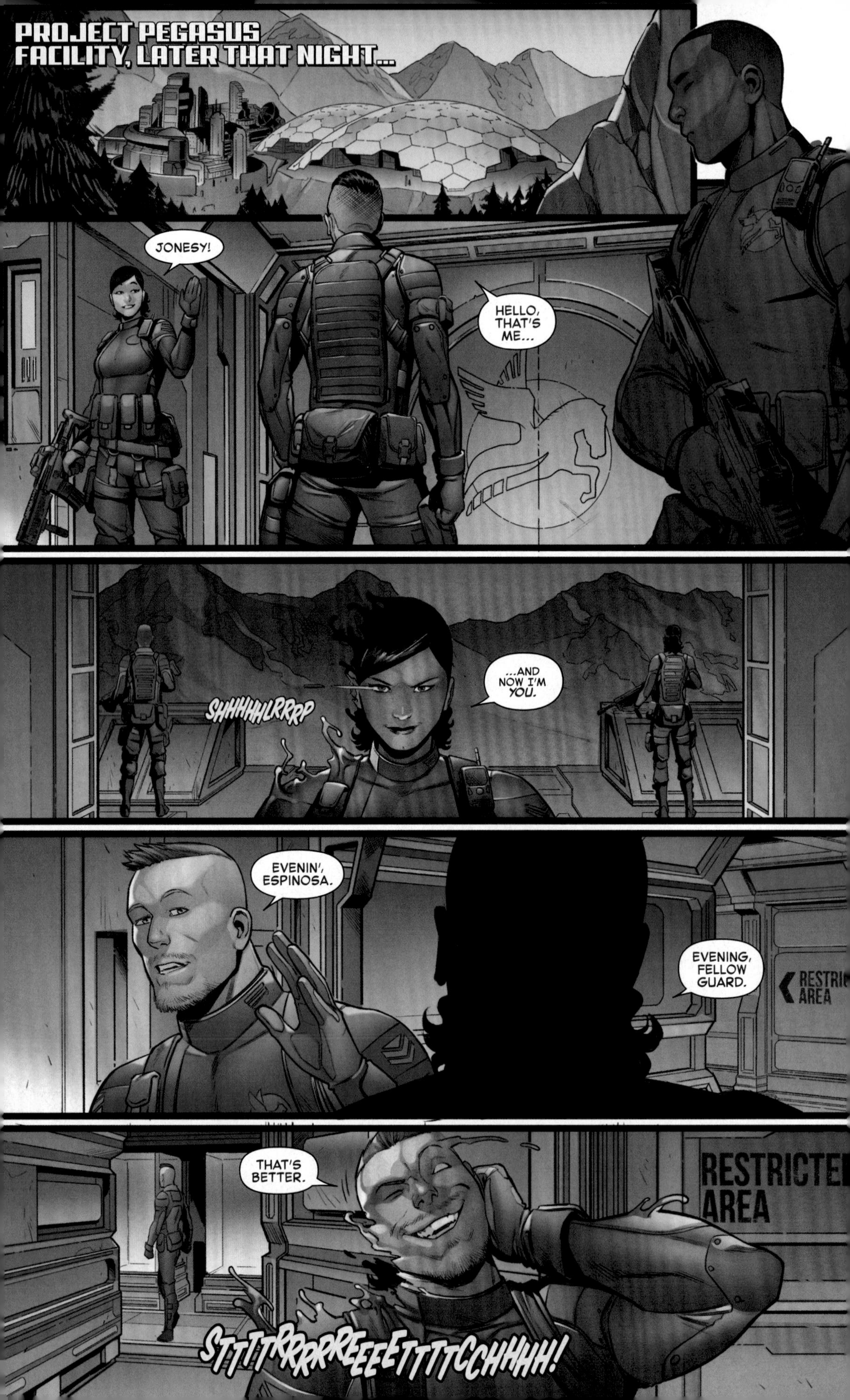
PROJECT PEGASUS FACILITY, LATER THAT NIGHT...
JONESY!
HELLO, THAT'S ME...
...AND NOW I'M YOU.
SHHHHHLRRRP
EVENIN', ESPINOSA.
EVENING, FELLOW GUARD.
RESTRIC AREA
THAT'S BETTER.
RESTRICTE AREA
STTTTRRRRREEEETTTTCCHHHH!

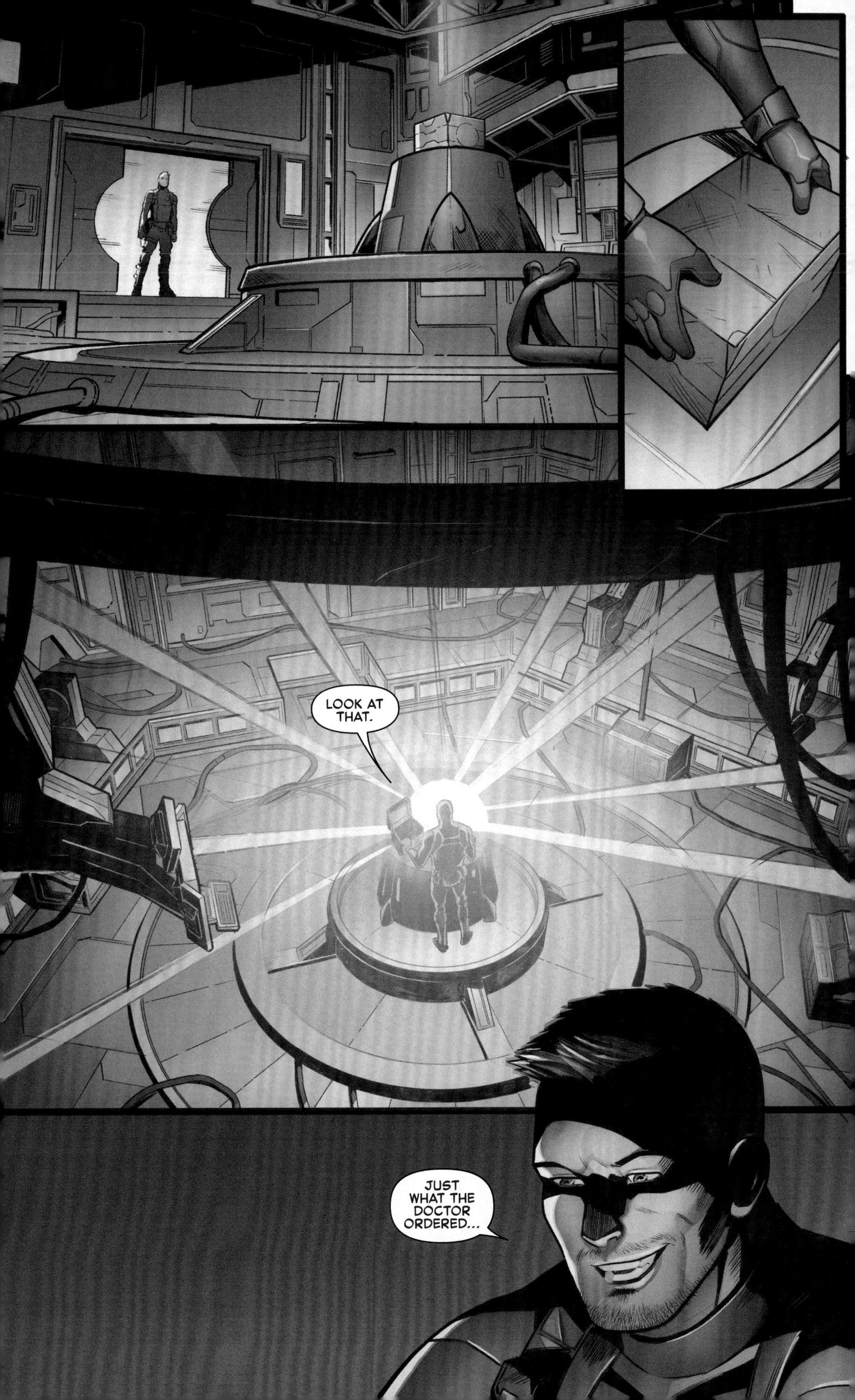
LOOK AT THAT.
JUST WHAT THE DOCTOR ORDERED...

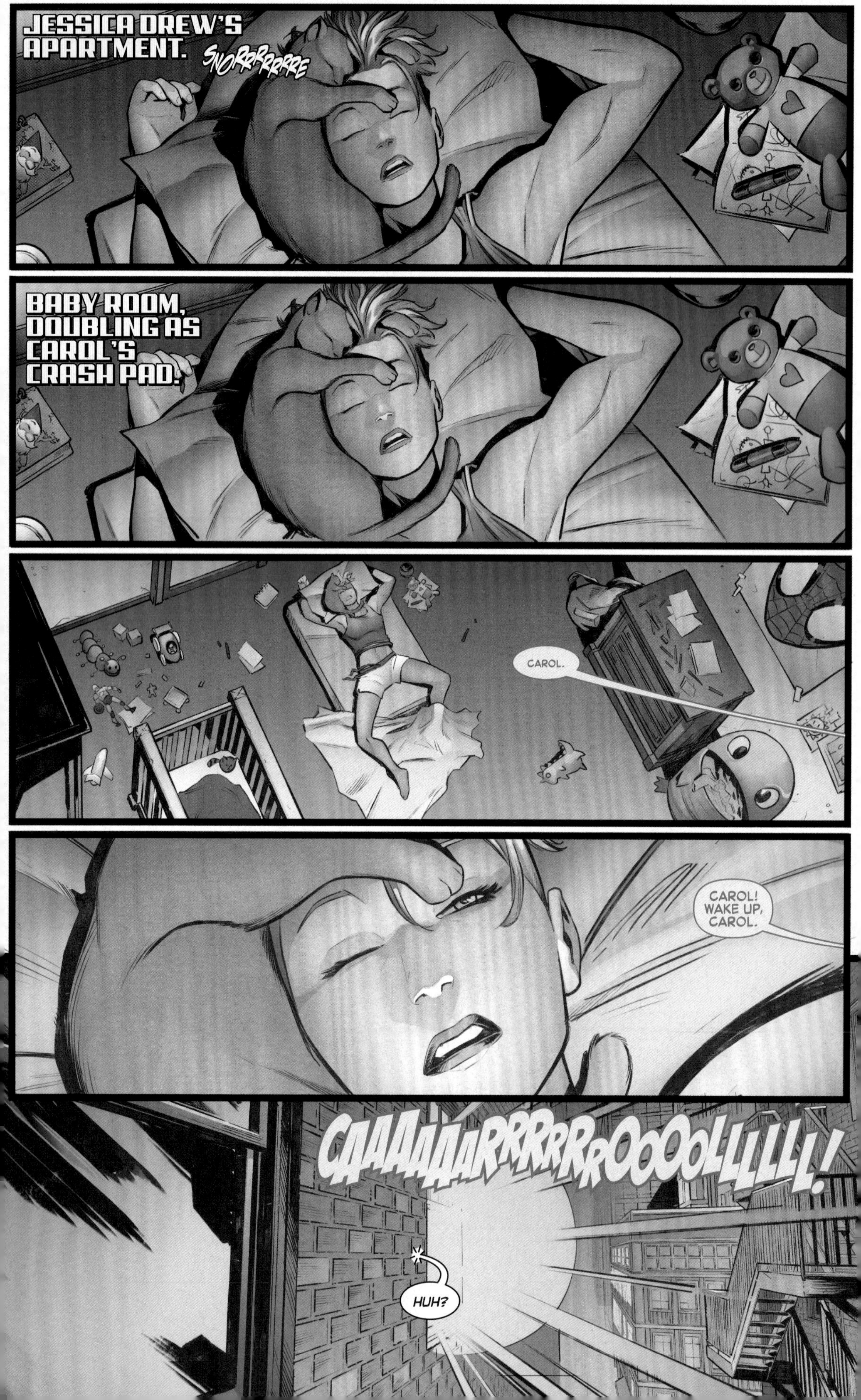
JESSICA DREW'S APARTMENT.
SNORRRRRRRE
BABY ROOM, DOUBLING AS CAROL'S CRASH PAD.
CAROL.
CAROL! WAKE UP, CAROL.
CAAAAAARRRRRROOOOLLLLLL!
HUH?

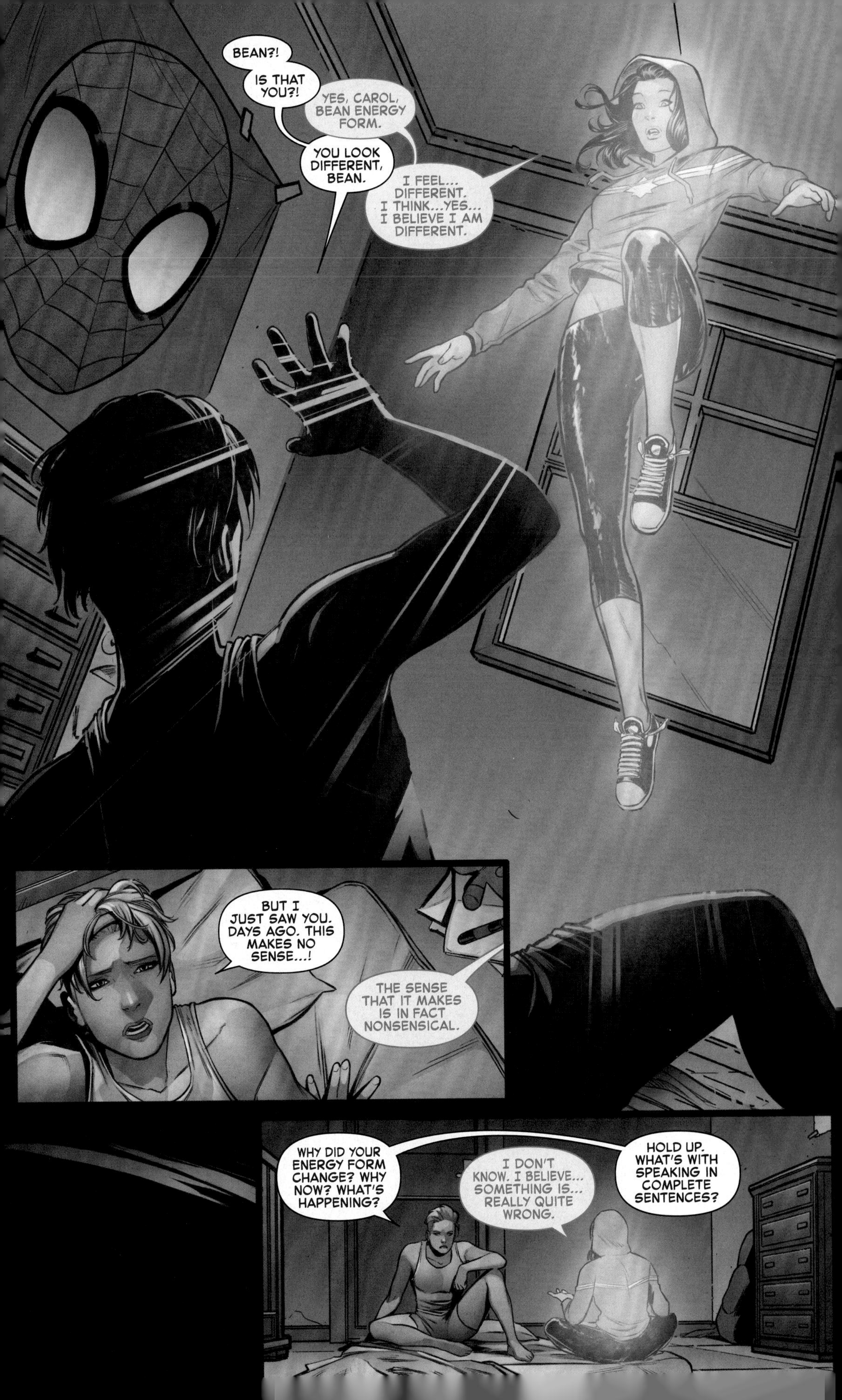
BEAN?!
IS THAT YOU?!
YES, CAROL, BEAN ENERGY FORM.
YOU LOOK DIFFERENT, BEAN.
I FEEL... DIFFERENT. I THINK...YES... I BELIEVE I AM DIFFERENT.
BUT I JUST SAW YOU. DAYS AGO. THIS MAKES NO SENSE...!
THE SENSE THAT IT MAKES IS IN FACT NONSENSICAL.
WHY DID YOUR ENERGY FORM CHANGE? WHY NOW? WHAT'S HAPPENING?
I DON'T KNOW. I BELIEVE... SOMETHING IS... REALLY QUITE WRONG.
HOLD UP. WHAT'S WITH SPEAKING IN COMPLETE SENTENCES?

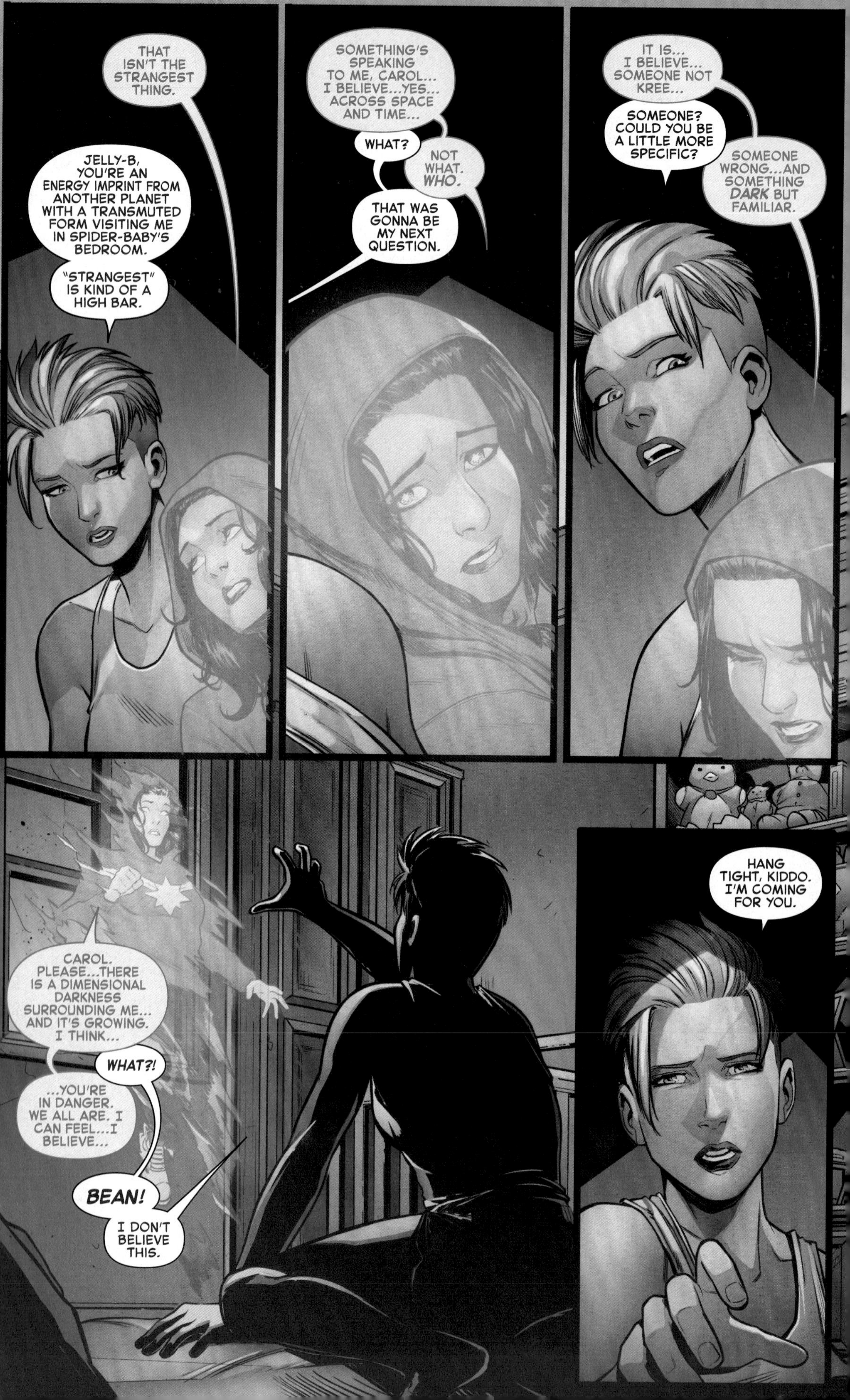

THAT ISN'T THE STRANGEST THING.
JELLY-B, YOU'RE AN ENERGY IMPRINT FROM ANOTHER PLANET WITH A TRANSMUTED FORM VISITING ME IN SPIDER-BABY'S BEDROOM.
"STRANGEST" IS KIND OF A HIGH BAR.
SOMETHING'S SPEAKING TO ME, CAROL... I BELIEVE...YES... ACROSS SPACE AND TIME...
WHAT?
NOT WHAT. *WHO.*
THAT WAS GONNA BE MY NEXT QUESTION.
IT IS... I BELIEVE... SOMEONE NOT KREE...
SOMEONE? COULD YOU BE A LITTLE MORE SPECIFIC?
SOMEONE WRONG...AND SOMETHING *DARK* BUT FAMILIAR.
CAROL. PLEASE...THERE IS A DIMENSIONAL DARKNESS SURROUNDING ME... AND IT'S GROWING. I THINK...
WHAT?!
...YOU'RE IN DANGER. WE ALL ARE. I CAN FEEL...I BELIEVE...
BEAN!
I DON'T BELIEVE THIS.
HANG TIGHT, KIDDO. I'M COMING FOR YOU.

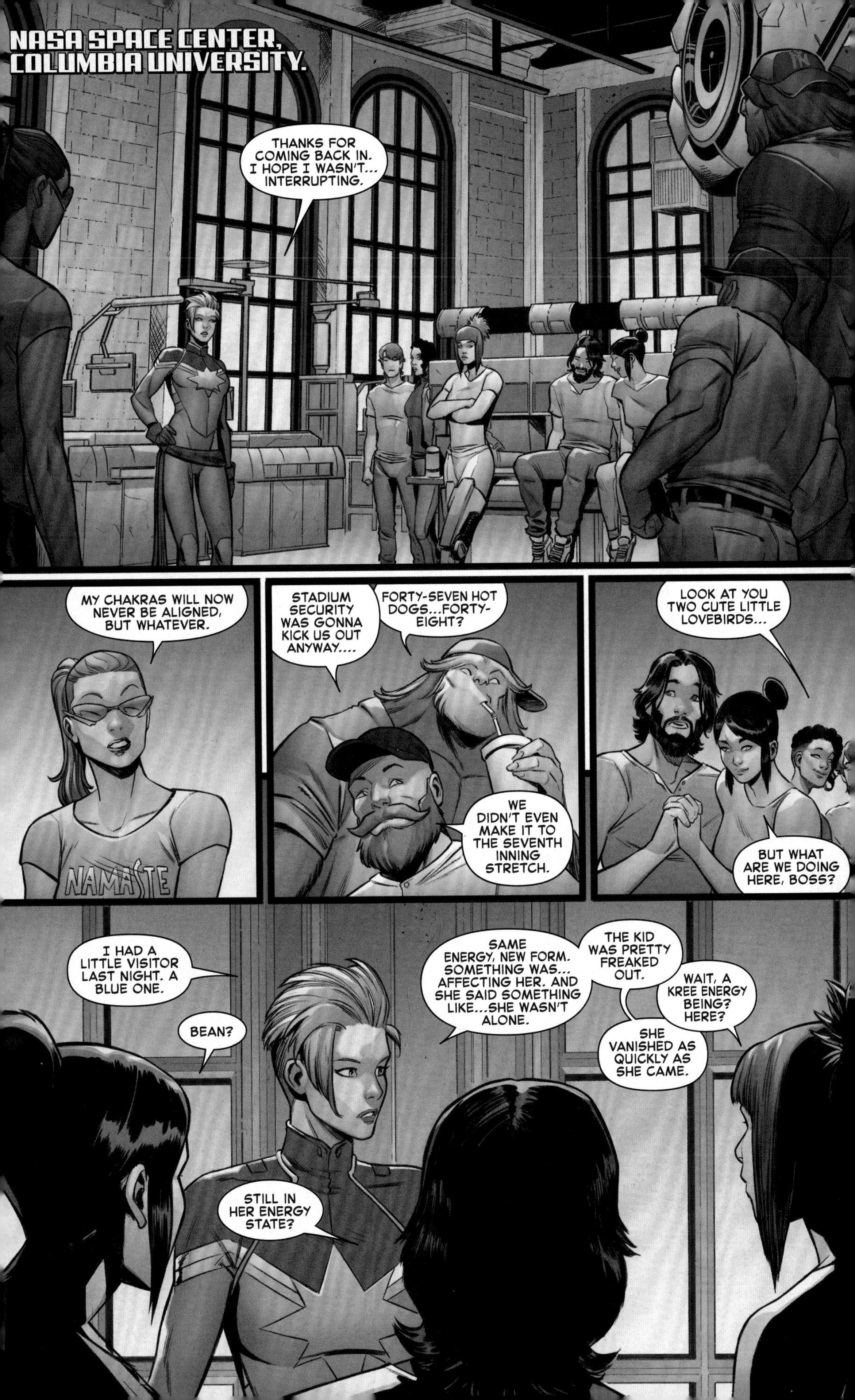
NASA SPACE CENTER, COLUMBIA UNIVERSITY.
THANKS FOR COMING BACK IN. I HOPE I WASN'T... INTERRUPTING.
MY CHAKRAS WILL NOW NEVER BE ALIGNED, BUT WHATEVER.
NAMASTE
STADIUM SECURITY WAS GONNA KICK US OUT ANYWAY....
FORTY-SEVEN HOT DOGS...FORTY-EIGHT?
WE DIDN'T EVEN MAKE IT TO THE SEVENTH INNING STRETCH.
LOOK AT YOU TWO CUTE LITTLE LOVEBIRDS...
BUT WHAT ARE WE DOING HERE, BOSS?
I HAD A LITTLE VISITOR LAST NIGHT. A BLUE ONE.
BEAN?
STILL IN HER ENERGY STATE?
SAME ENERGY, NEW FORM. SOMETHING WAS... AFFECTING HER. AND SHE SAID SOMETHING LIKE...SHE WASN'T ALONE.
THE KID WAS PRETTY FREAKED OUT.
SHE VANISHED AS QUICKLY AS SHE CAME.
WAIT, A KREE ENERGY BEING? HERE?

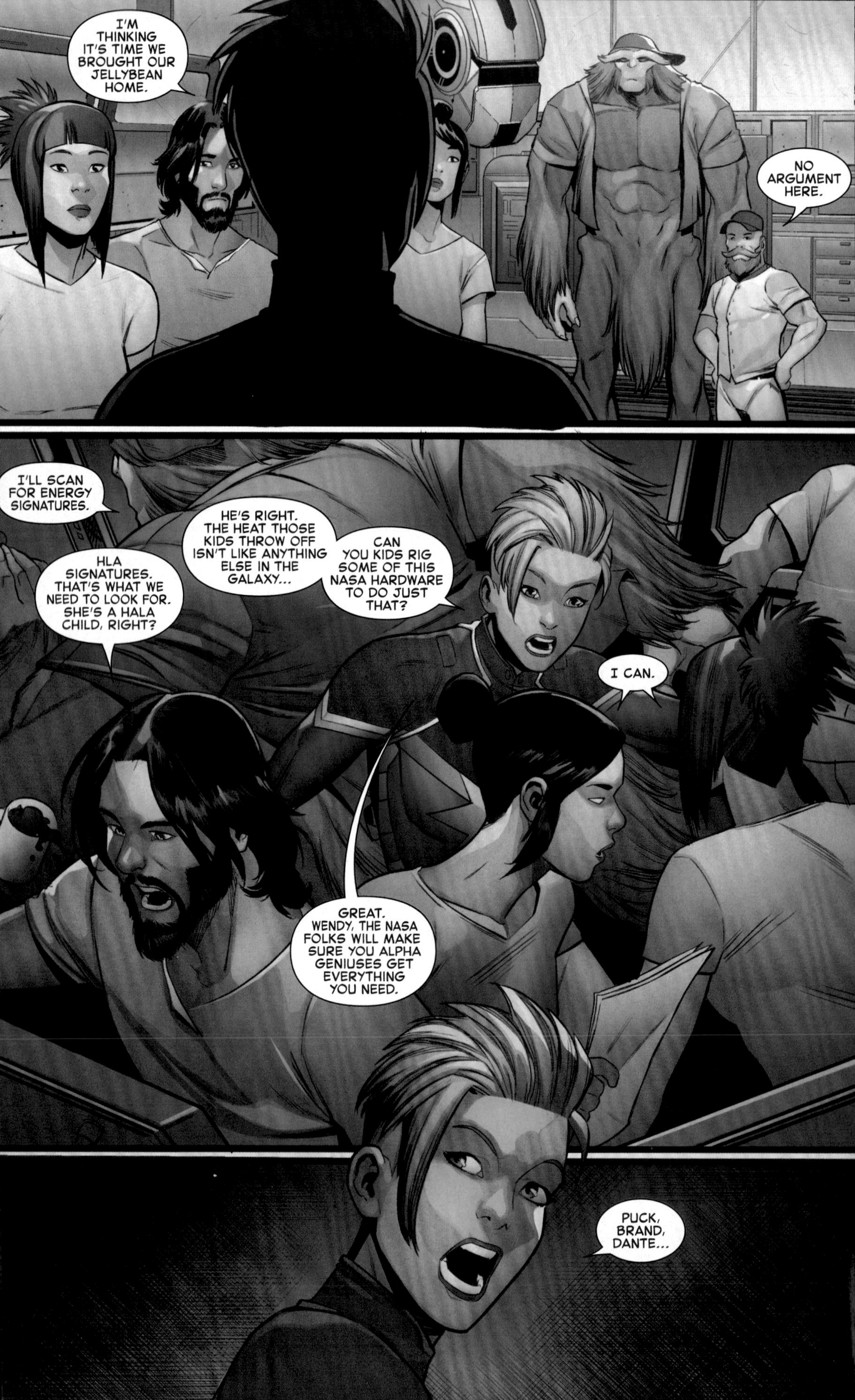
I'M THINKING IT'S TIME WE BROUGHT OUR JELLYBEAN HOME.
NO ARGUMENT HERE.
I'LL SCAN FOR ENERGY SIGNATURES.
HLA SIGNATURES. THAT'S WHAT WE NEED TO LOOK FOR. SHE'S A HALA CHILD, RIGHT?
HE'S RIGHT. THE HEAT THOSE KIDS THROW OFF ISN'T LIKE ANYTHING ELSE IN THE GALAXY...
CAN YOU KIDS RIG SOME OF THIS NASA HARDWARE TO DO JUST THAT?
I CAN.
GREAT. WENDY, THE NASA FOLKS WILL MAKE SURE YOU ALPHA GENIUSES GET EVERYTHING YOU NEED.
PUCK, BRAND, DANTE...

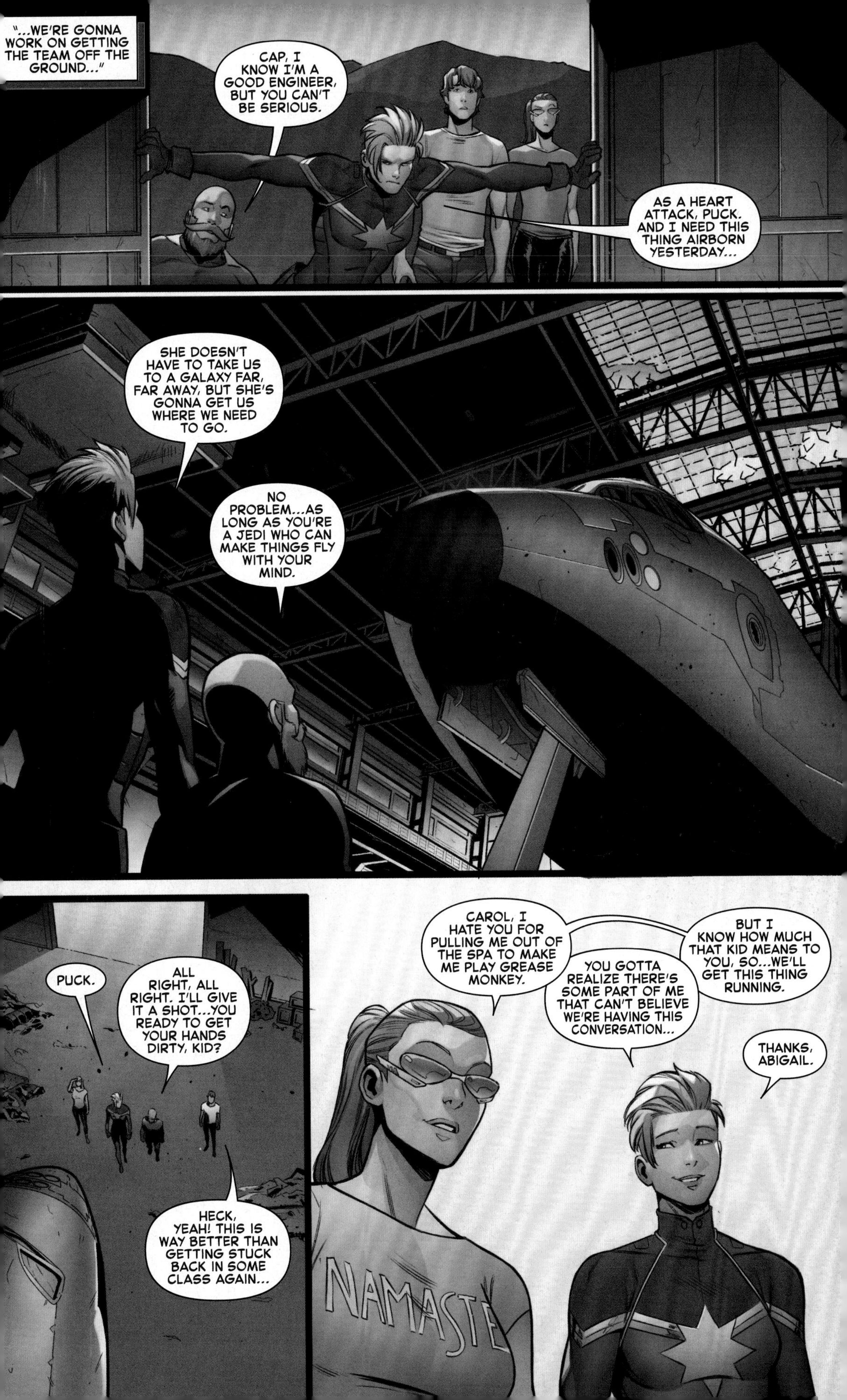
"...WE'RE GONNA WORK ON GETTING THE TEAM OFF THE GROUND..."
CAP, I KNOW I'M A GOOD ENGINEER, BUT YOU CAN'T BE SERIOUS.
AS A HEART ATTACK, PUCK. AND I NEED THIS THING AIRBORN YESTERDAY...
SHE DOESN'T HAVE TO TAKE US TO A GALAXY FAR, FAR AWAY, BUT SHE'S GONNA GET US WHERE WE NEED TO GO.
NO PROBLEM...AS LONG AS YOU'RE A JEDI WHO CAN MAKE THINGS FLY WITH YOUR MIND.
PUCK.
ALL RIGHT, ALL RIGHT. I'LL GIVE IT A SHOT...YOU READY TO GET YOUR HANDS DIRTY, KID?
HECK, YEAH! THIS IS WAY BETTER THAN GETTING STUCK BACK IN SOME CLASS AGAIN...
CAROL, I HATE YOU FOR PULLING ME OUT OF THE SPA TO MAKE ME PLAY GREASE MONKEY.
BUT I KNOW HOW MUCH THAT KID MEANS TO YOU, SO...WE'LL GET THIS THING RUNNING.
YOU GOTTA REALIZE THERE'S SOME PART OF ME THAT CAN'T BELIEVE WE'RE HAVING THIS CONVERSATION...
THANKS, ABIGAIL.
NAMASTE

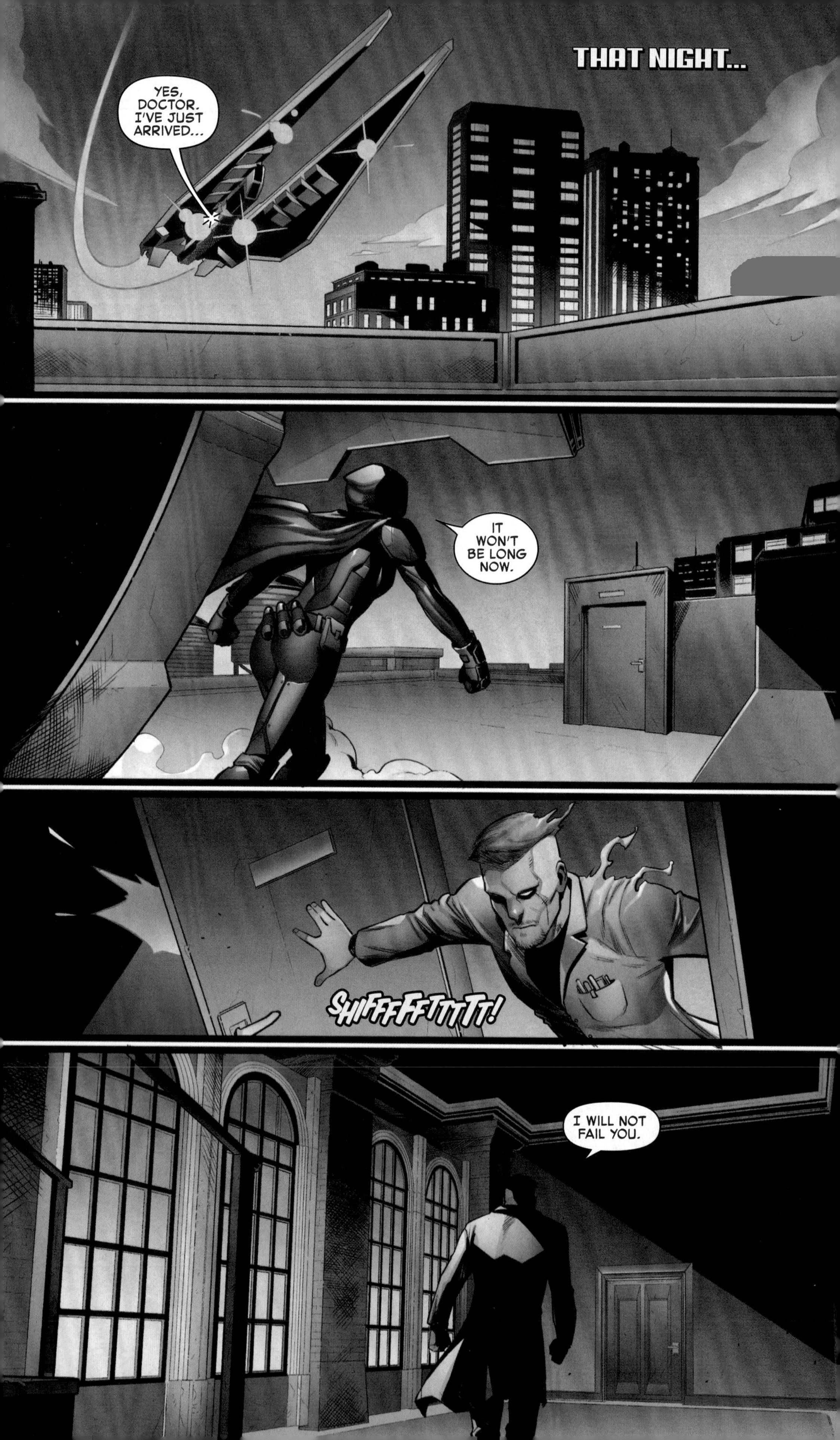
THAT NIGHT...
YES, DOCTOR. I'VE JUST ARRIVED...
IT WON'T BE LONG NOW.
SHIFFFFFTTTTT!
I WILL NOT FAIL YOU.

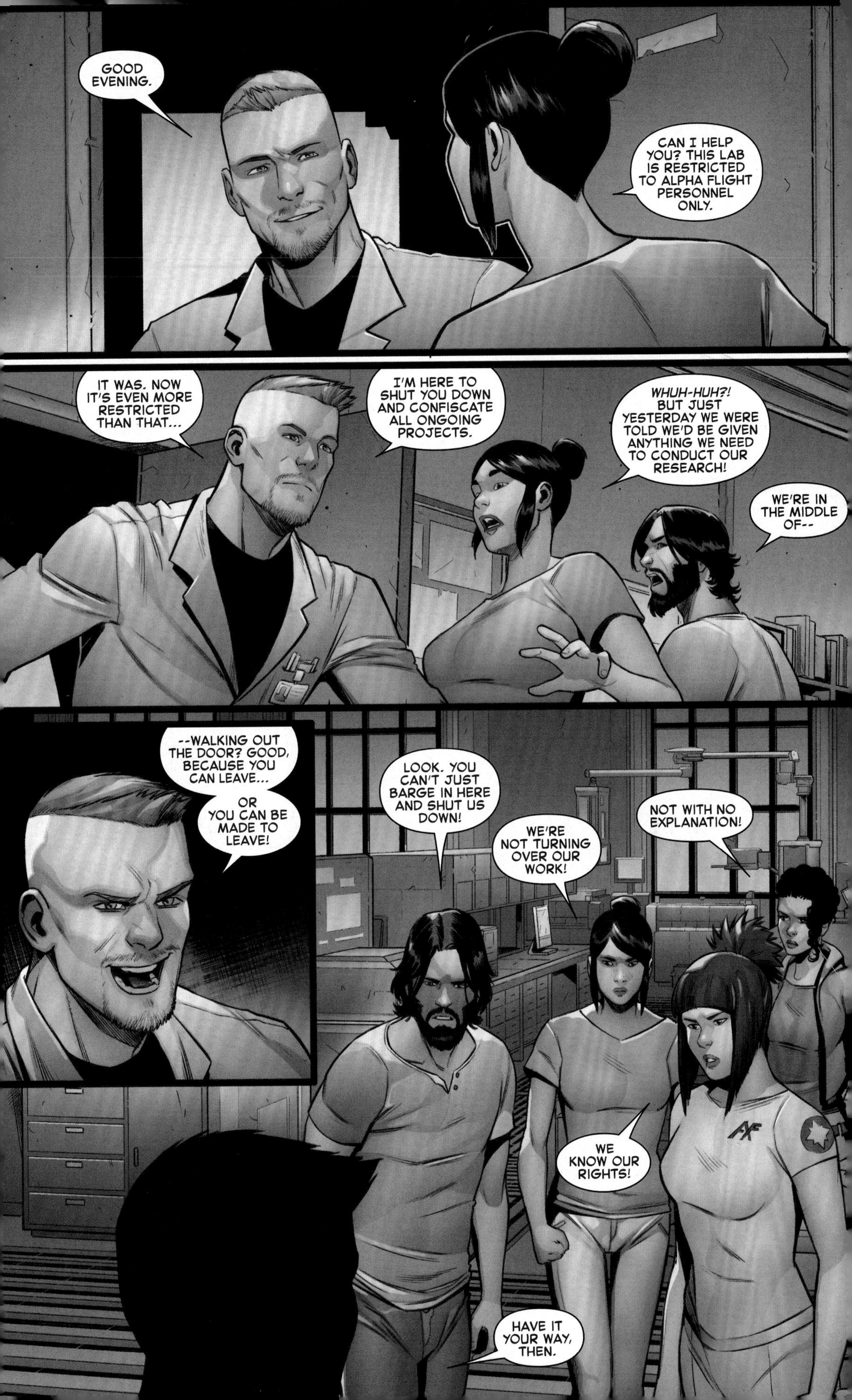
GOOD EVENING.
CAN I HELP YOU? THIS LAB IS RESTRICTED TO ALPHA FLIGHT PERSONNEL ONLY.
IT WAS. NOW IT'S EVEN MORE RESTRICTED THAN THAT...
I'M HERE TO SHUT YOU DOWN AND CONFISCATE ALL ONGOING PROJECTS.
WHUH-HUH?! BUT JUST YESTERDAY WE WERE TOLD WE'D BE GIVEN ANYTHING WE NEED TO CONDUCT OUR RESEARCH!
WE'RE IN THE MIDDLE OF--
--WALKING OUT THE DOOR? GOOD, BECAUSE YOU CAN LEAVE...
OR YOU CAN BE MADE TO LEAVE!
LOOK. YOU CAN'T JUST BARGE IN HERE AND SHUT US DOWN!
WE'RE NOT TURNING OVER OUR WORK!
NOT WITH NO EXPLANATION!
WE KNOW OUR RIGHTS!
HAVE IT YOUR WAY, THEN.

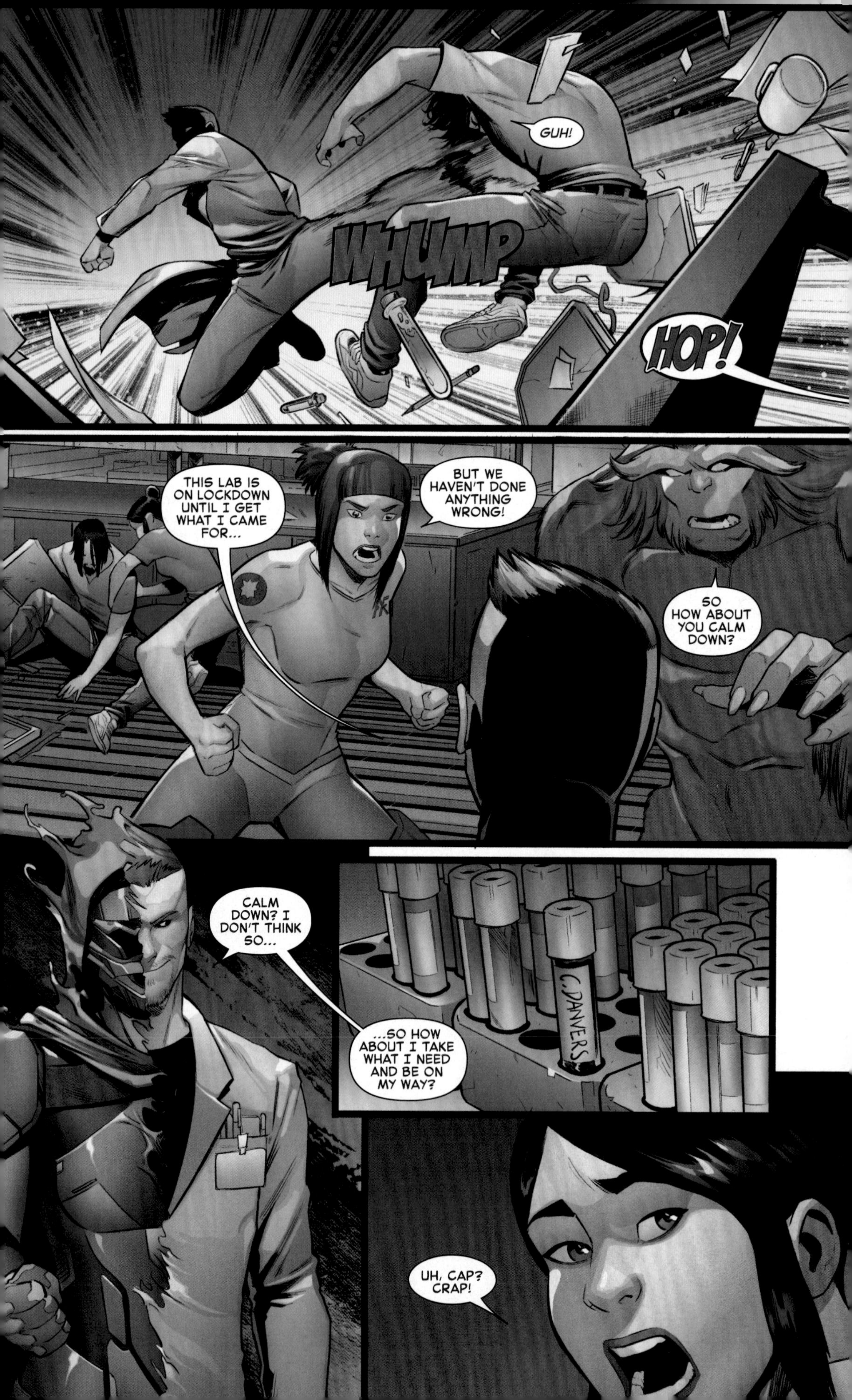
GUH!
WHUMP
HOP!
THIS LAB IS ON LOCKDOWN UNTIL I GET WHAT I CAME FOR...
BUT WE HAVEN'T DONE ANYTHING WRONG!
SO HOW ABOUT YOU CALM DOWN?
CALM DOWN? I DON'T THINK SO...
...SO HOW ABOUT I TAKE WHAT I NEED AND BE ON MY WAY?
C. DANVERS
UH, CAP? CRAP!

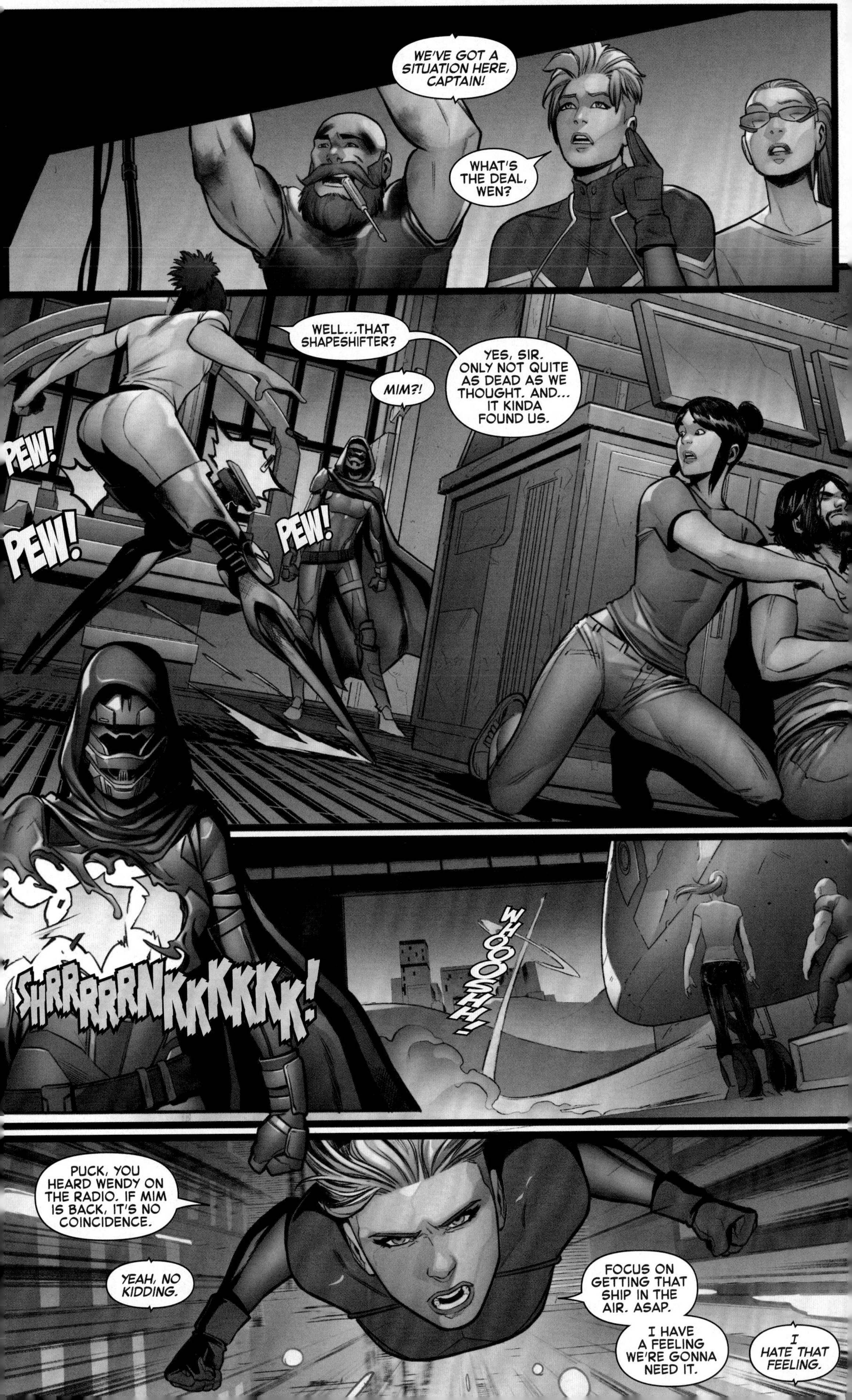
WE'VE GOT A SITUATION HERE, CAPTAIN!
WHAT'S THE DEAL, WEN?
WELL...THAT SHAPESHIFTER?
MIM?!
YES, SIR. ONLY NOT QUITE AS DEAD AS WE THOUGHT. AND... IT KINDA FOUND US.
PEW!
PEW!
PEW!
SHRRRRRNKKKKKK!
WHOOOOSHH!
PUCK, YOU HEARD WENDY ON THE RADIO. IF MIM IS BACK, IT'S NO COINCIDENCE.
YEAH, NO KIDDING.
FOCUS ON GETTING THAT SHIP IN THE AIR. ASAP.
I HAVE A FEELING WE'RE GONNA NEED IT.
I HATE THAT FEELING.

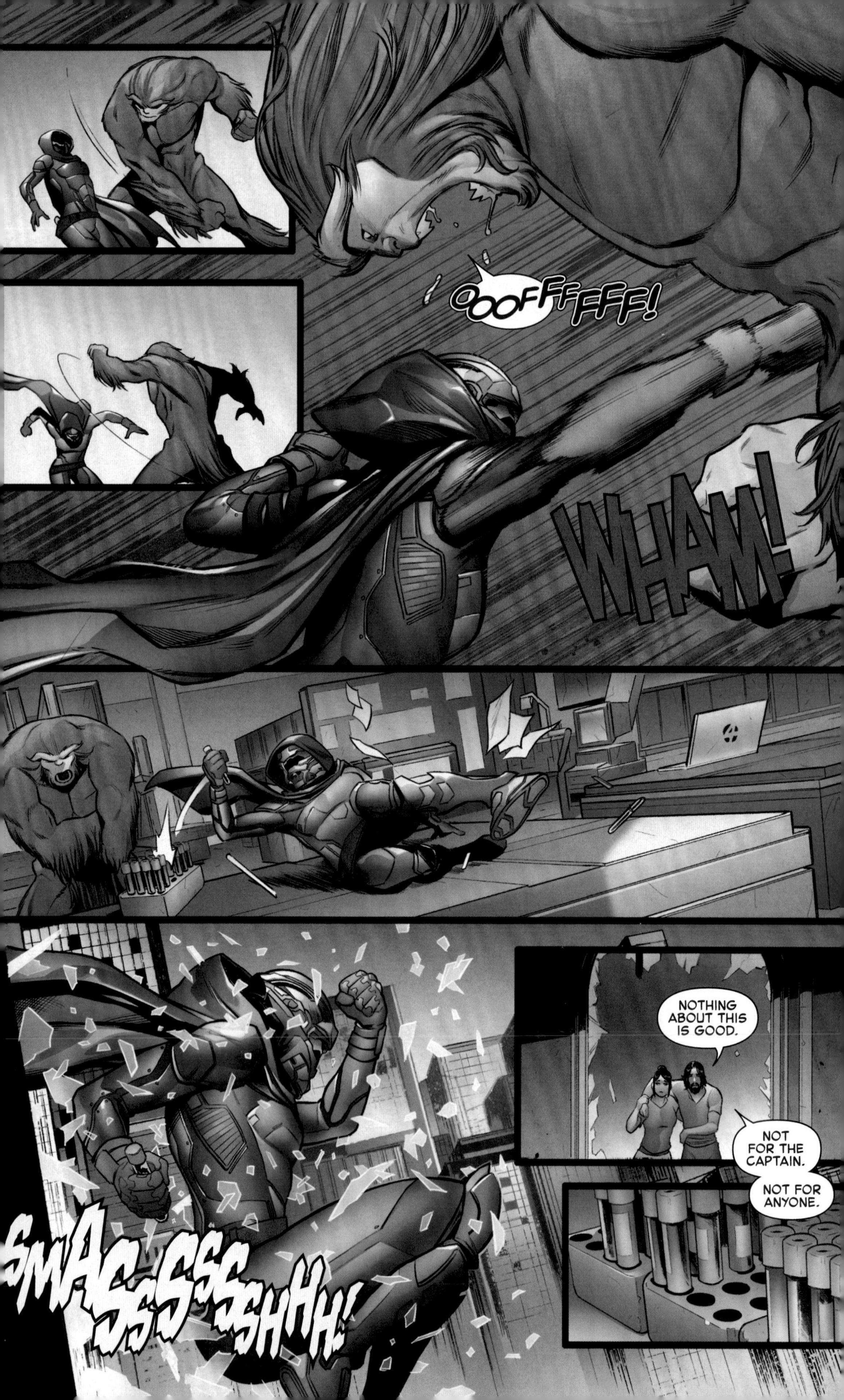
OOOFFFFFFF!
WHAM!
SMASSSSSSHHH!
NOTHING ABOUT THIS IS GOOD.
NOT FOR THE CAPTAIN.
NOT FOR ANYONE.

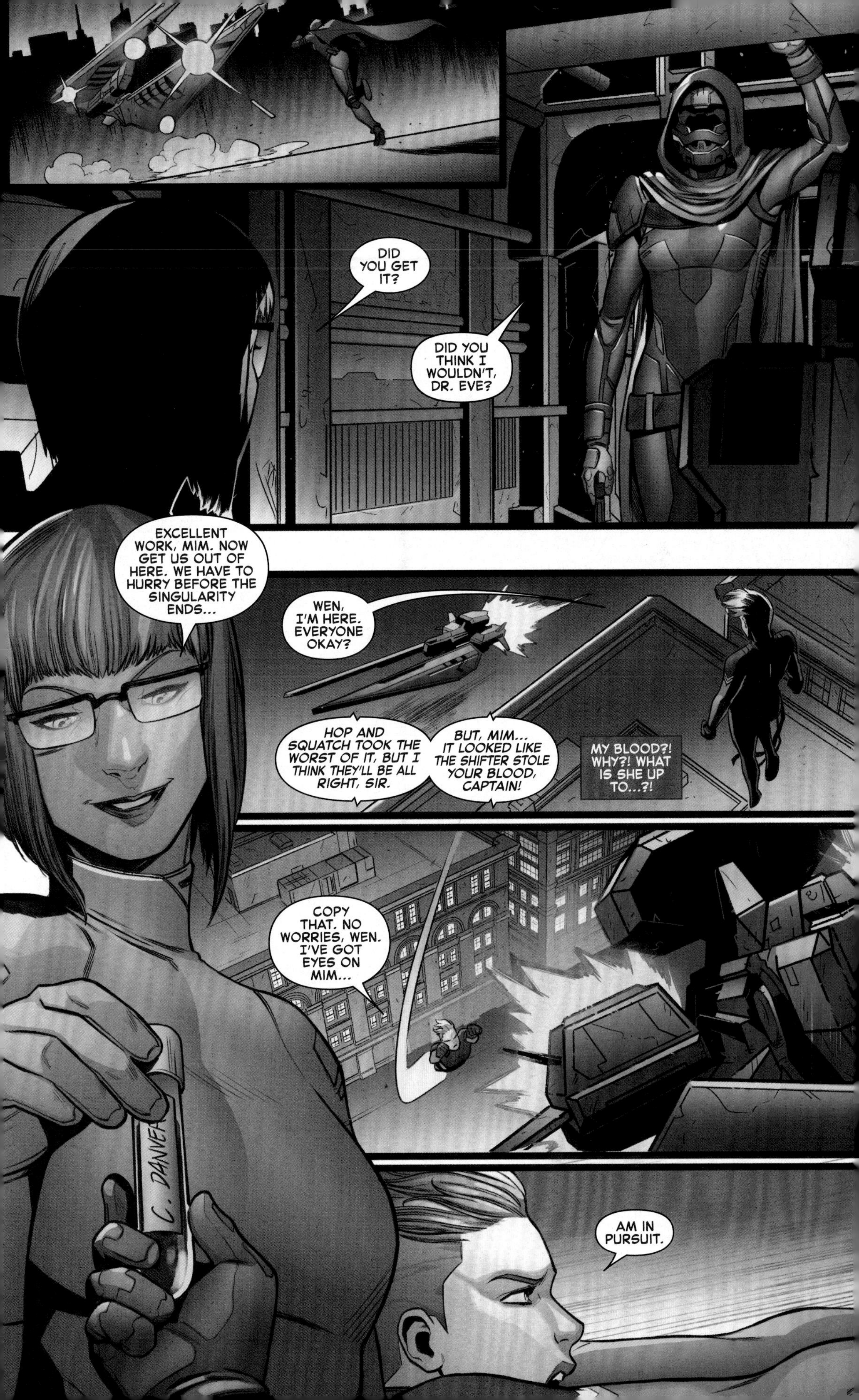
DID YOU GET IT?
DID YOU THINK I WOULDN'T, DR. EVE?
EXCELLENT WORK, MIM. NOW GET US OUT OF HERE. WE HAVE TO HURRY BEFORE THE SINGULARITY ENDS...
WEN, I'M HERE. EVERYONE OKAY?
HOP AND SQUATCH TOOK THE WORST OF IT, BUT I THINK THEY'LL BE ALL RIGHT, SIR.
BUT, MIM... IT LOOKED LIKE THE SHIFTER STOLE YOUR BLOOD, CAPTAIN!
MY BLOOD?! WHY?! WHAT IS SHE UP TO...?!
COPY THAT. NO WORRIES, WEN. I'VE GOT EYES ON MIM...
AM IN PURSUIT.
C. DANVER

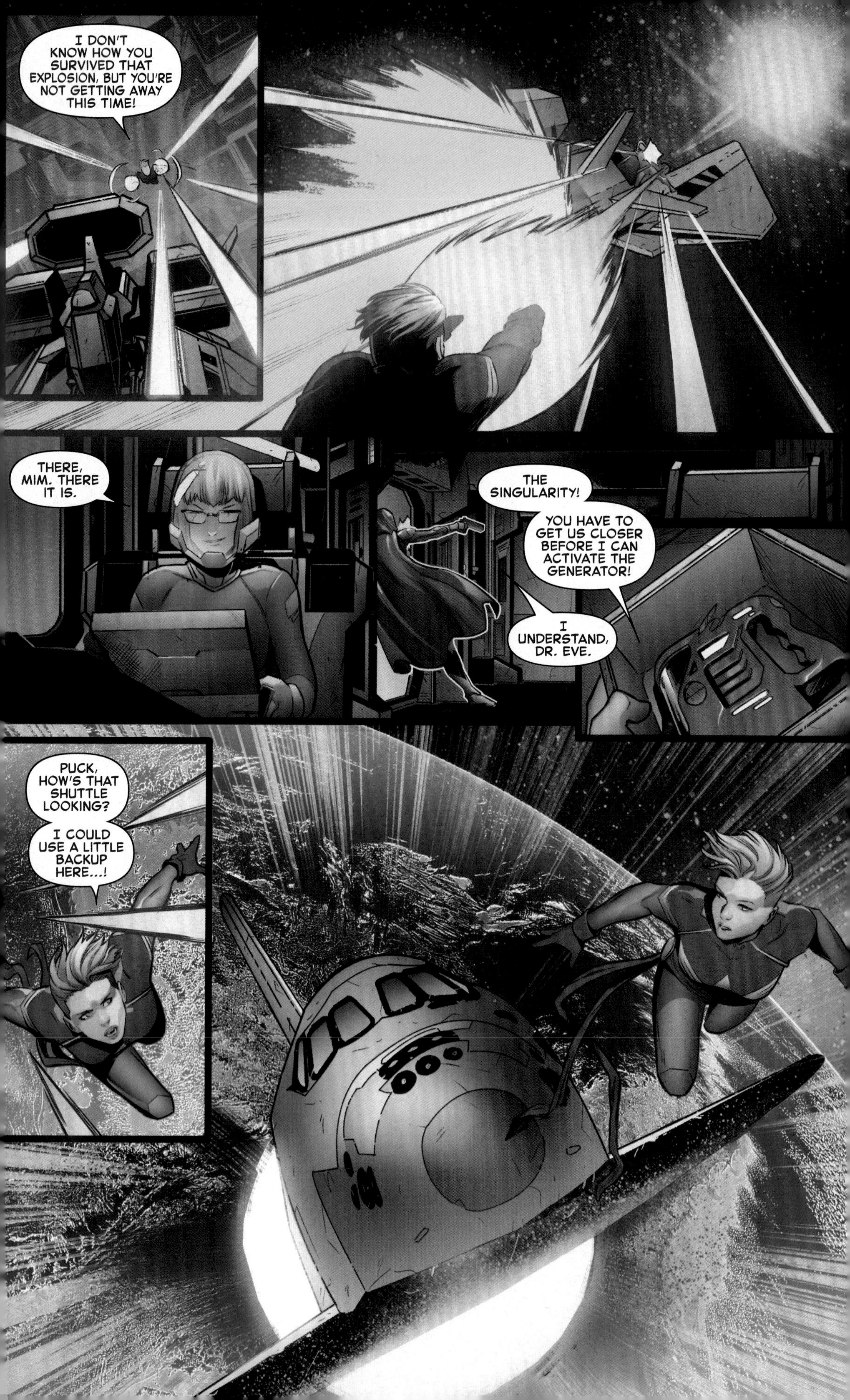
I DON'T KNOW HOW YOU SURVIVED THAT EXPLOSION, BUT YOU'RE NOT GETTING AWAY THIS TIME!
THERE, MIM. THERE IT IS.
THE SINGULARITY!
YOU HAVE TO GET US CLOSER BEFORE I CAN ACTIVATE THE GENERATOR!
I UNDERSTAND, DR. EVE.
PUCK, HOW'S THAT SHUTTLE LOOKING?
I COULD USE A LITTLE BACKUP HERE...!

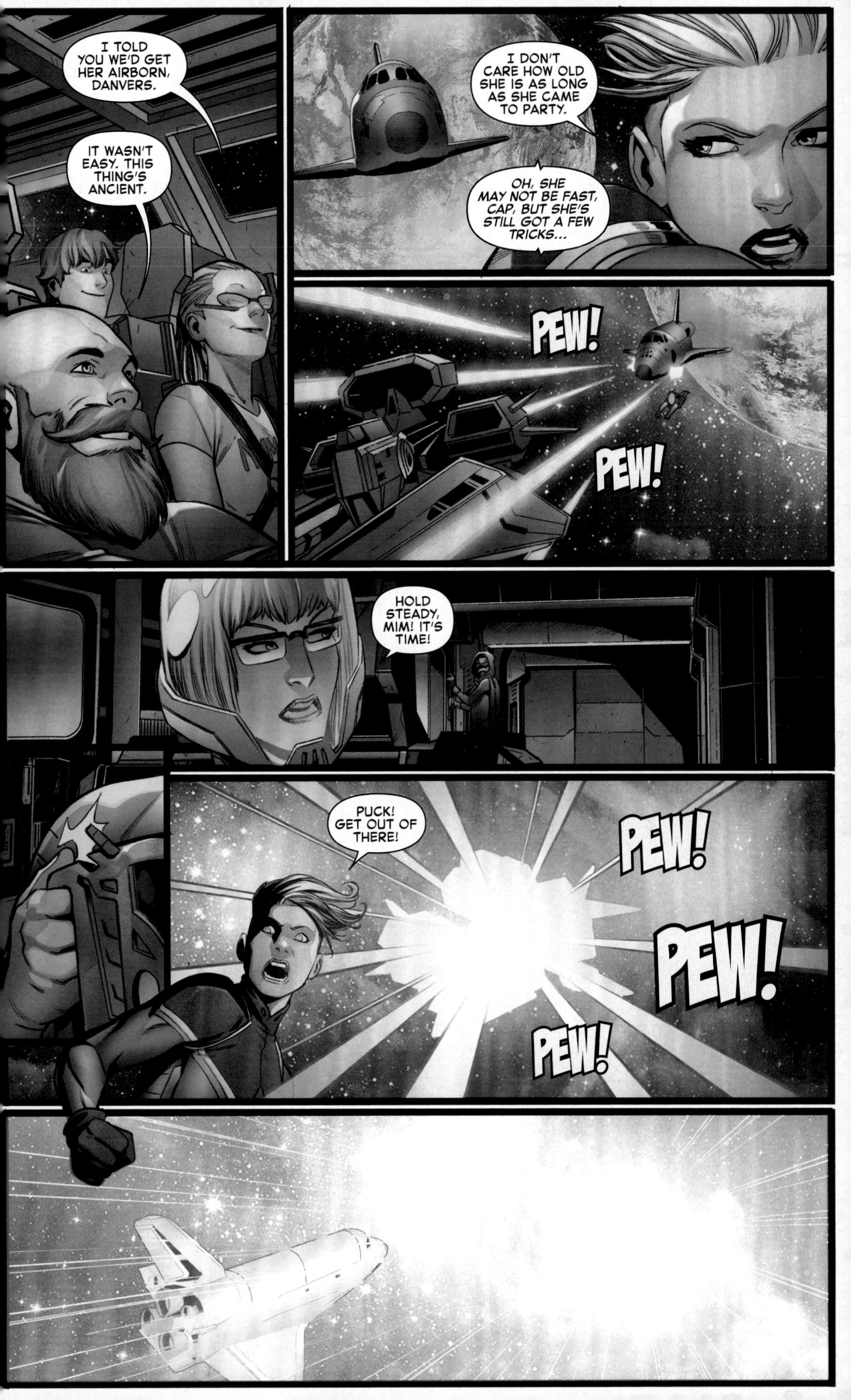
I TOLD YOU WE'D GET HER AIRBORN, DANVERS.
IT WASN'T EASY. THIS THING'S ANCIENT.
I DON'T CARE HOW OLD SHE IS AS LONG AS SHE CAME TO PARTY.
OH, SHE MAY NOT BE FAST, CAP, BUT SHE'S STILL GOT A FEW TRICKS...
PEW!
PEW!
HOLD STEADY, MIM! IT'S TIME!
PUCK! GET OUT OF THERE!
PEW!
PEW!
PEW!

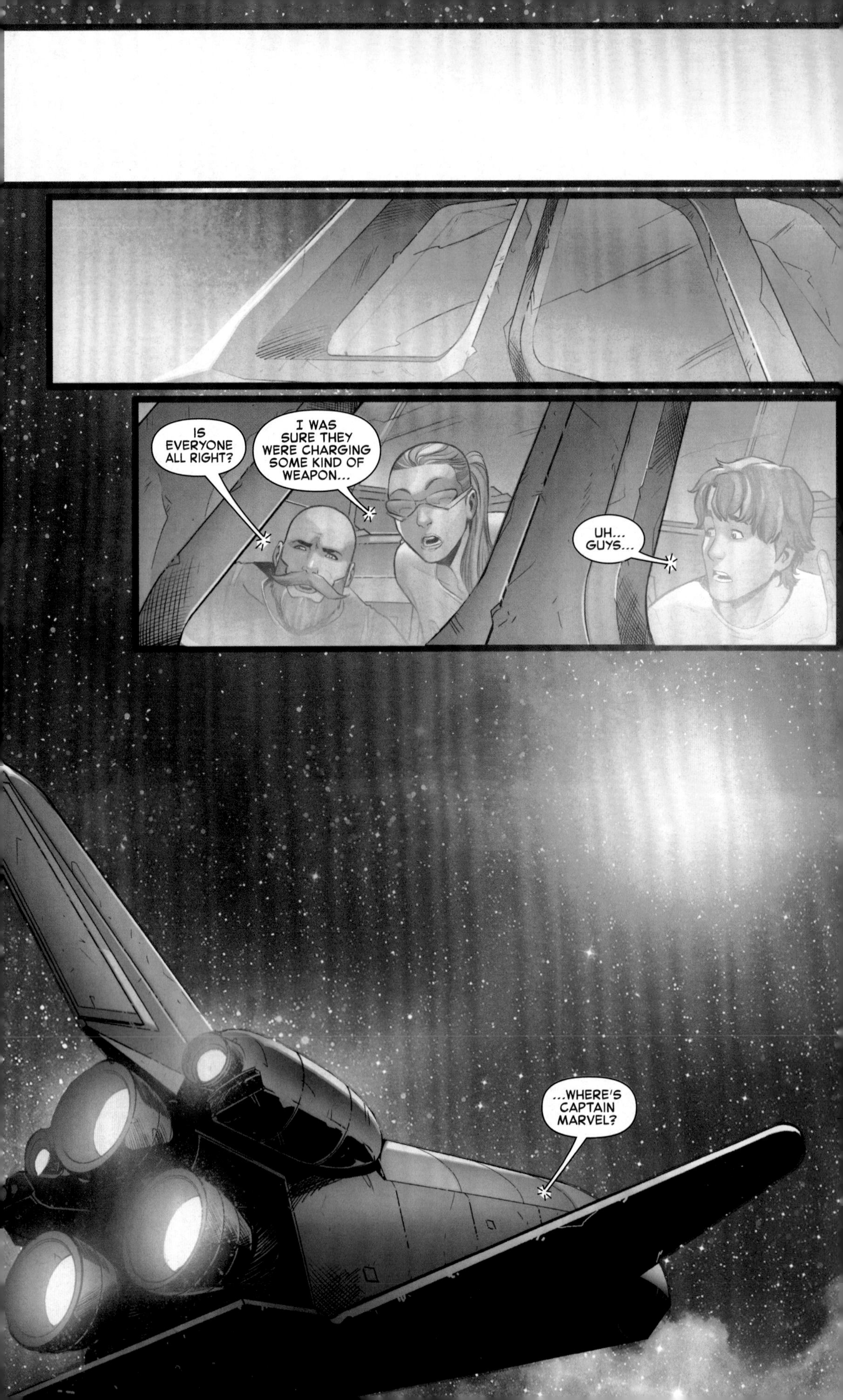
IS EVERYONE ALL RIGHT?
I WAS SURE THEY WERE CHARGING SOME KIND OF WEAPON...
UH... GUYS...
...WHERE'S CAPTAIN MARVEL?

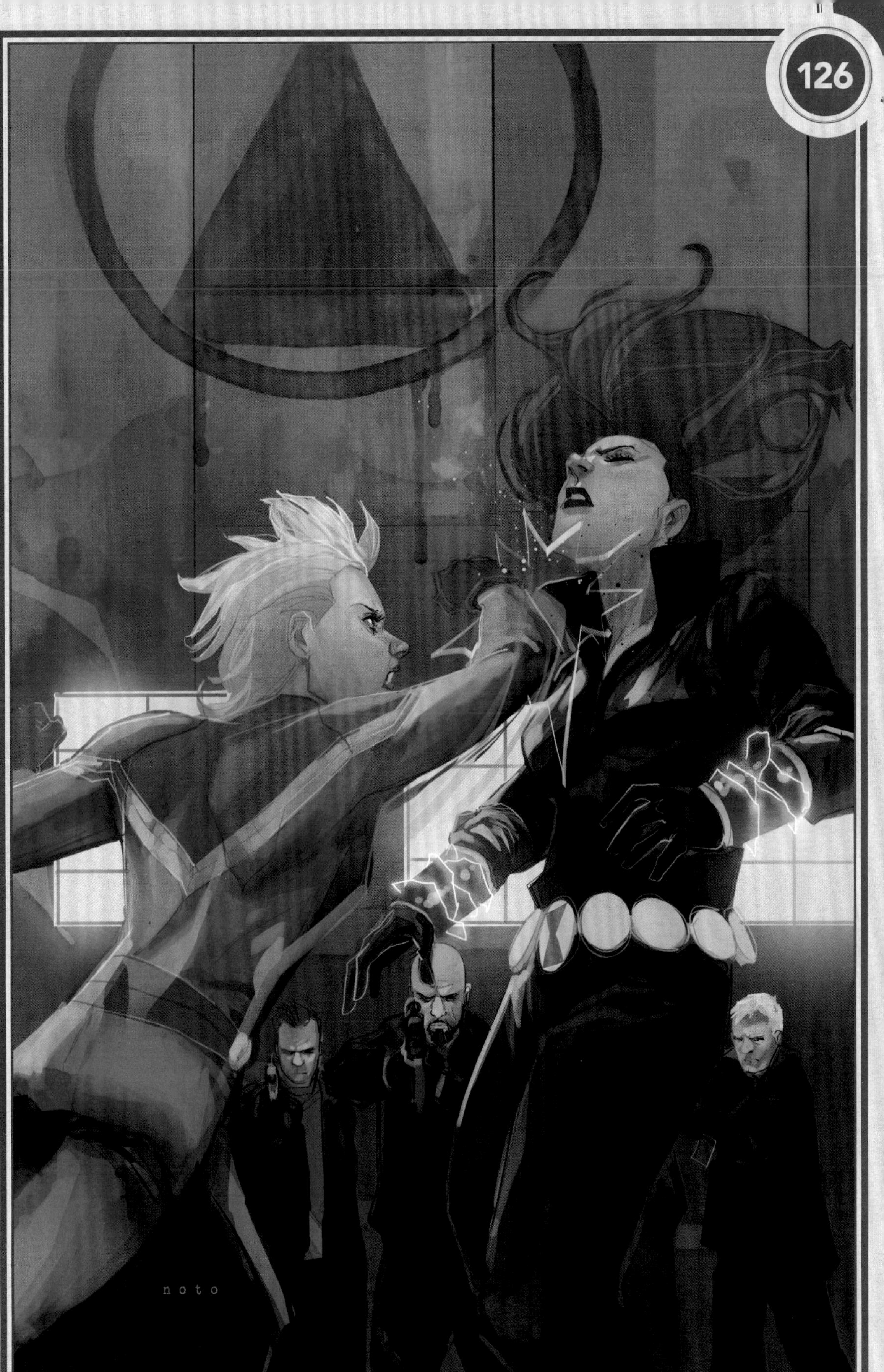
126
noto

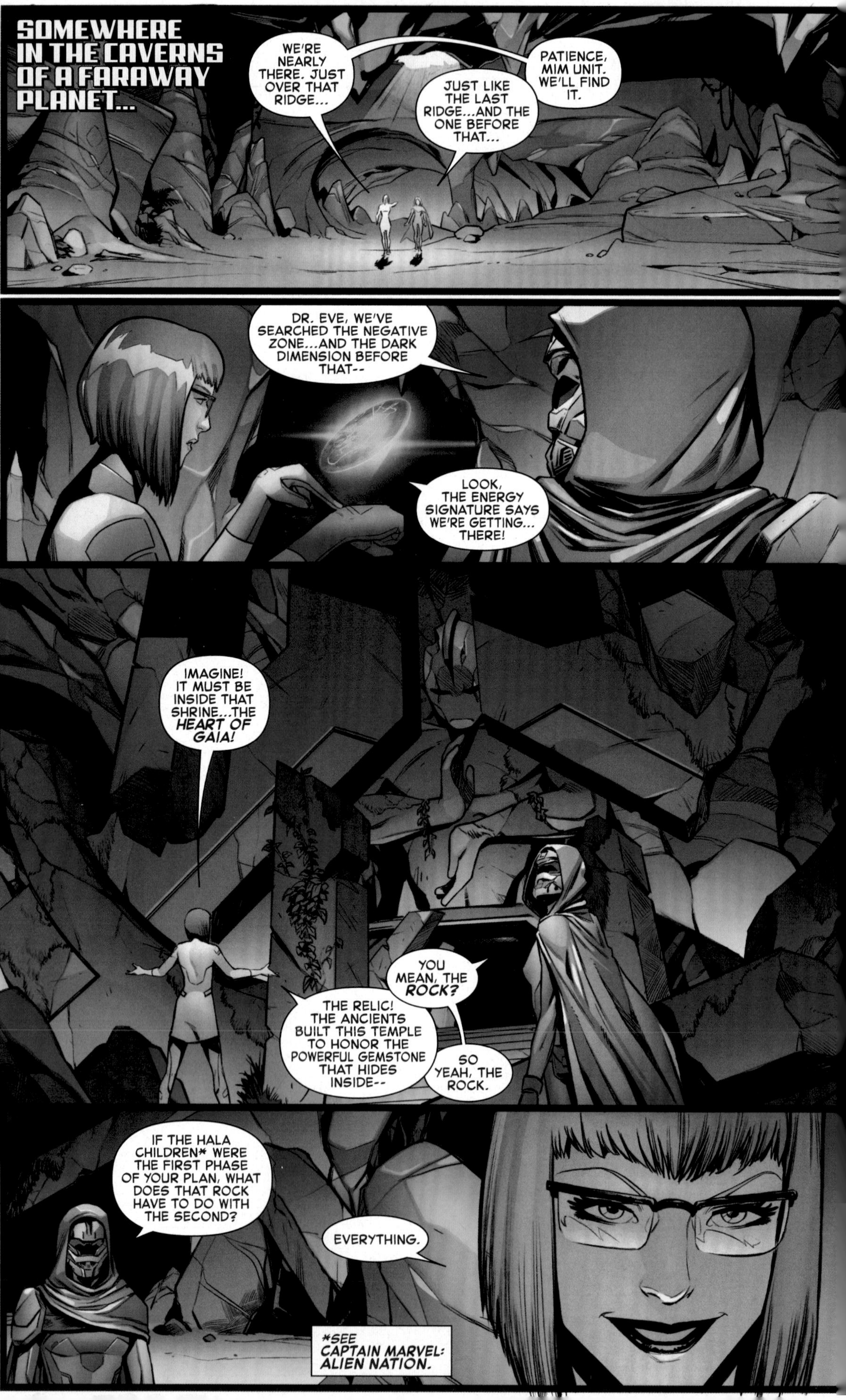
SOMEWHERE IN THE CAVERNS OF A FARAWAY PLANET...
WE'RE NEARLY THERE. JUST OVER THAT RIDGE...
JUST LIKE THE LAST RIDGE...AND THE ONE BEFORE THAT...
PATIENCE, MIM UNIT. WE'LL FIND IT.
DR. EVE, WE'VE SEARCHED THE NEGATIVE ZONE...AND THE DARK DIMENSION BEFORE THAT--
LOOK, THE ENERGY SIGNATURE SAYS WE'RE GETTING... THERE!
IMAGINE! IT MUST BE INSIDE THAT SHRINE...THE HEART OF GAIA!
YOU MEAN, THE ROCK?
THE RELIC! THE ANCIENTS BUILT THIS TEMPLE TO HONOR THE POWERFUL GEMSTONE THAT HIDES INSIDE--
SO YEAH, THE ROCK.
IF THE HALA CHILDREN* WERE THE FIRST PHASE OF YOUR PLAN, WHAT DOES THAT ROCK HAVE TO DO WITH THE SECOND?
EVERYTHING.
*SEE CAPTAIN MARVEL: ALIEN NATION.

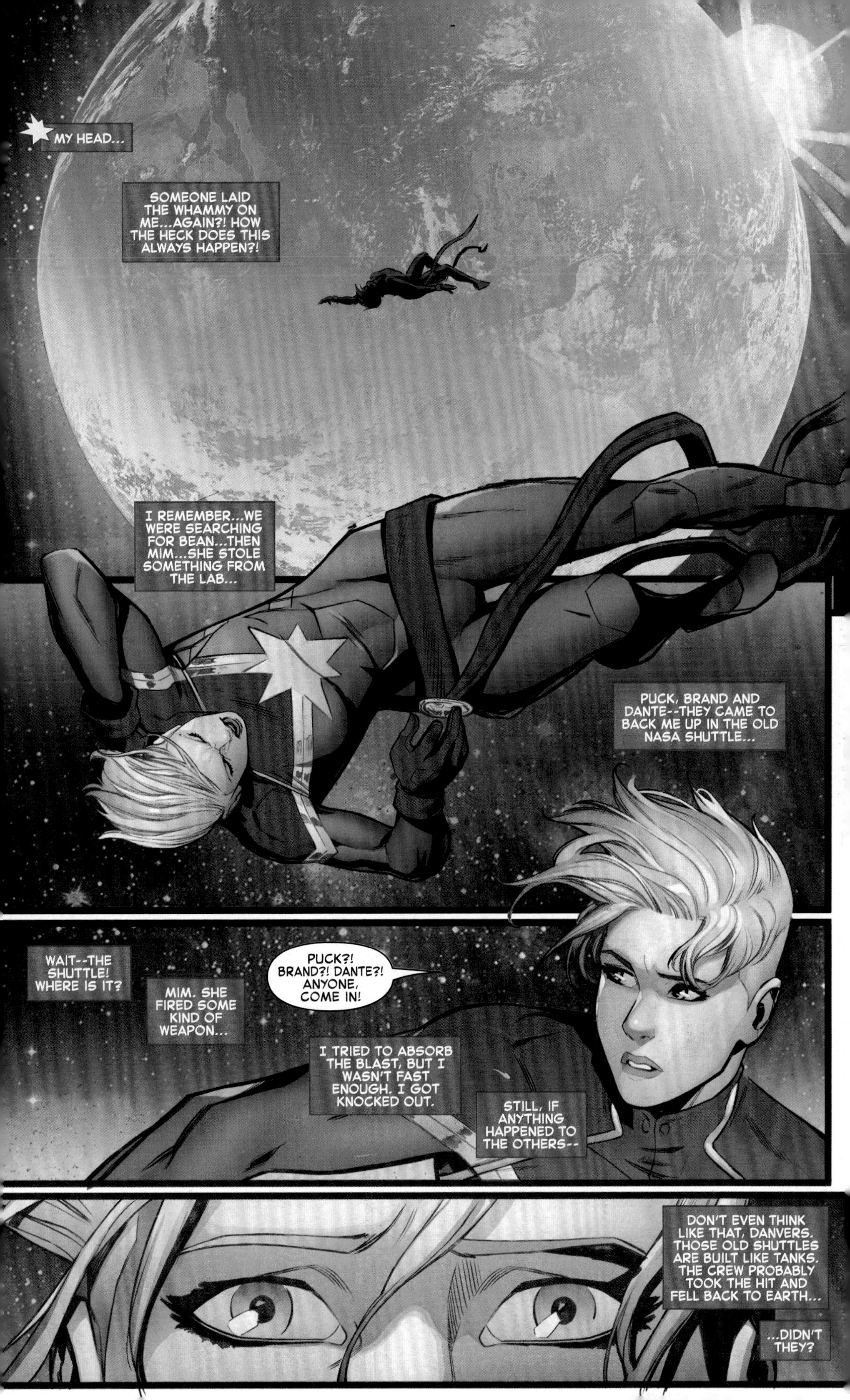
MY HEAD...
SOMEONE LAID THE WHAMMY ON ME...AGAIN?! HOW THE HECK DOES THIS ALWAYS HAPPEN?!
I REMEMBER...WE WERE SEARCHING FOR BEAN...THEN MIM...SHE STOLE SOMETHING FROM THE LAB...
PUCK, BRAND AND DANTE--THEY CAME TO BACK ME UP IN THE OLD NASA SHUTTLE...
WAIT--THE SHUTTLE! WHERE IS IT?
MIM. SHE FIRED SOME KIND OF WEAPON...
PUCK?! BRAND?! DANTE?! ANYONE, COME IN!
I TRIED TO ABSORB THE BLAST, BUT I WASN'T FAST ENOUGH. I GOT KNOCKED OUT.
STILL, IF ANYTHING HAPPENED TO THE OTHERS--
DON'T EVEN THINK LIKE THAT, DANVERS. THOSE OLD SHUTTLES ARE BUILT LIKE TANKS. THE CREW PROBABLY TOOK THE HIT AND FELL BACK TO EARTH...
...DIDN'T THEY?

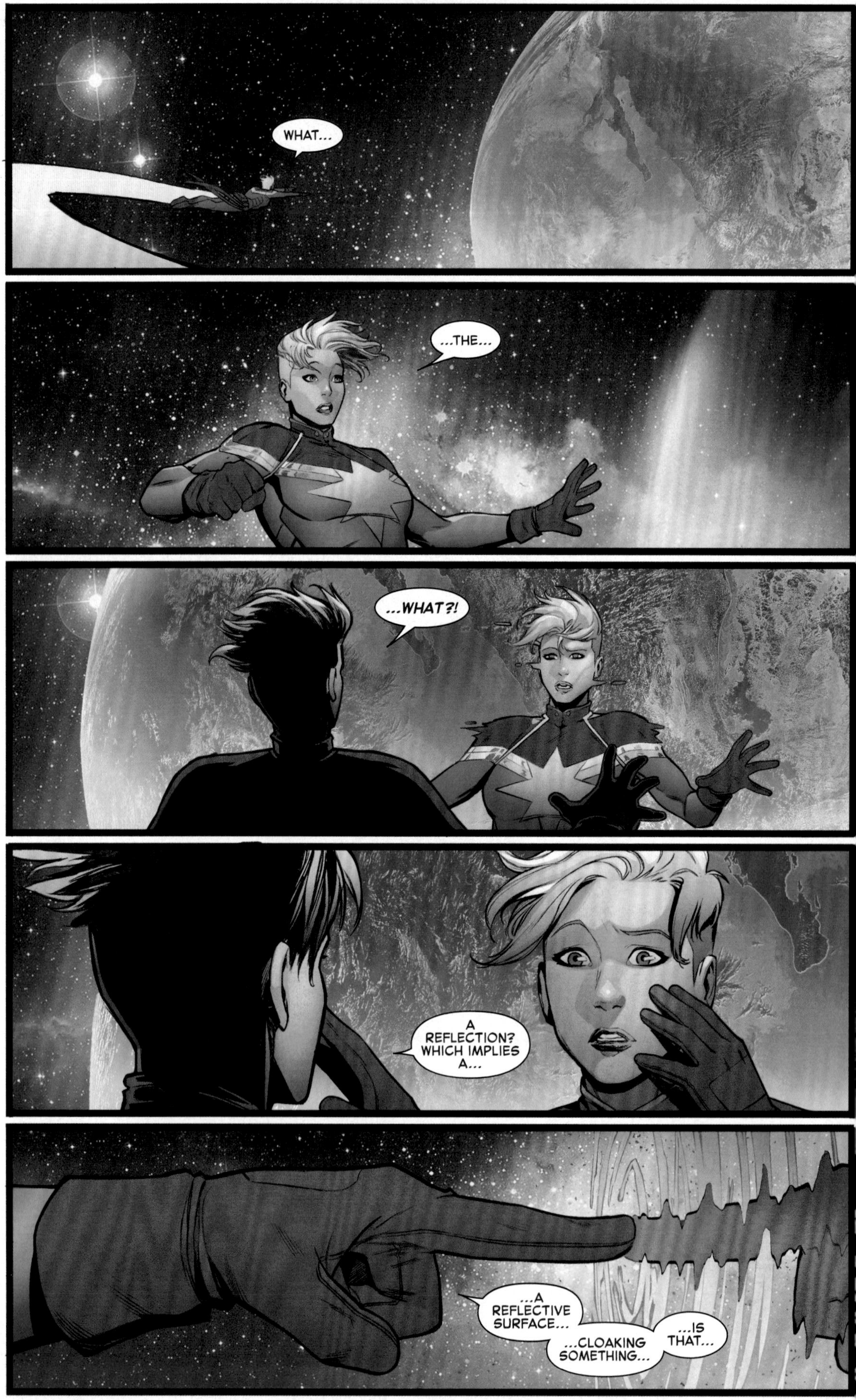
WHAT...
...THE...
...WHAT?!
A REFLECTION? WHICH IMPLIES A...
...A REFLECTIVE SURFACE...
...CLOAKING SOMETHING...
...IS THAT...

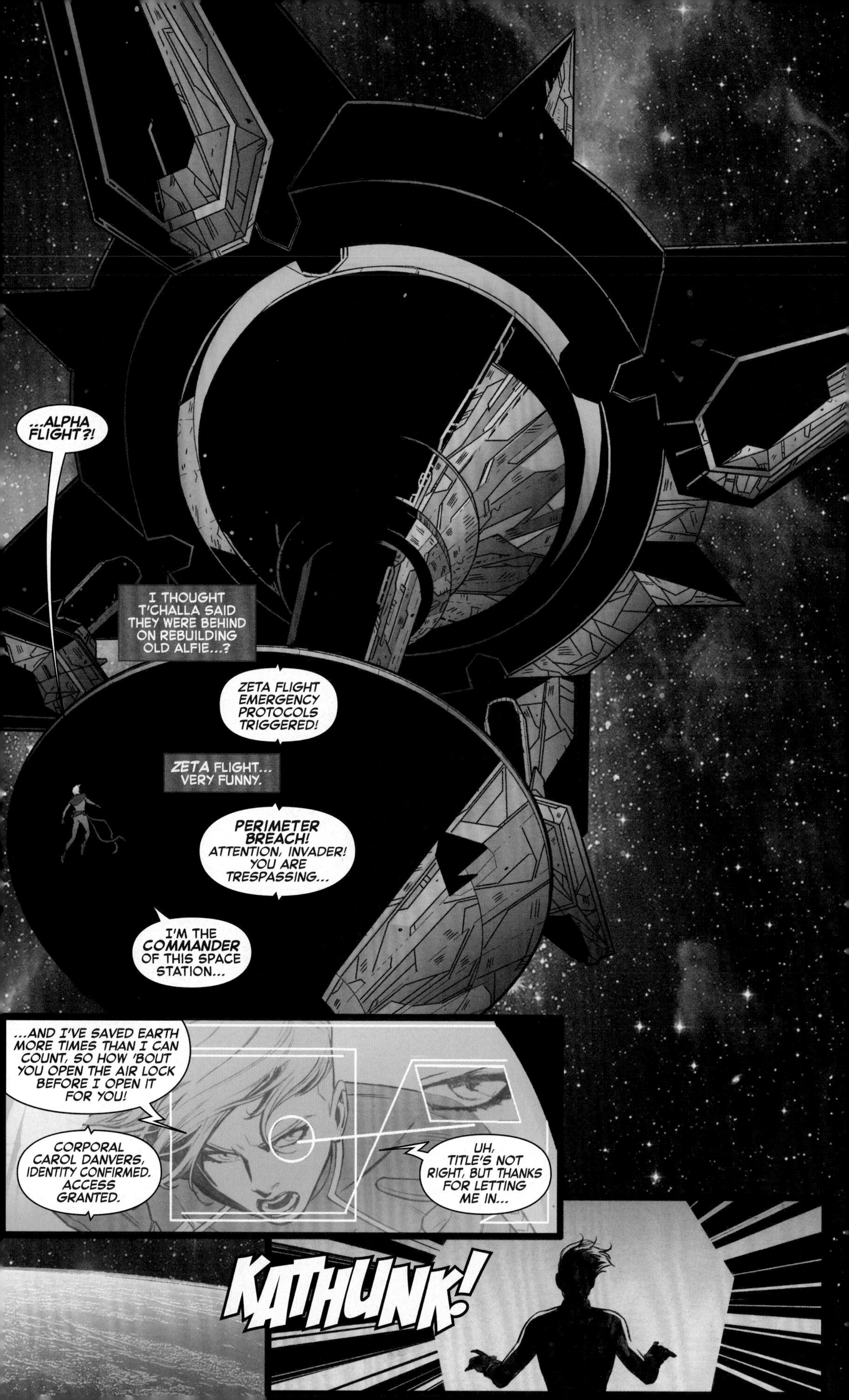
...ALPHA FLIGHT?!
I THOUGHT T'CHALLA SAID THEY WERE BEHIND ON REBUILDING OLD ALFIE...?
ZETA FLIGHT EMERGENCY PROTOCOLS TRIGGERED!
ZETA FLIGHT... VERY FUNNY.
PERIMETER BREACH! ATTENTION, INVADER! YOU ARE TRESPASSING...
I'M THE COMMANDER OF THIS SPACE STATION...
...AND I'VE SAVED EARTH MORE TIMES THAN I CAN COUNT, SO HOW 'BOUT YOU OPEN THE AIR LOCK BEFORE I OPEN IT FOR YOU!
CORPORAL CAROL DANVERS, IDENTITY CONFIRMED. ACCESS GRANTED.
UH, TITLE'S NOT RIGHT, BUT THANKS FOR LETTING ME IN...
KATHUNK!

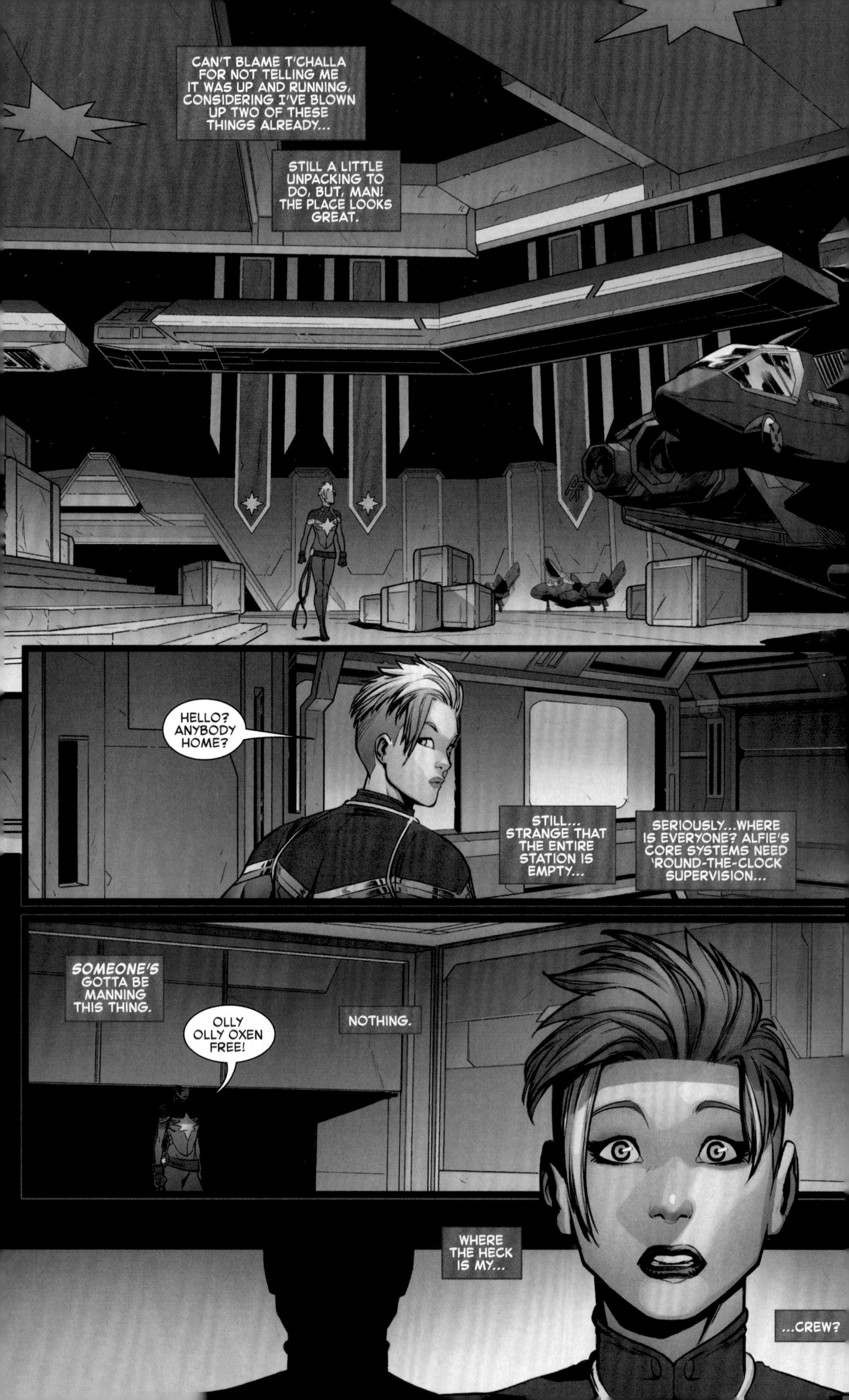
CAN'T BLAME T'CHALLA FOR NOT TELLING ME IT WAS UP AND RUNNING, CONSIDERING I'VE BLOWN UP TWO OF THESE THINGS ALREADY...
STILL A LITTLE UNPACKING TO DO, BUT, MAN! THE PLACE LOOKS GREAT.
HELLO? ANYBODY HOME?
STILL... STRANGE THAT THE ENTIRE STATION IS EMPTY...
SERIOUSLY...WHERE IS EVERYONE? ALFIE'S CORE SYSTEMS NEED 'ROUND-THE-CLOCK SUPERVISION...
SOMEONE'S GOTTA BE MANNING THIS THING.
OLLY OLLY OXEN FREE!
NOTHING.
WHERE THE HECK IS MY...
...CREW?

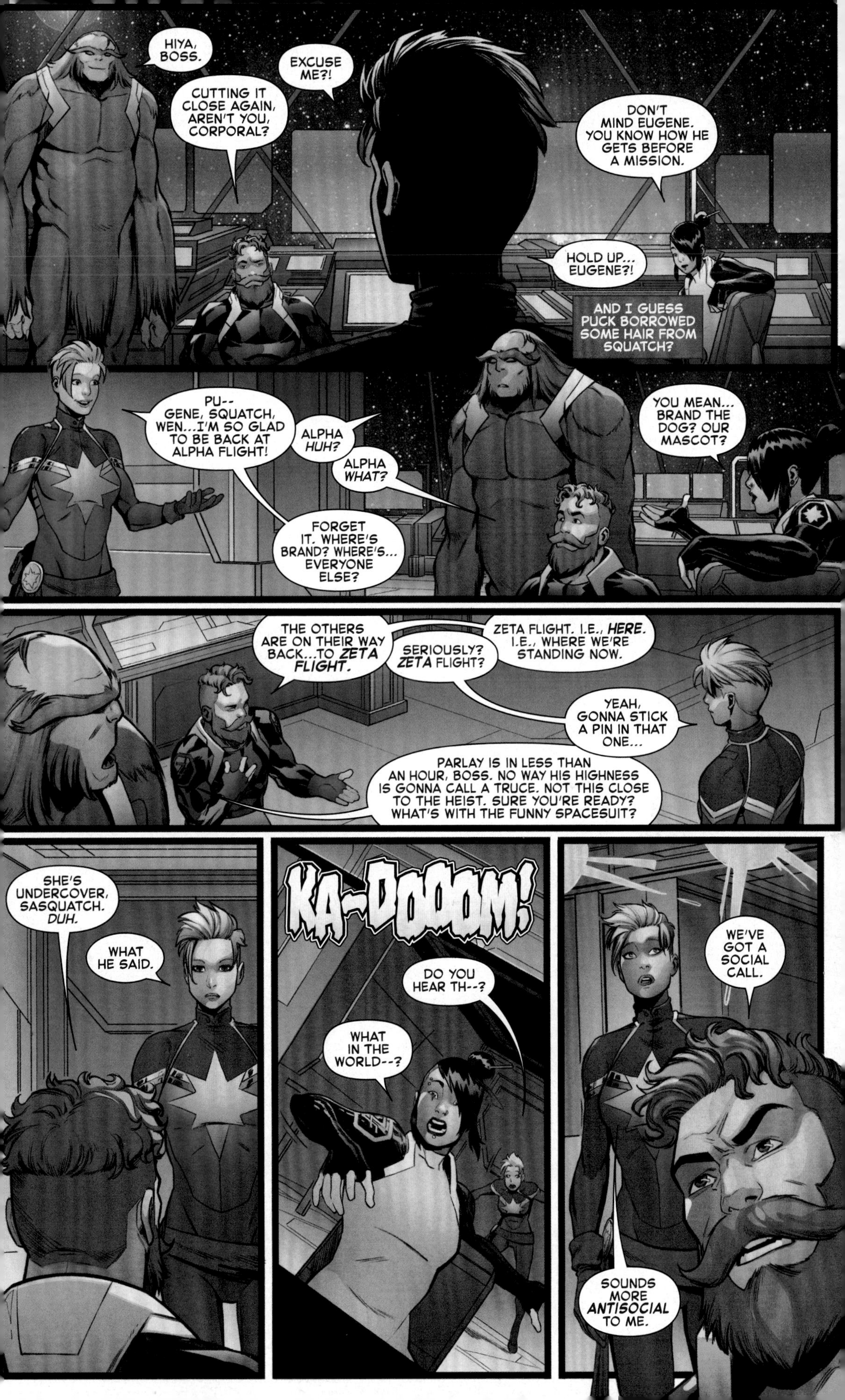
HIYA, BOSS.
CUTTING IT CLOSE AGAIN, AREN'T YOU, CORPORAL?
EXCUSE ME?!
DON'T MIND EUGENE. YOU KNOW HOW HE GETS BEFORE A MISSION.
HOLD UP... EUGENE?!
AND I GUESS PUCK BORROWED SOME HAIR FROM SQUATCH?
PU-- GENE, SQUATCH, WEN...I'M SO GLAD TO BE BACK AT ALPHA FLIGHT!
ALPHA *HUH?*
ALPHA *WHAT?*
YOU MEAN... BRAND THE DOG? OUR MASCOT?
FORGET IT. WHERE'S BRAND? WHERE'S... EVERYONE ELSE?
THE OTHERS ARE ON THEIR WAY BACK...TO *ZETA FLIGHT.*
SERIOUSLY? *ZETA* FLIGHT?
ZETA FLIGHT. I.E., *HERE.* I.E., WHERE WE'RE STANDING NOW.
YEAH, GONNA STICK A PIN IN THAT ONE...
PARLAY IS IN LESS THAN AN HOUR, BOSS. NO WAY HIS HIGHNESS IS GONNA CALL A TRUCE. NOT THIS CLOSE TO THE HEIST. SURE YOU'RE READY? WHAT'S WITH THE FUNNY SPACESUIT?
SHE'S UNDERCOVER, SASQUATCH. *DUH.*
WHAT HE SAID.
KA-DOOOM!
DO YOU HEAR TH--?
WHAT IN THE WORLD--?
WE'VE GOT A SOCIAL CALL.
SOUNDS MORE *ANTISOCIAL* TO ME.

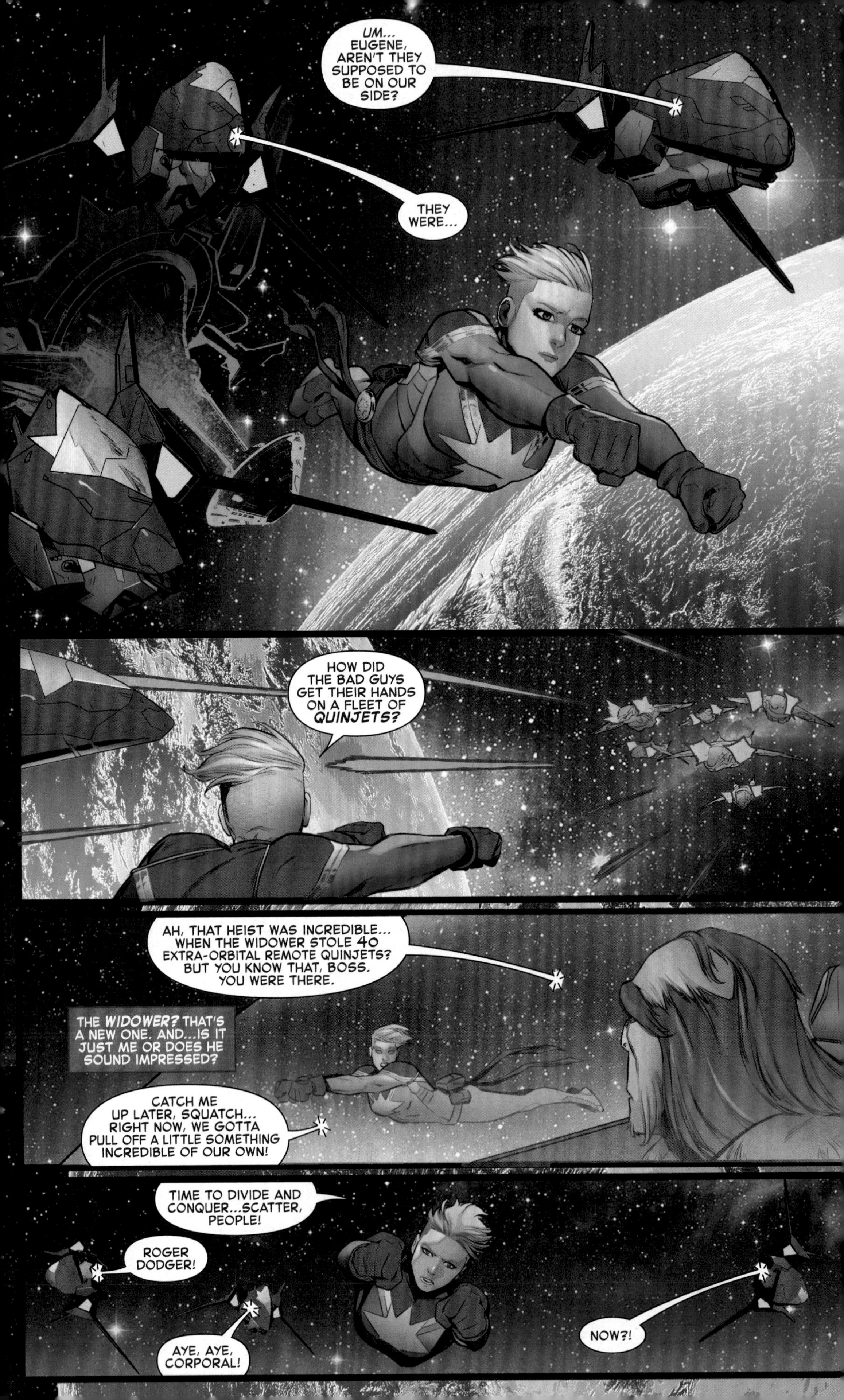
UM... EUGENE, AREN'T THEY SUPPOSED TO BE ON OUR SIDE?
THEY WERE...
HOW DID THE BAD GUYS GET THEIR HANDS ON A FLEET OF *QUINJETS?*
AH, THAT HEIST WAS INCREDIBLE... WHEN THE WIDOWER STOLE 40 EXTRA-ORBITAL REMOTE QUINJETS? BUT YOU KNOW THAT, BOSS. YOU WERE THERE.
THE *WIDOWER?* THAT'S A NEW ONE. AND...IS IT JUST ME OR DOES HE SOUND IMPRESSED?
CATCH ME UP LATER, SQUATCH... RIGHT NOW, WE GOTTA PULL OFF A LITTLE SOMETHING INCREDIBLE OF OUR OWN!
TIME TO DIVIDE AND CONQUER...SCATTER, PEOPLE!
ROGER DODGER!
AYE, AYE, CORPORAL!
NOW?!

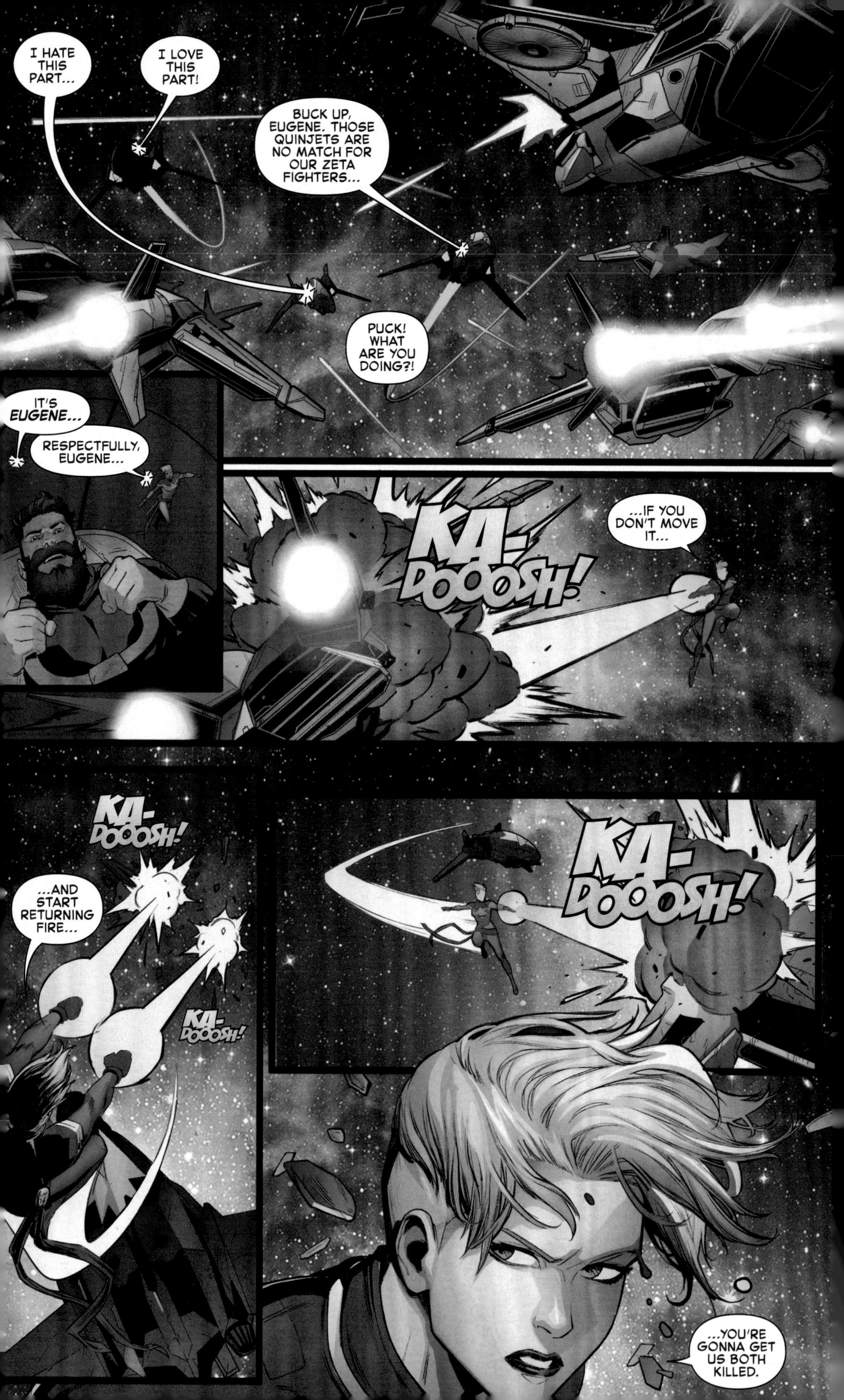
I HATE THIS PART...
I LOVE THIS PART!
BUCK UP, EUGENE. THOSE QUINJETS ARE NO MATCH FOR OUR ZETA FIGHTERS...
PUCK! WHAT ARE YOU DOING?!
IT'S *EUGENE*...
RESPECTFULLY, EUGENE...
KA-DOOOSH!
...IF YOU DON'T MOVE IT...
KA-DOOOSH!
...AND START RETURNING FIRE...
KA-DOOOSH!
KA-DOOOSH!
...YOU'RE GONNA GET US BOTH KILLED.

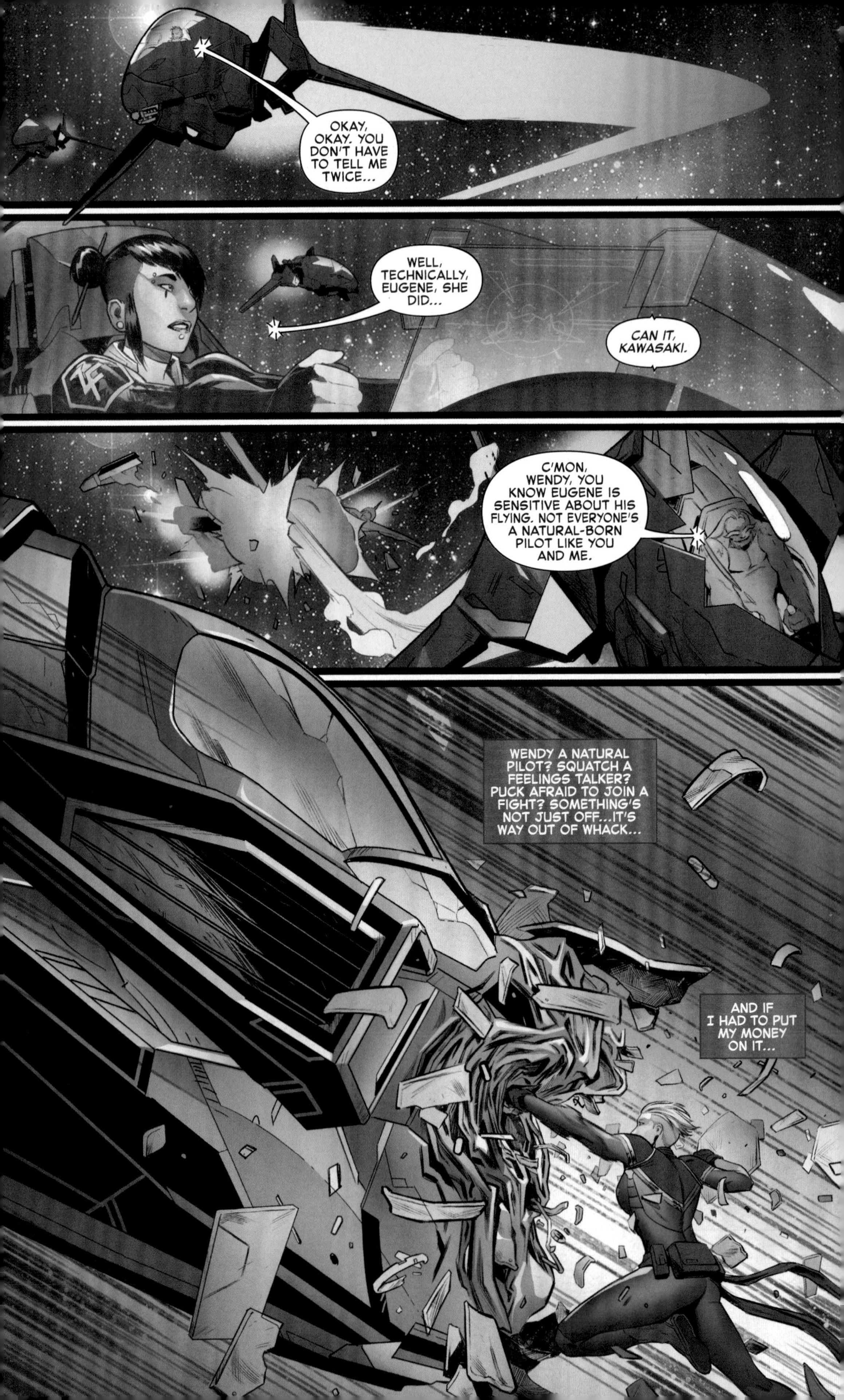
OKAY, OKAY. YOU DON'T HAVE TO TELL ME TWICE...
WELL, TECHNICALLY, EUGENE, SHE DID...
CAN IT, KAWASAKI.
C'MON, WENDY, YOU KNOW EUGENE IS SENSITIVE ABOUT HIS FLYING. NOT EVERYONE'S A NATURAL-BORN PILOT LIKE YOU AND ME.
WENDY A NATURAL PILOT? SQUATCH A FEELINGS TALKER? PUCK AFRAID TO JOIN A FIGHT? SOMETHING'S NOT JUST OFF...IT'S WAY OUT OF WHACK...
AND IF I HAD TO PUT MY MONEY ON IT...

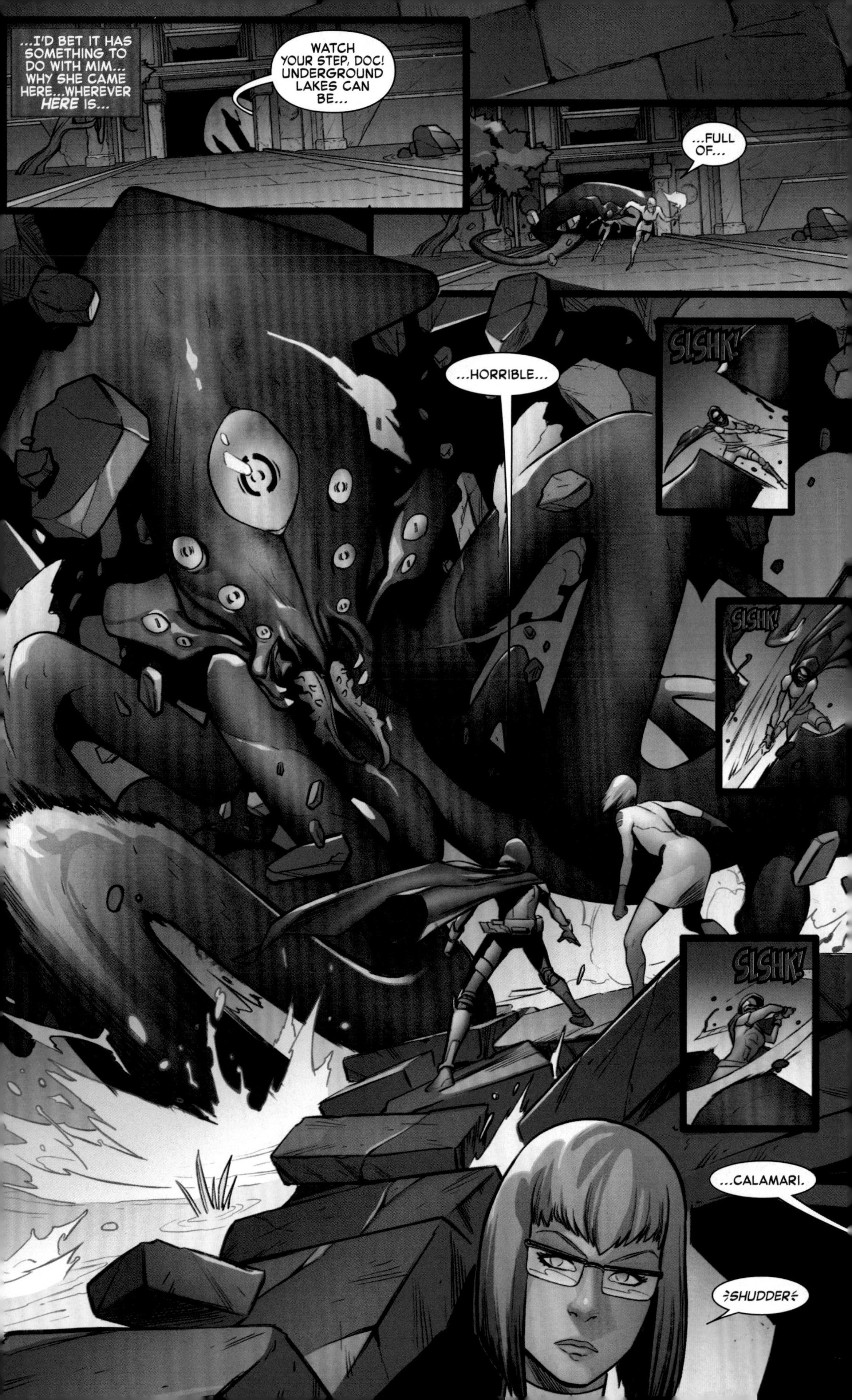
...I'D BET IT HAS SOMETHING TO DO WITH MIM... WHY SHE CAME HERE...WHEREVER HERE IS...
WATCH YOUR STEP, DOC! UNDERGROUND LAKES CAN BE...
...FULL OF...
...HORRIBLE...
SLSHK!
SLSHK!
SLSHK!
...CALAMARI.
SHUDDER

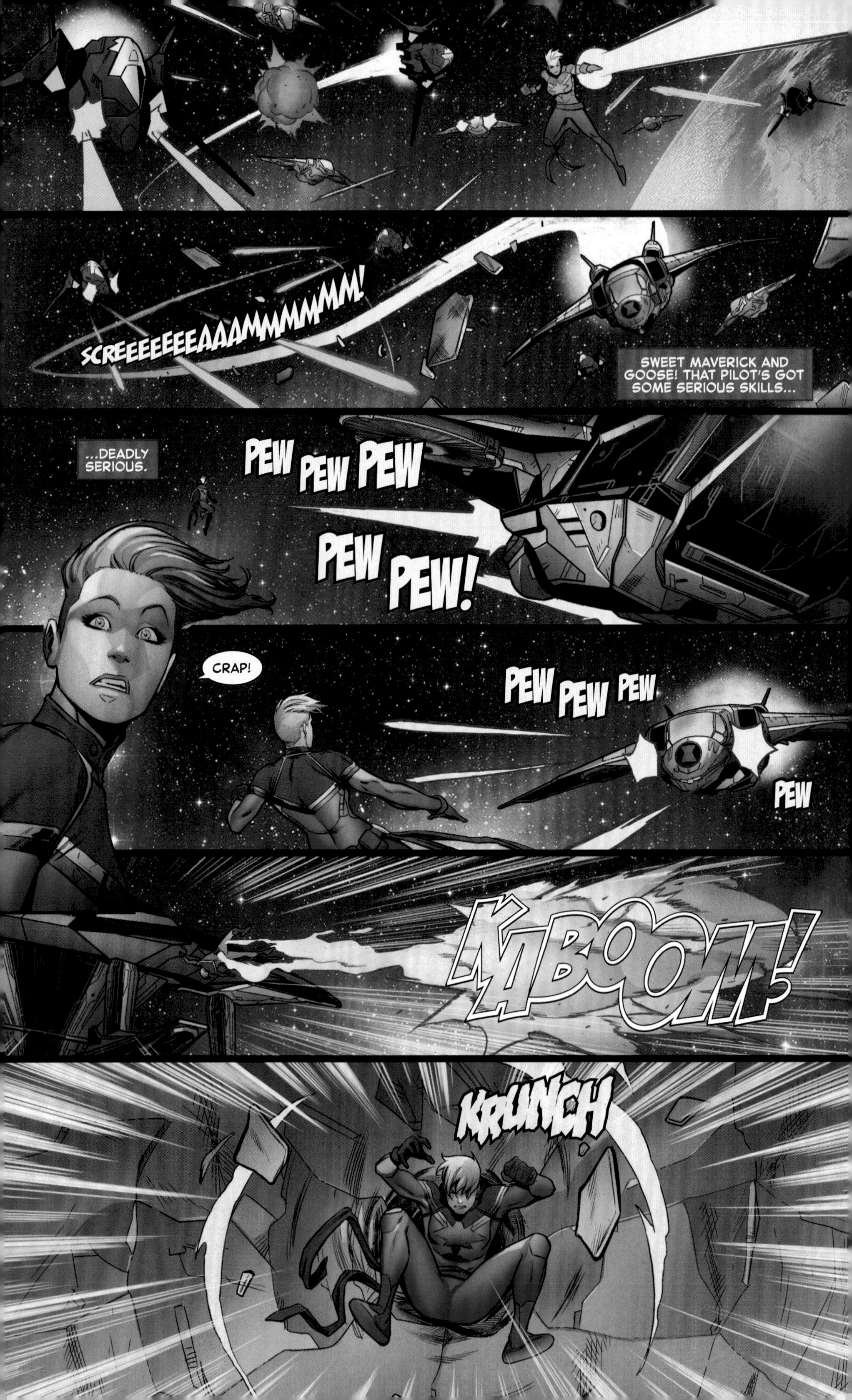
SCREEEEEEEAAAMMMMMM!
SWEET MAVERICK AND GOOSE! THAT PILOT'S GOT SOME SERIOUS SKILLS...
...DEADLY SERIOUS.
PEW PEW PEW
PEW PEW!
CRAP!
PEW PEW PEW
PEW
KABOOM!
KRUNCH

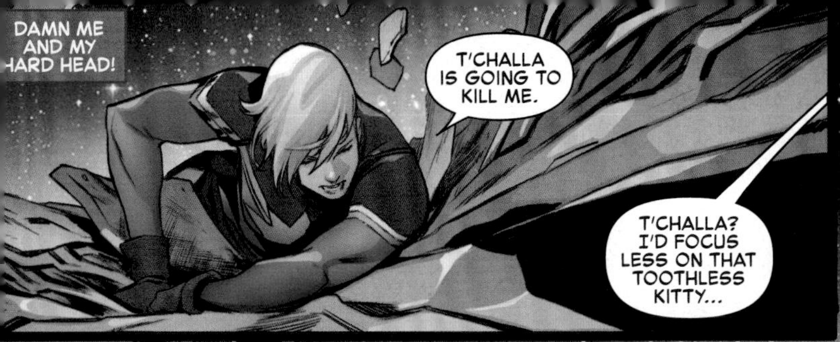
DAMN ME AND MY HARD HEAD!
T'CHALLA IS GOING TO KILL ME.
T'CHALLA? I'D FOCUS LESS ON THAT TOOTHLESS KITTY...

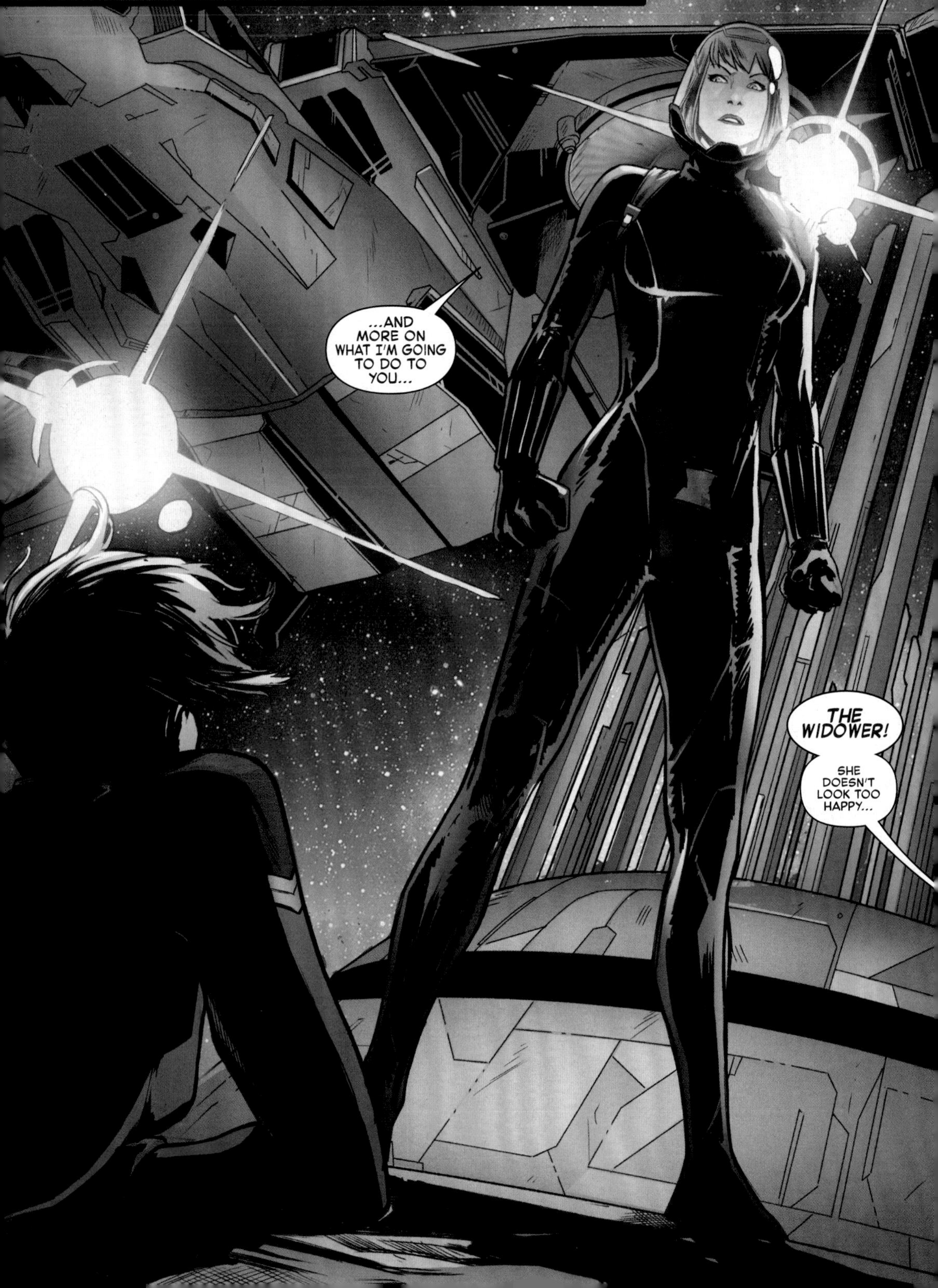
...AND MORE ON WHAT I'M GOING TO DO TO YOU...
THE WIDOWER!
SHE DOESN'T LOOK TOO HAPPY...

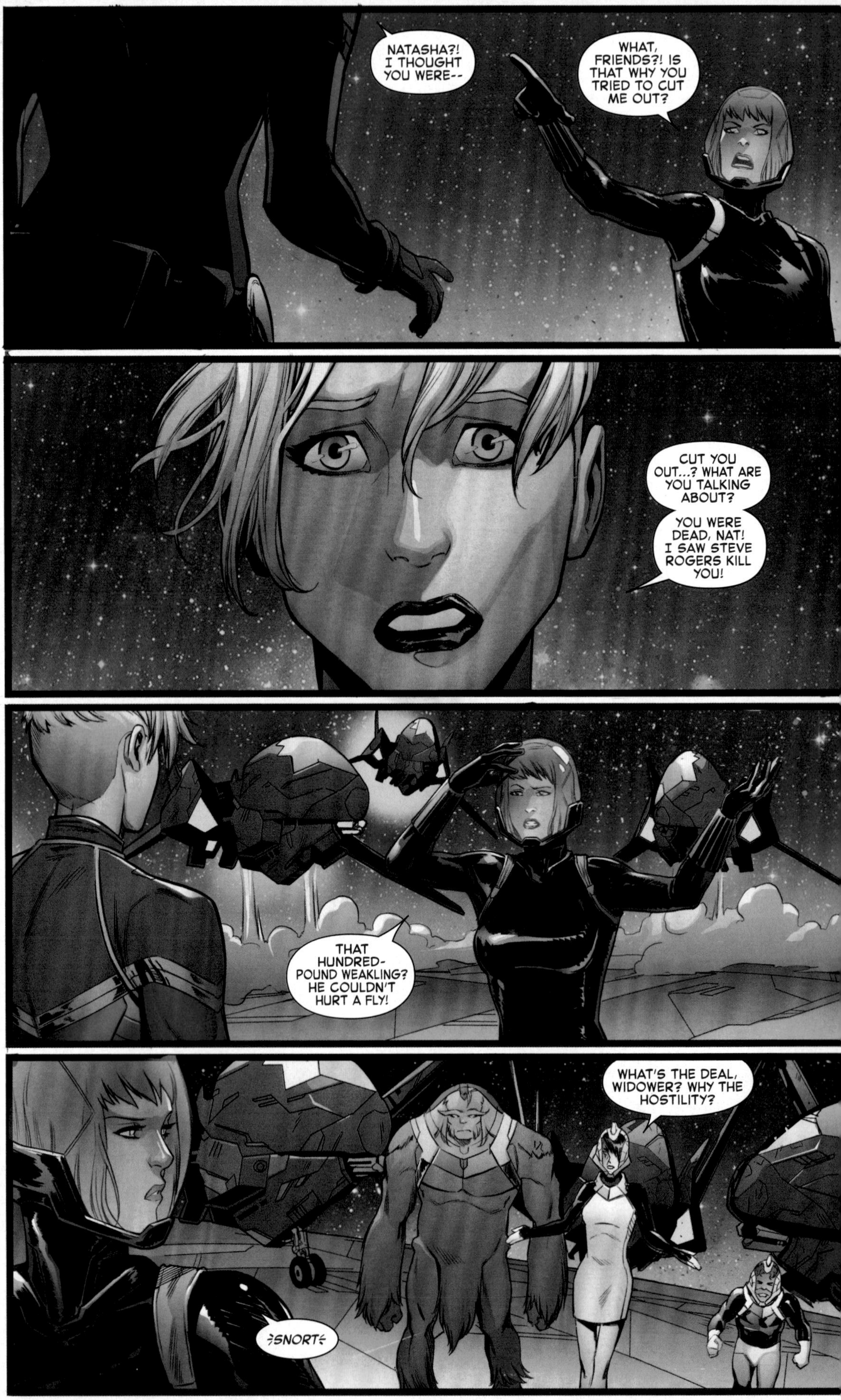
NATASHA?! I THOUGHT YOU WERE--
WHAT, FRIENDS?! IS THAT WHY YOU TRIED TO CUT ME OUT?
CUT YOU OUT...? WHAT ARE YOU TALKING ABOUT?
YOU WERE DEAD, NAT! I SAW STEVE ROGERS KILL YOU!
THAT HUNDRED-POUND WEAKLING? HE COULDN'T HURT A FLY!
WHAT'S THE DEAL, WIDOWER? WHY THE HOSTILITY?
SNORT

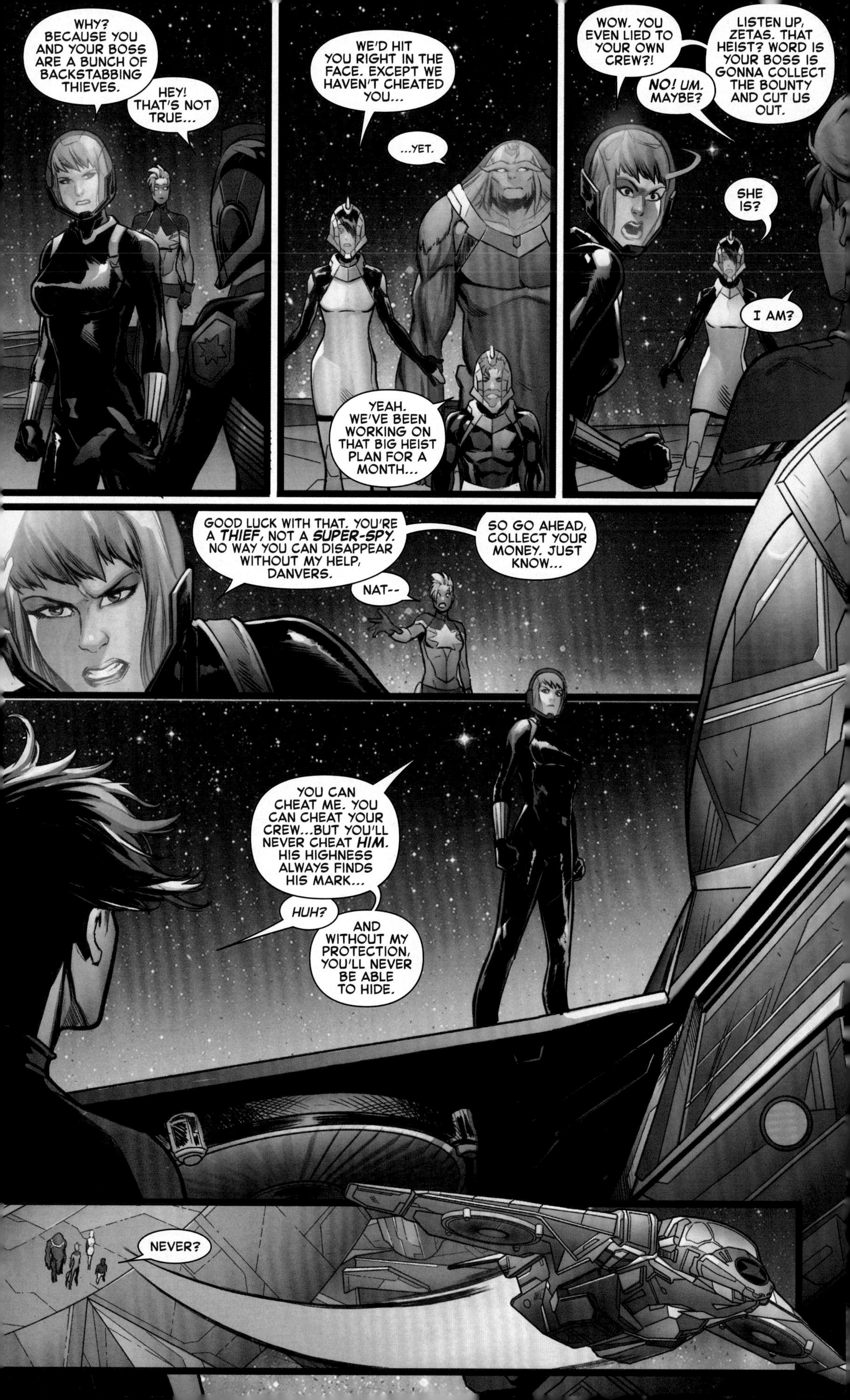
WHY? BECAUSE YOU AND YOUR BOSS ARE A BUNCH OF BACKSTABBING THIEVES.
HEY! THAT'S NOT TRUE...
WE'D HIT YOU RIGHT IN THE FACE. EXCEPT WE HAVEN'T CHEATED YOU...
...YET.
YEAH. WE'VE BEEN WORKING ON THAT BIG HEIST PLAN FOR A MONTH...
WOW. YOU EVEN LIED TO YOUR OWN CREW?!
NO! UM. MAYBE?
LISTEN UP, ZETAS. THAT HEIST? WORD IS YOUR BOSS IS GONNA COLLECT THE BOUNTY AND CUT US OUT.
SHE IS?
I AM?
GOOD LUCK WITH THAT. YOU'RE A THIEF, NOT A SUPER-SPY. NO WAY YOU CAN DISAPPEAR WITHOUT MY HELP, DANVERS.
SO GO AHEAD, COLLECT YOUR MONEY. JUST KNOW...
NAT--
YOU CAN CHEAT ME. YOU CAN CHEAT YOUR CREW...BUT YOU'LL NEVER CHEAT HIM. HIS HIGHNESS ALWAYS FINDS HIS MARK...
HUH?
AND WITHOUT MY PROTECTION, YOU'LL NEVER BE ABLE TO HIDE.
NEVER?

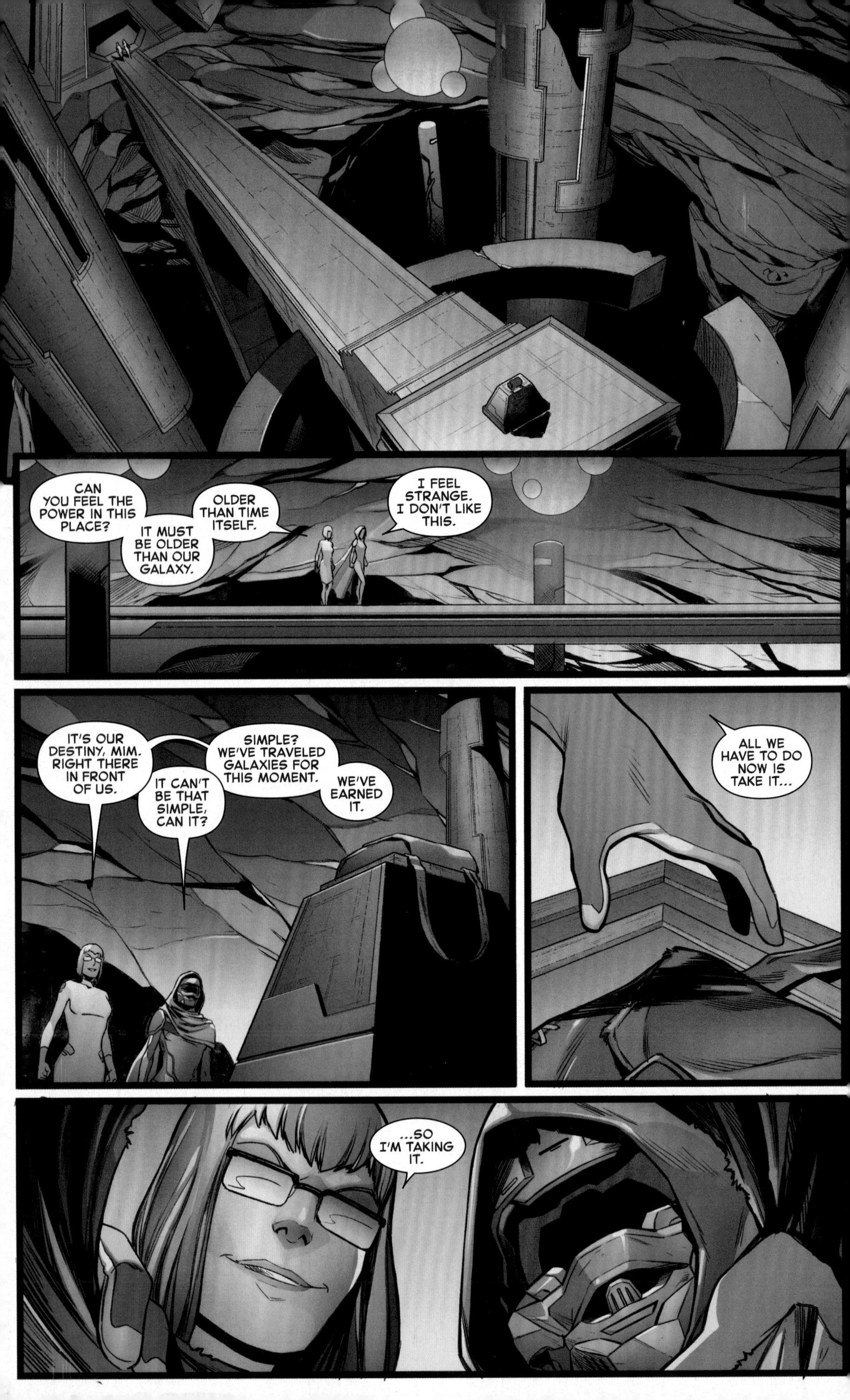
CAN YOU FEEL THE POWER IN THIS PLACE?
IT MUST BE OLDER THAN OUR GALAXY.
OLDER THAN TIME ITSELF.
I FEEL STRANGE. I DON'T LIKE THIS.
IT'S OUR DESTINY, MIM. RIGHT THERE IN FRONT OF US.
IT CAN'T BE THAT SIMPLE, CAN IT?
SIMPLE? WE'VE TRAVELED GALAXIES FOR THIS MOMENT.
WE'VE EARNED IT.
ALL WE HAVE TO DO NOW IS TAKE IT...
...SO I'M TAKING IT.

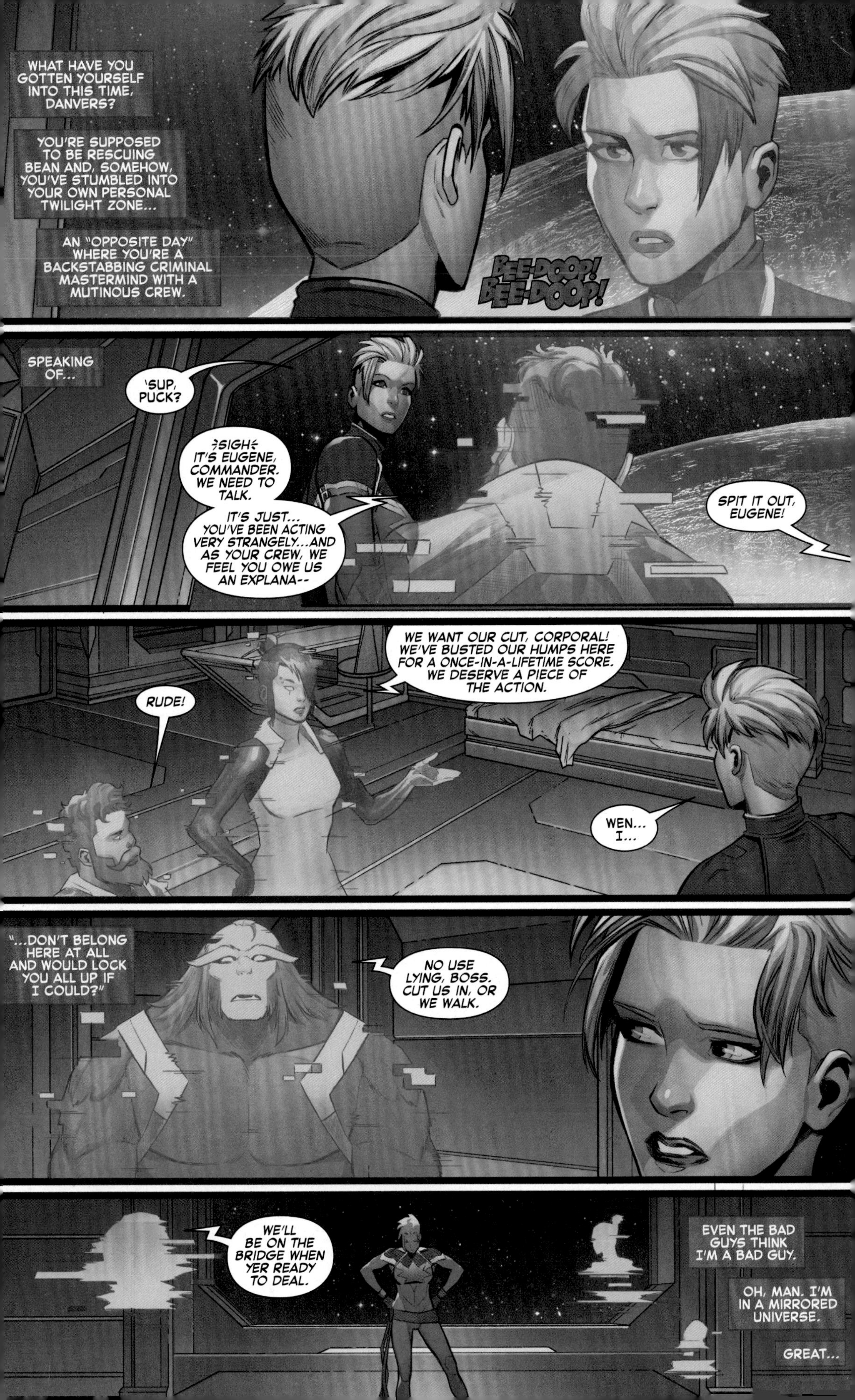

WHAT HAVE YOU GOTTEN YOURSELF INTO THIS TIME, DANVERS?
YOU'RE SUPPOSED TO BE RESCUING BEAN AND, SOMEHOW, YOU'VE STUMBLED INTO YOUR OWN PERSONAL TWILIGHT ZONE...
AN "OPPOSITE DAY" WHERE YOU'RE A BACKSTABBING CRIMINAL MASTERMIND WITH A MUTINOUS CREW.
BEE-DOOP! BEE-DOOP!
SPEAKING OF...
'SUP, PUCK?
SIGH IT'S EUGENE, COMMANDER. WE NEED TO TALK.
IT'S JUST... YOU'VE BEEN ACTING VERY STRANGELY...AND AS YOUR CREW, WE FEEL YOU OWE US AN EXPLANA--
SPIT IT OUT, EUGENE!
WE WANT OUR CUT, CORPORAL! WE'VE BUSTED OUR HUMPS HERE FOR A ONCE-IN-A-LIFETIME SCORE. WE DESERVE A PIECE OF THE ACTION.
RUDE!
WEN... I...
"...DON'T BELONG HERE AT ALL AND WOULD LOCK YOU ALL UP IF I COULD?"
NO USE LYING, BOSS. CUT US IN, OR WE WALK.
WE'LL BE ON THE BRIDGE WHEN YER READY TO DEAL.
EVEN THE BAD GUYS THINK I'M A BAD GUY.
OH, MAN. I'M IN A MIRRORED UNIVERSE.
GREAT...

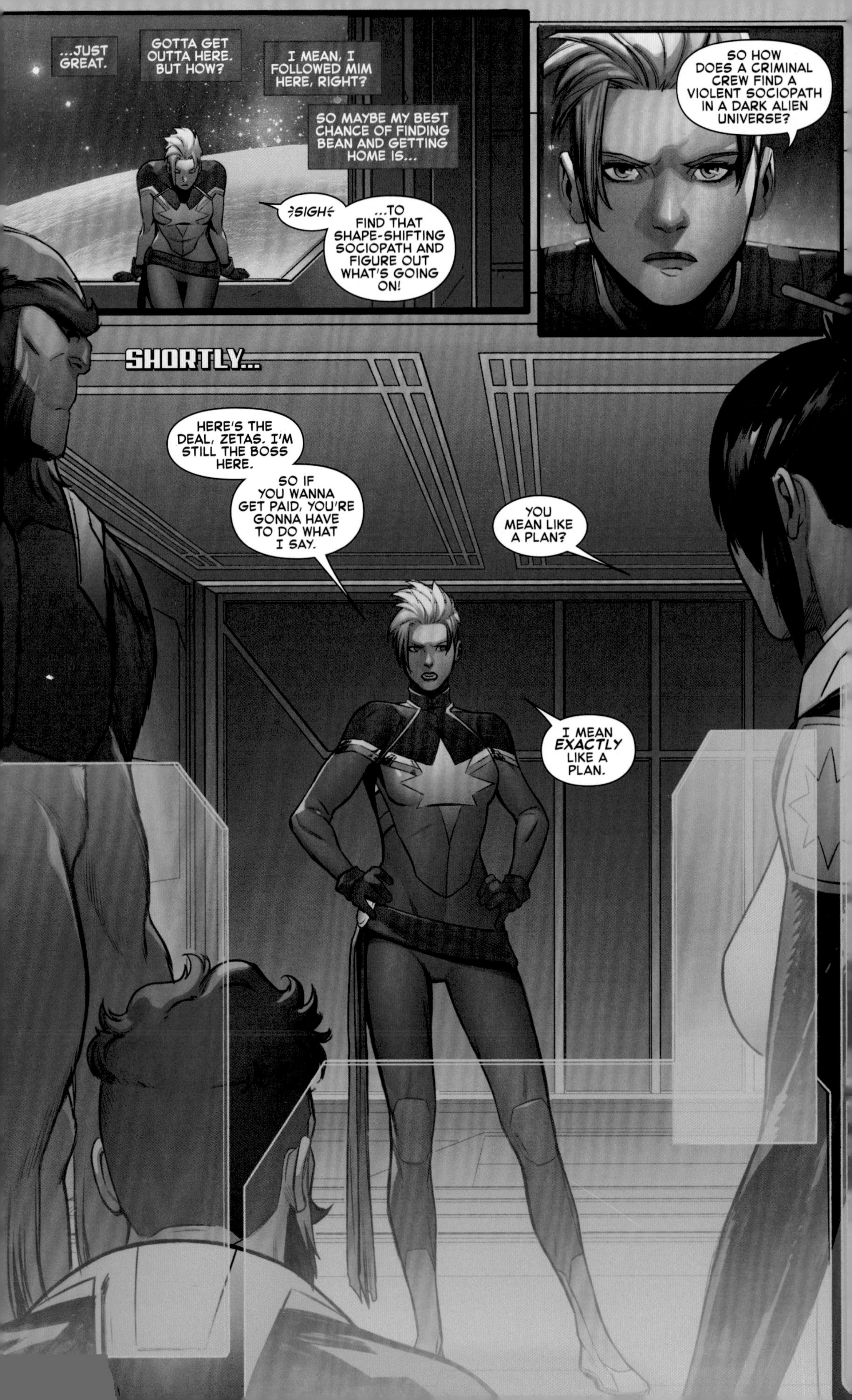

...JUST GREAT.
GOTTA GET OUTTA HERE. BUT HOW?
I MEAN, I FOLLOWED MIM HERE, RIGHT?
SO MAYBE MY BEST CHANCE OF FINDING BEAN AND GETTING HOME IS...
SIGH
...TO FIND THAT SHAPE-SHIFTING SOCIOPATH AND FIGURE OUT WHAT'S GOING ON!
SO HOW DOES A CRIMINAL CREW FIND A VIOLENT SOCIOPATH IN A DARK ALIEN UNIVERSE?
SHORTLY...
HERE'S THE DEAL, ZETAS. I'M STILL THE BOSS HERE.
SO IF YOU WANNA GET PAID, YOU'RE GONNA HAVE TO DO WHAT I SAY.
YOU MEAN LIKE A PLAN?
I MEAN *EXACTLY* LIKE A PLAN.

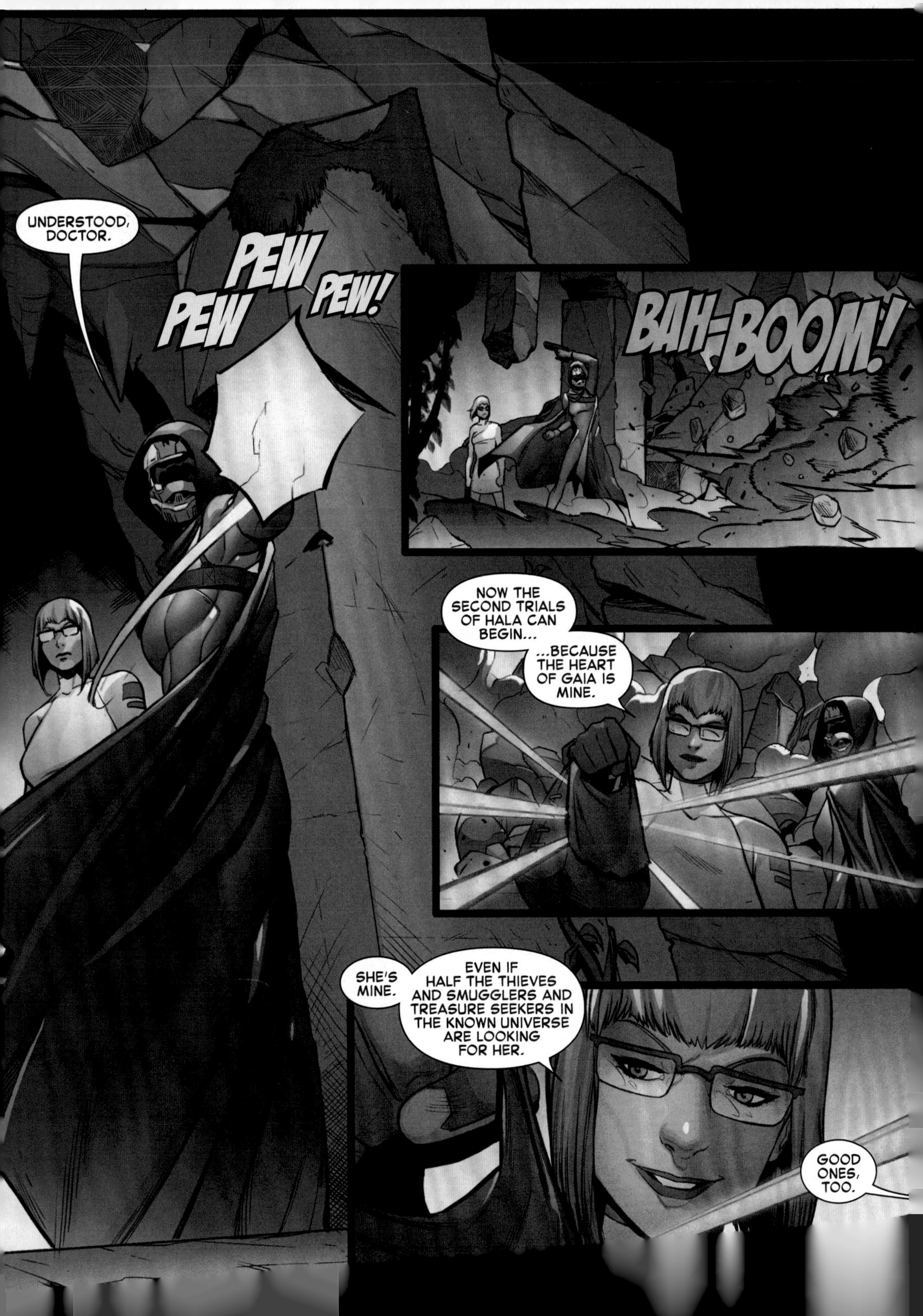
UNDERSTOOD, DOCTOR.
PEW PEW PEW!
BAH-BOOM!
NOW THE SECOND TRIALS OF HALA CAN BEGIN...
...BECAUSE THE HEART OF GAIA IS MINE.
SHE'S MINE.
EVEN IF HALF THE THIEVES AND SMUGGLERS AND TREASURE SEEKERS IN THE KNOWN UNIVERSE ARE LOOKING FOR HER.
GOOD ONES, TOO.

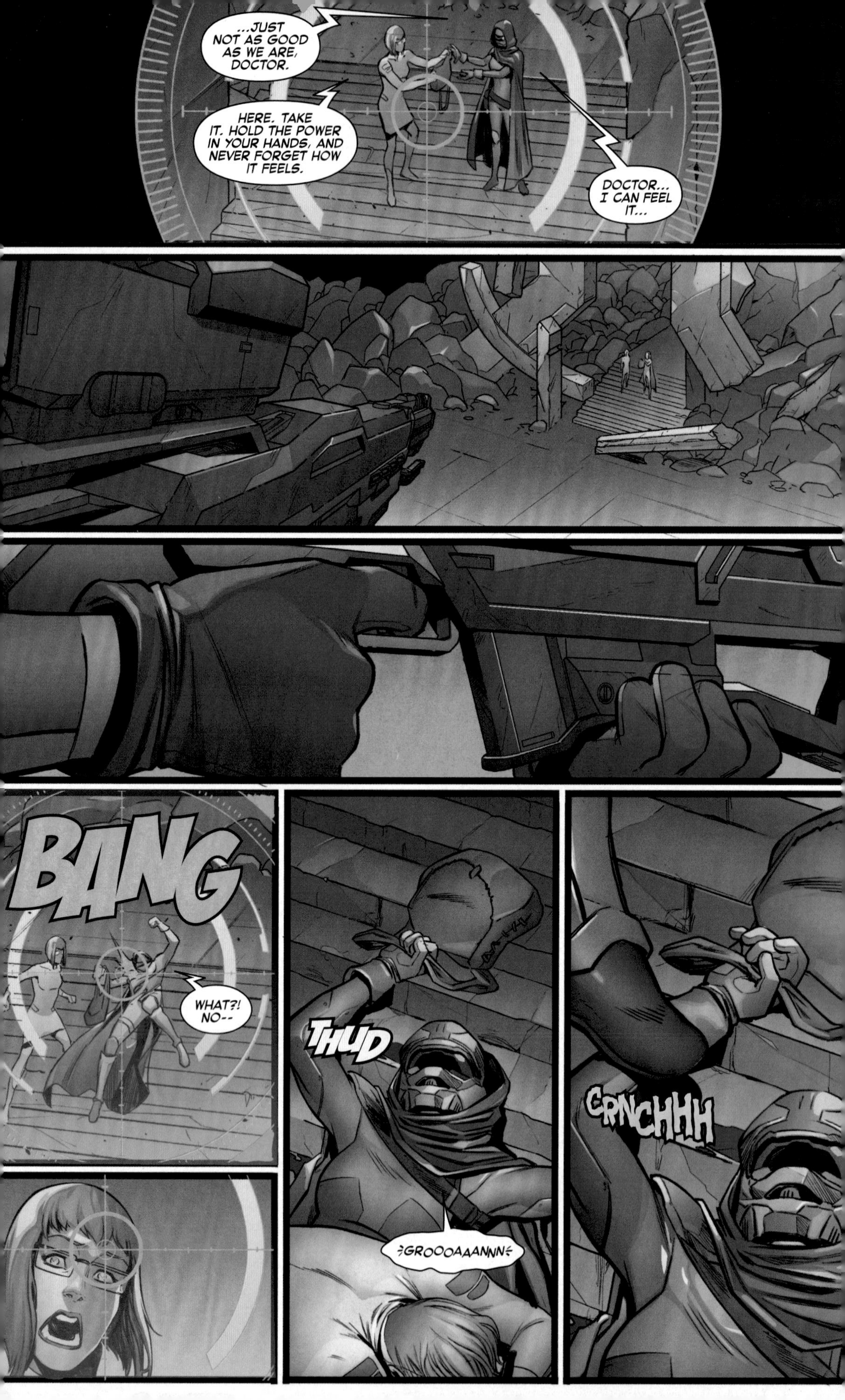
...JUST NOT AS GOOD AS WE ARE, DOCTOR.
HERE. TAKE IT. HOLD THE POWER IN YOUR HANDS, AND NEVER FORGET HOW IT FEELS.
DOCTOR... I CAN FEEL IT...
BANG
WHAT?! NO--
THUD
GROOOAAANNN
CRNCHHH

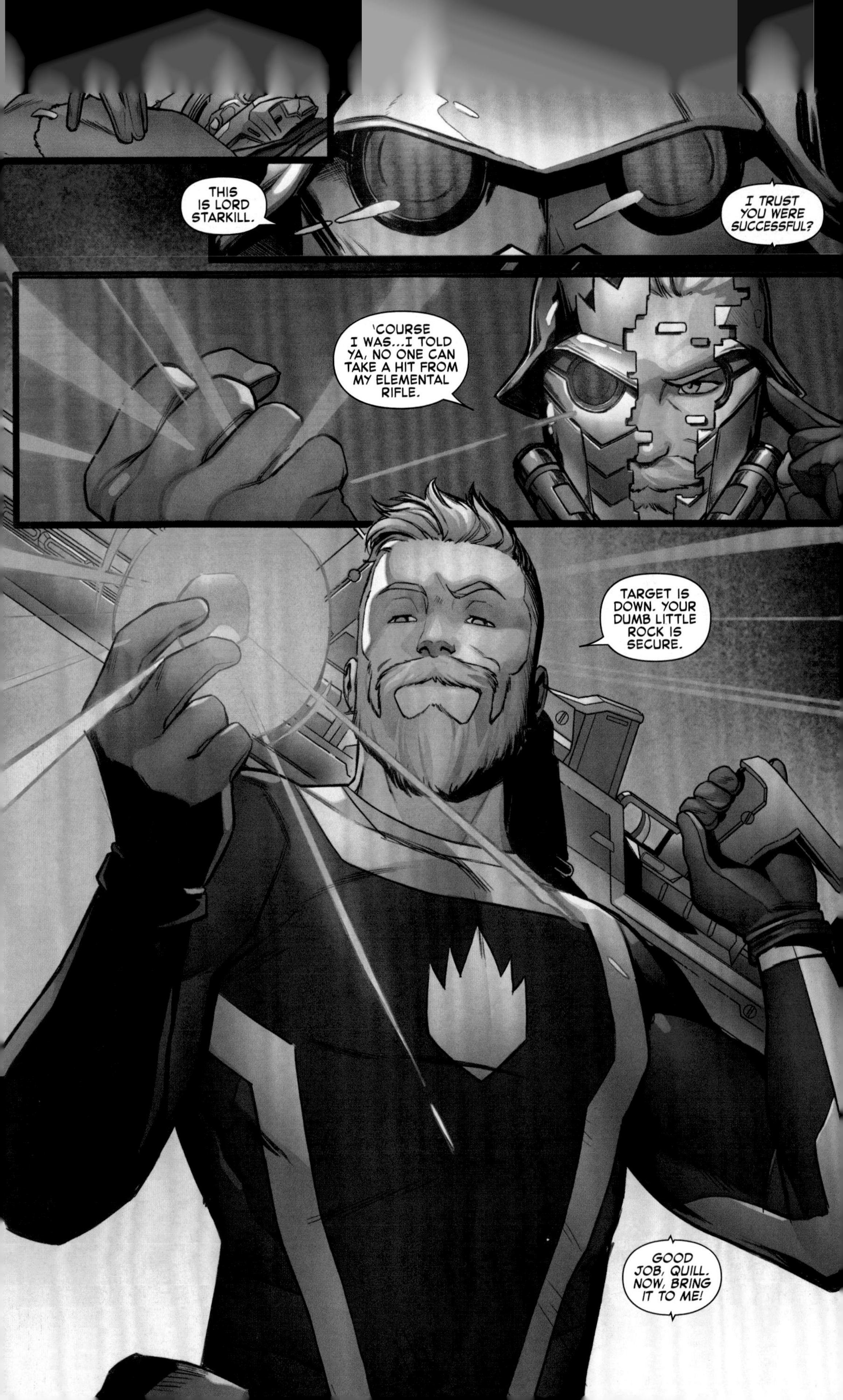
THIS IS LORD STARKILL.
I TRUST YOU WERE SUCCESSFUL?
'COURSE I WAS...I TOLD YA, NO ONE CAN TAKE A HIT FROM MY ELEMENTAL RIFLE.
TARGET IS DOWN. YOUR DUMB LITTLE ROCK IS SECURE.
GOOD JOB, QUILL. NOW, BRING IT TO ME!

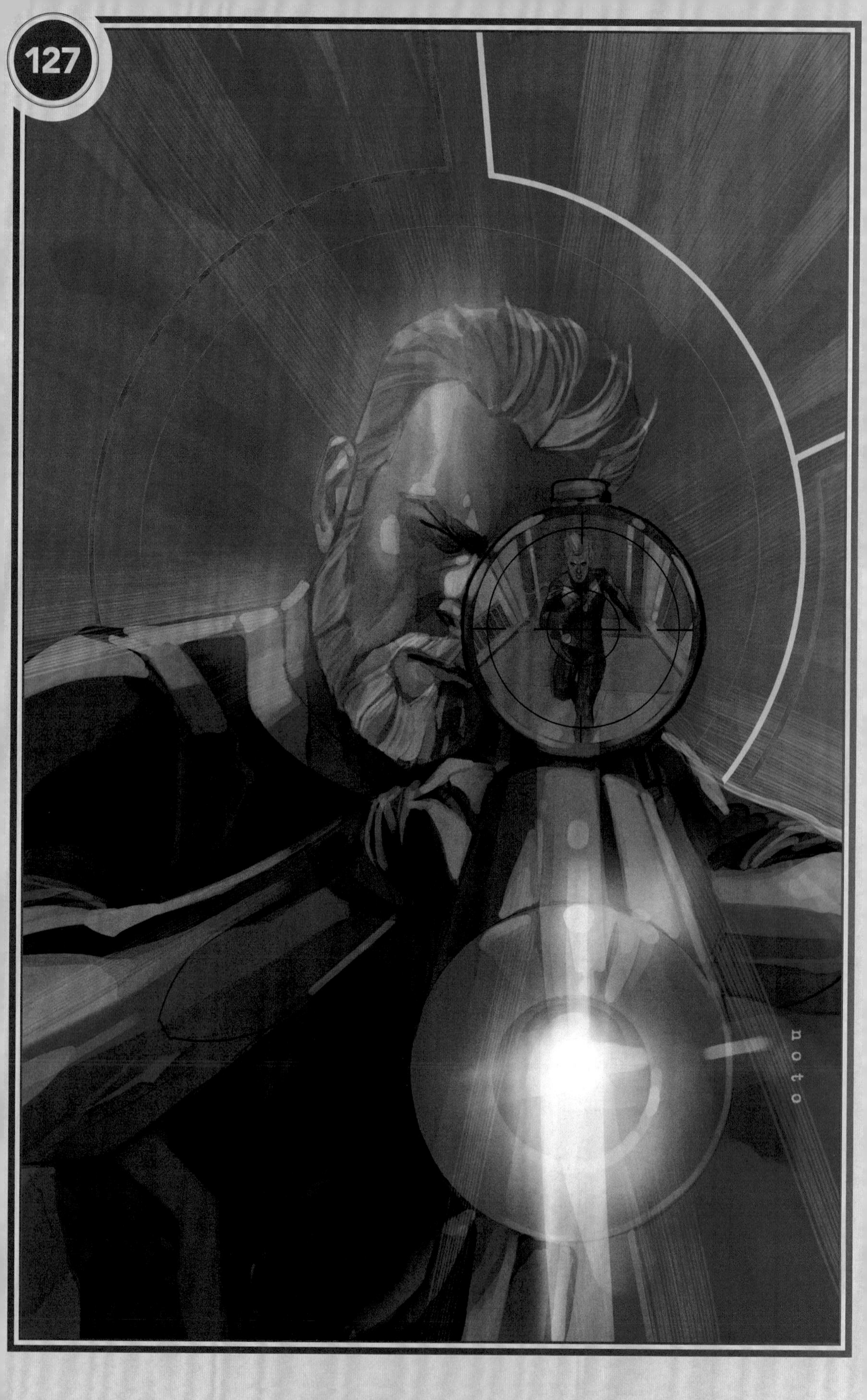
127
noto

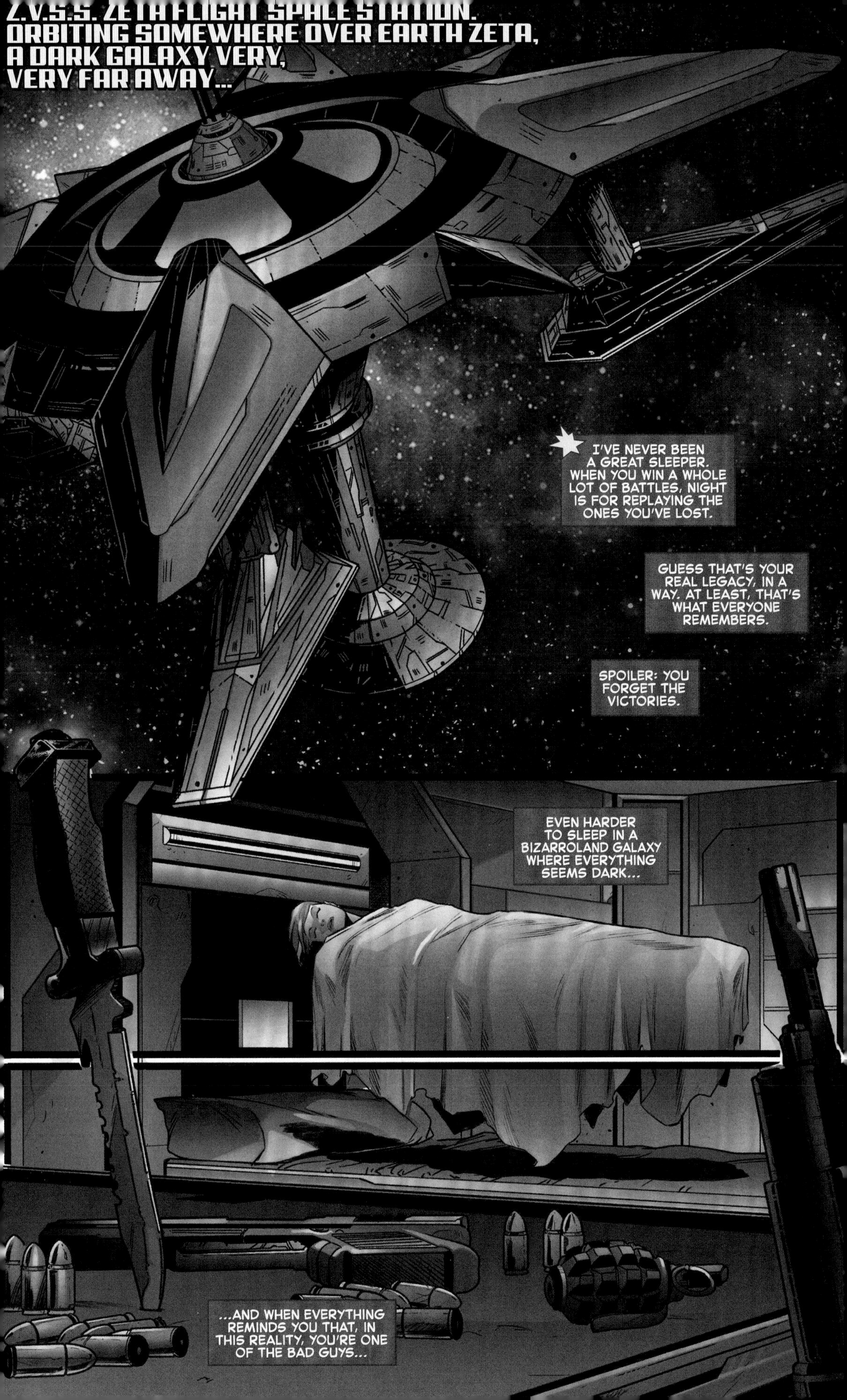
Z.V.S.S. ZETA FLIGHT SPACE STATION.
ORBITING SOMEWHERE OVER EARTH ZETA, A DARK GALAXY VERY, VERY FAR AWAY...
I'VE NEVER BEEN A GREAT SLEEPER. WHEN YOU WIN A WHOLE LOT OF BATTLES, NIGHT IS FOR REPLAYING THE ONES YOU'VE LOST.
GUESS THAT'S YOUR REAL LEGACY, IN A WAY. AT LEAST, THAT'S WHAT EVERYONE REMEMBERS.
SPOILER: YOU FORGET THE VICTORIES.
EVEN HARDER TO SLEEP IN A BIZARROLAND GALAXY WHERE EVERYTHING SEEMS DARK...
...AND WHEN EVERYTHING REMINDS YOU THAT, IN THIS REALITY, YOU'RE ONE OF THE BAD GUYS...

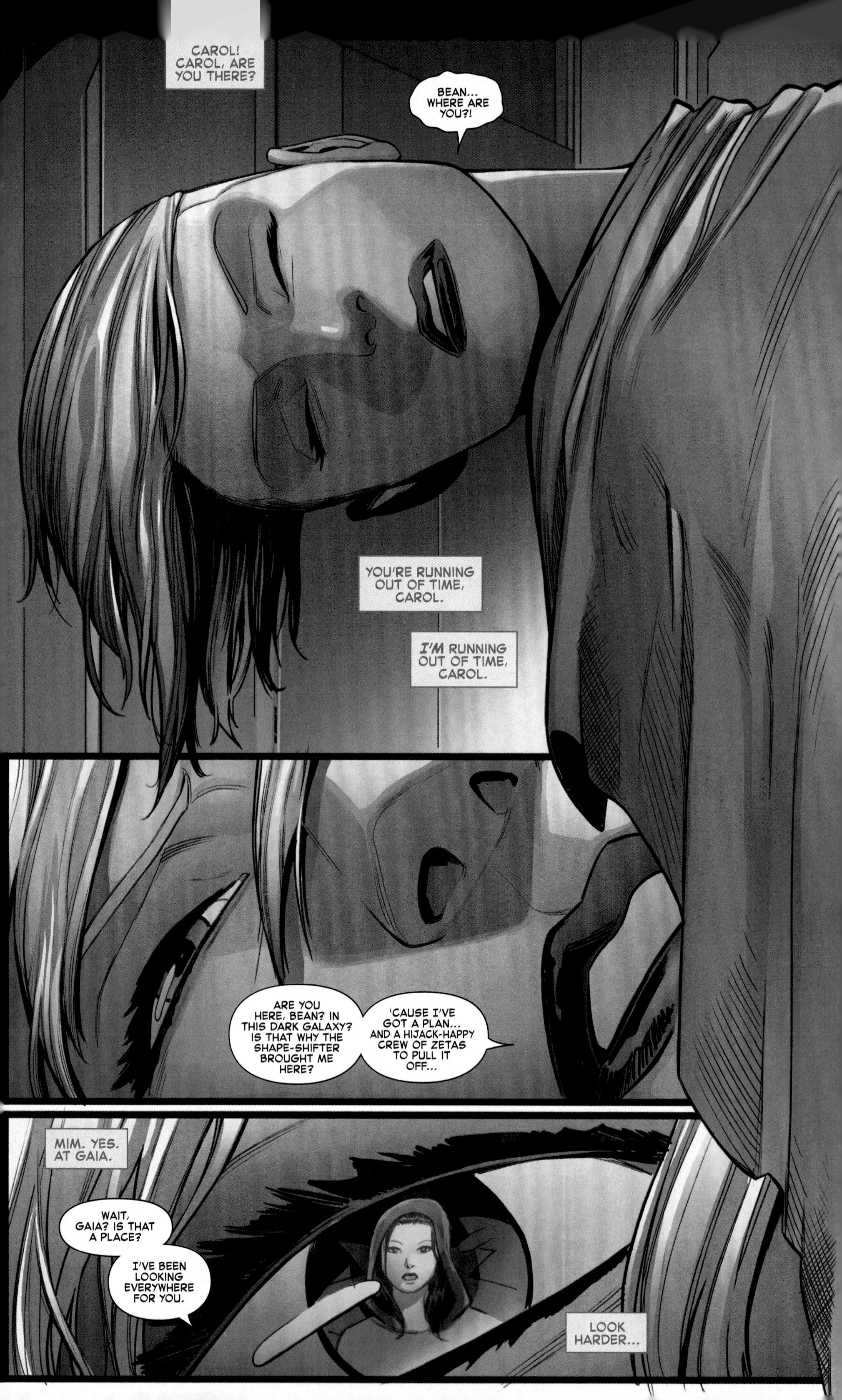

CAROL! CAROL, ARE YOU THERE?
BEAN... WHERE ARE YOU?!
YOU'RE RUNNING OUT OF TIME, CAROL.
I'M RUNNING OUT OF TIME, CAROL.
ARE YOU HERE, BEAN? IN THIS DARK GALAXY? IS THAT WHY THE SHAPE-SHIFTER BROUGHT ME HERE?
'CAUSE I'VE GOT A PLAN... AND A HIJACK-HAPPY CREW OF ZETAS TO PULL IT OFF...
MIM. YES. AT GAIA.
WAIT, GAIA? IS THAT A PLACE?
I'VE BEEN LOOKING EVERYWHERE FOR YOU.
LOOK HARDER...

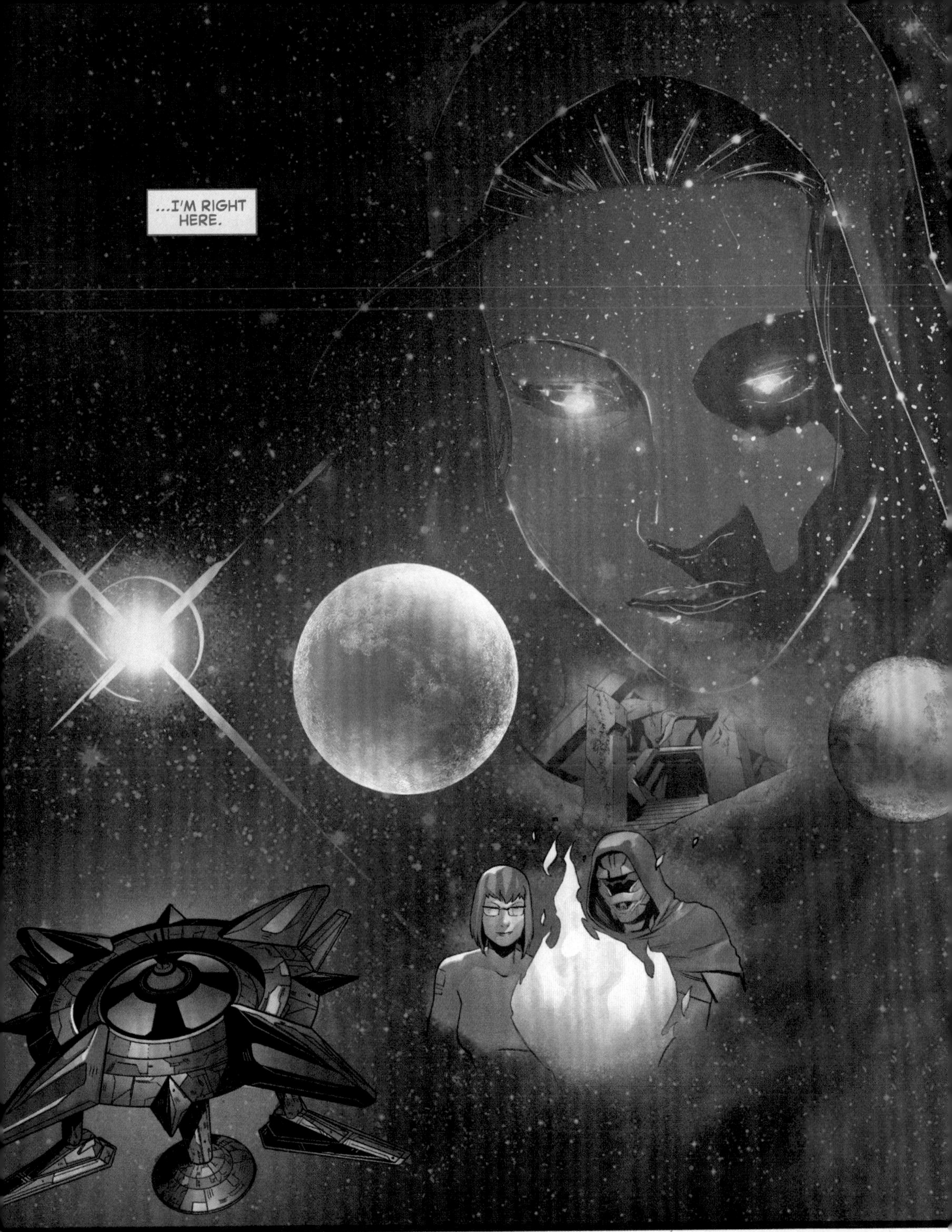
...I'M RIGHT HERE.

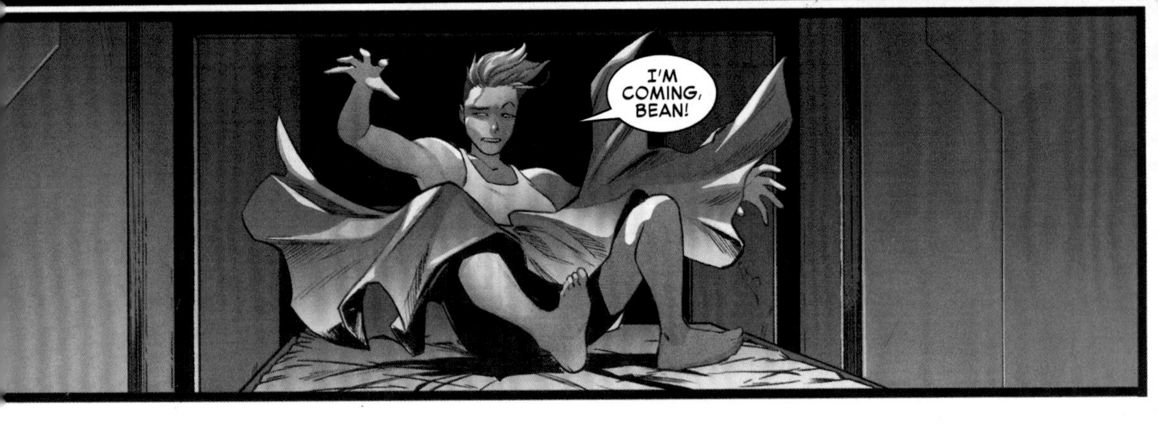
I'M COMING, BEAN!

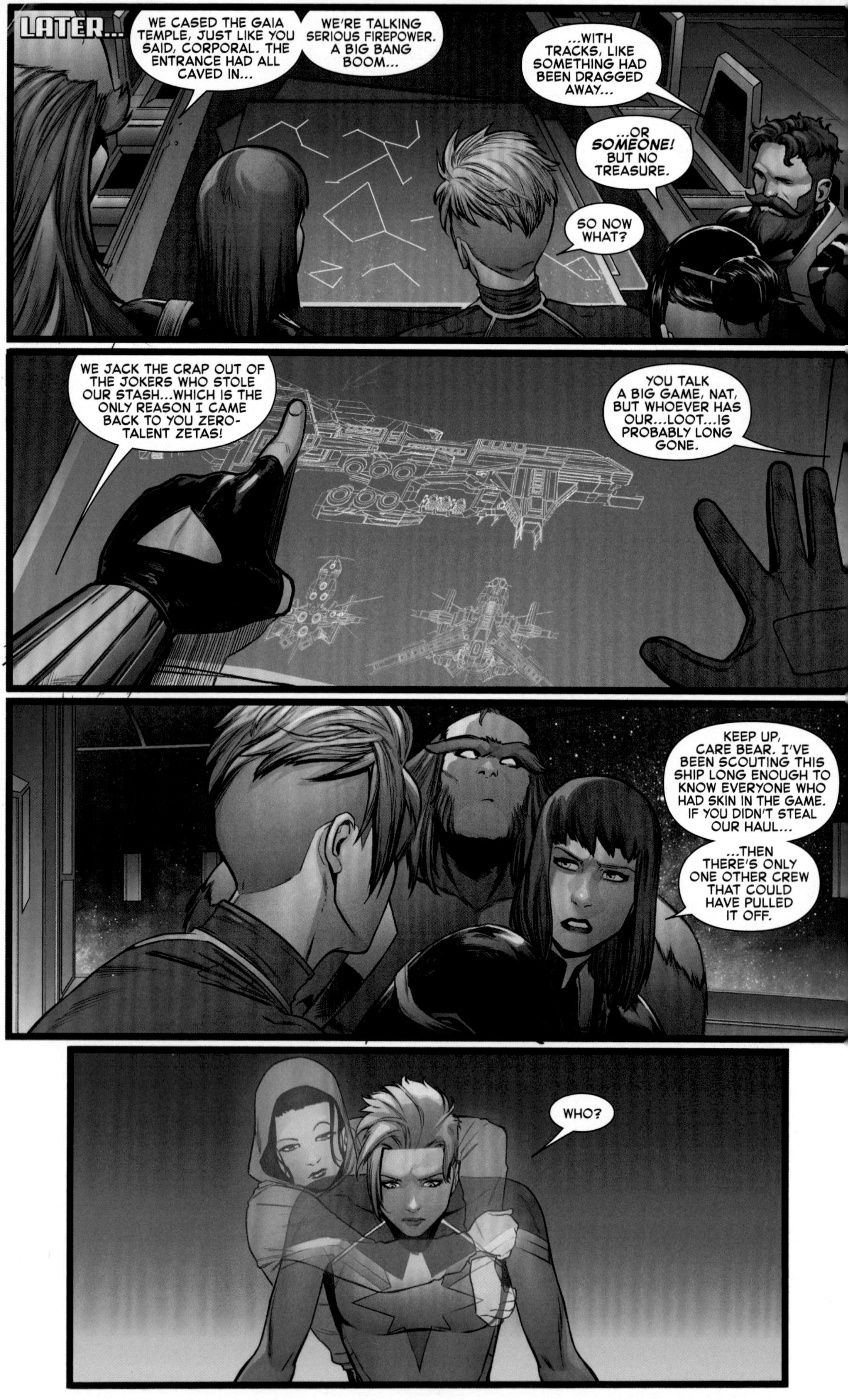
LATER...
WE CASED THE GAIA TEMPLE, JUST LIKE YOU SAID, CORPORAL. THE ENTRANCE HAD ALL CAVED IN...
WE'RE TALKING SERIOUS FIREPOWER. A BIG BANG BOOM...
...WITH TRACKS, LIKE SOMETHING HAD BEEN DRAGGED AWAY...
...OR SOMEONE! BUT NO TREASURE.
SO NOW WHAT?
WE JACK THE CRAP OUT OF THE JOKERS WHO STOLE OUR STASH...WHICH IS THE ONLY REASON I CAME BACK TO YOU ZERO-TALENT ZETAS!
YOU TALK A BIG GAME, NAT, BUT WHOEVER HAS OUR...LOOT...IS PROBABLY LONG GONE.
KEEP UP, CARE BEAR. I'VE BEEN SCOUTING THIS SHIP LONG ENOUGH TO KNOW EVERYONE WHO HAD SKIN IN THE GAME. IF YOU DIDN'T STEAL OUR HAUL...
...THEN THERE'S ONLY ONE OTHER CREW THAT COULD HAVE PULLED IT OFF.
WHO?

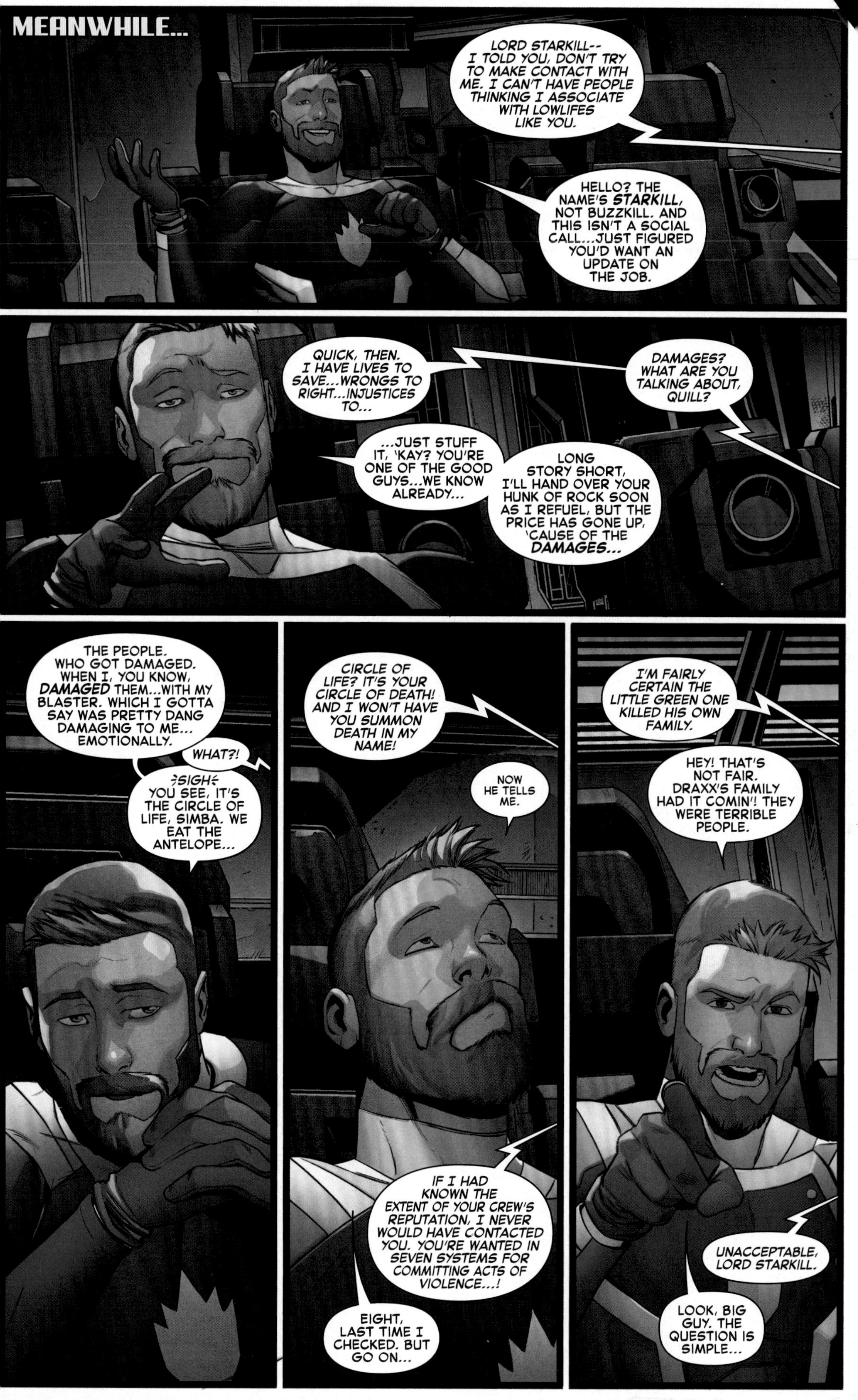
MEANWHILE...
LORD STARKILL-- I TOLD YOU, DON'T TRY TO MAKE CONTACT WITH ME. I CAN'T HAVE PEOPLE THINKING I ASSOCIATE WITH LOWLIFES LIKE YOU.
HELLO? THE NAME'S STARKILL, NOT BUZZKILL. AND THIS ISN'T A SOCIAL CALL...JUST FIGURED YOU'D WANT AN UPDATE ON THE JOB.
QUICK, THEN. I HAVE LIVES TO SAVE...WRONGS TO RIGHT...INJUSTICES TO...
...JUST STUFF IT, 'KAY? YOU'RE ONE OF THE GOOD GUYS...WE KNOW ALREADY...
LONG STORY SHORT, I'LL HAND OVER YOUR HUNK OF ROCK SOON AS I REFUEL, BUT THE PRICE HAS GONE UP, 'CAUSE OF THE DAMAGES...
DAMAGES? WHAT ARE YOU TALKING ABOUT, QUILL?
THE PEOPLE. WHO GOT DAMAGED. WHEN I, YOU KNOW, DAMAGED THEM...WITH MY BLASTER. WHICH I GOTTA SAY WAS PRETTY DANG DAMAGING TO ME... EMOTIONALLY.
WHAT?!
SIGH YOU SEE, IT'S THE CIRCLE OF LIFE, SIMBA. WE EAT THE ANTELOPE...
CIRCLE OF LIFE? IT'S YOUR CIRCLE OF DEATH! AND I WON'T HAVE YOU SUMMON DEATH IN MY NAME!
NOW HE TELLS ME.
IF I HAD KNOWN THE EXTENT OF YOUR CREW'S REPUTATION, I NEVER WOULD HAVE CONTACTED YOU. YOU'RE WANTED IN SEVEN SYSTEMS FOR COMMITTING ACTS OF VIOLENCE...!
EIGHT, LAST TIME I CHECKED. BUT GO ON...
I'M FAIRLY CERTAIN THE LITTLE GREEN ONE KILLED HIS OWN FAMILY.
HEY! THAT'S NOT FAIR. DRAXX'S FAMILY HAD IT COMIN'! THEY WERE TERRIBLE PEOPLE.
UNACCEPTABLE, LORD STARKILL.
LOOK, BIG GUY. THE QUESTION IS SIMPLE...

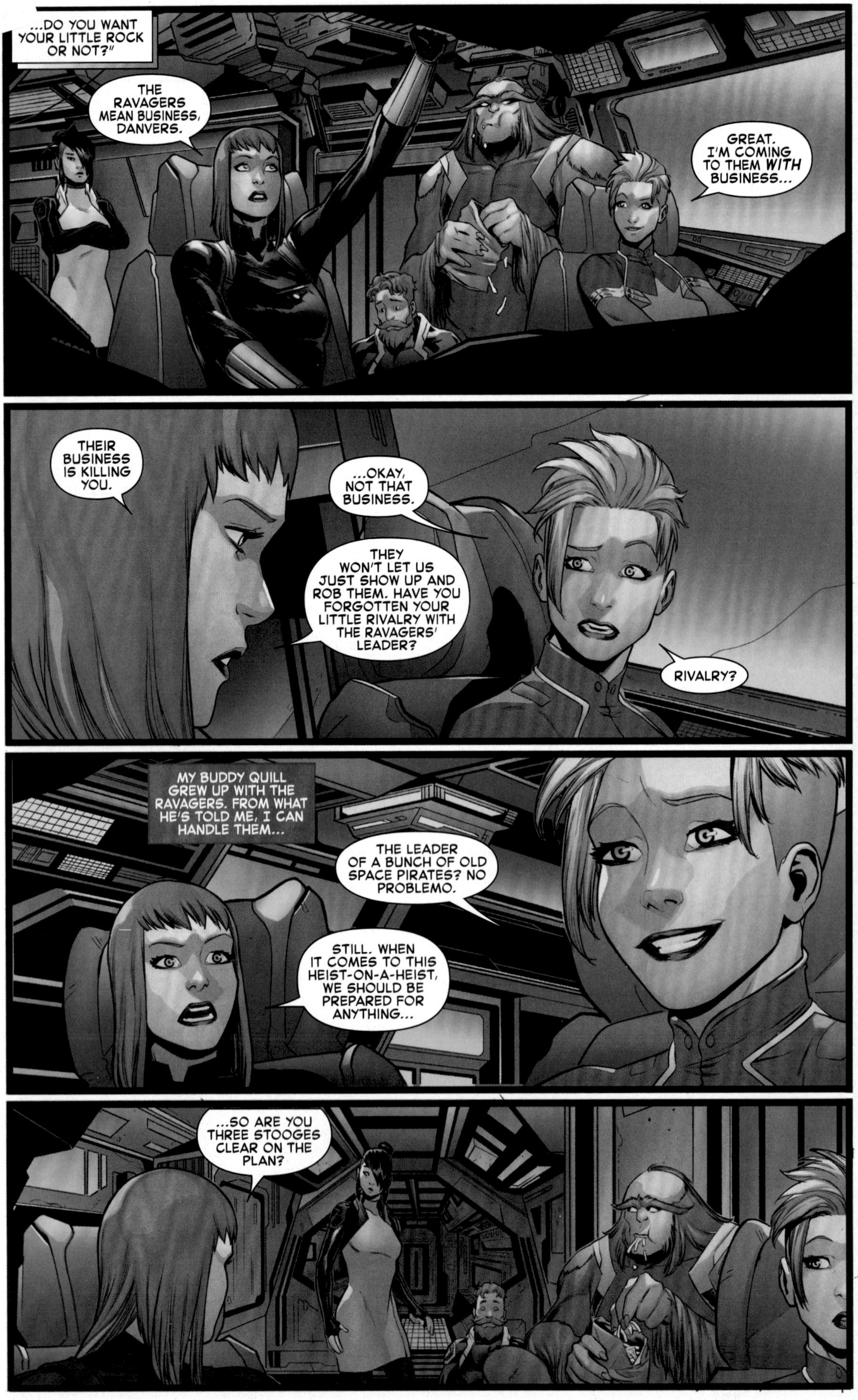

...DO YOU WANT YOUR LITTLE ROCK OR NOT?"
THE RAVAGERS MEAN BUSINESS, DANVERS.
GREAT. I'M COMING TO THEM *WITH* BUSINESS...
THEIR BUSINESS IS KILLING YOU.
...OKAY, NOT THAT BUSINESS.
THEY WON'T LET US JUST SHOW UP AND ROB THEM. HAVE YOU FORGOTTEN YOUR LITTLE RIVALRY WITH THE RAVAGERS' LEADER?
RIVALRY?
MY BUDDY QUILL GREW UP WITH THE RAVAGERS. FROM WHAT HE'S TOLD ME, I CAN HANDLE THEM...
THE LEADER OF A BUNCH OF OLD SPACE PIRATES? NO PROBLEMO.
STILL. WHEN IT COMES TO THIS HEIST-ON-A-HEIST, WE SHOULD BE PREPARED FOR ANYTHING...
...SO ARE YOU THREE STOOGES CLEAR ON THE PLAN?

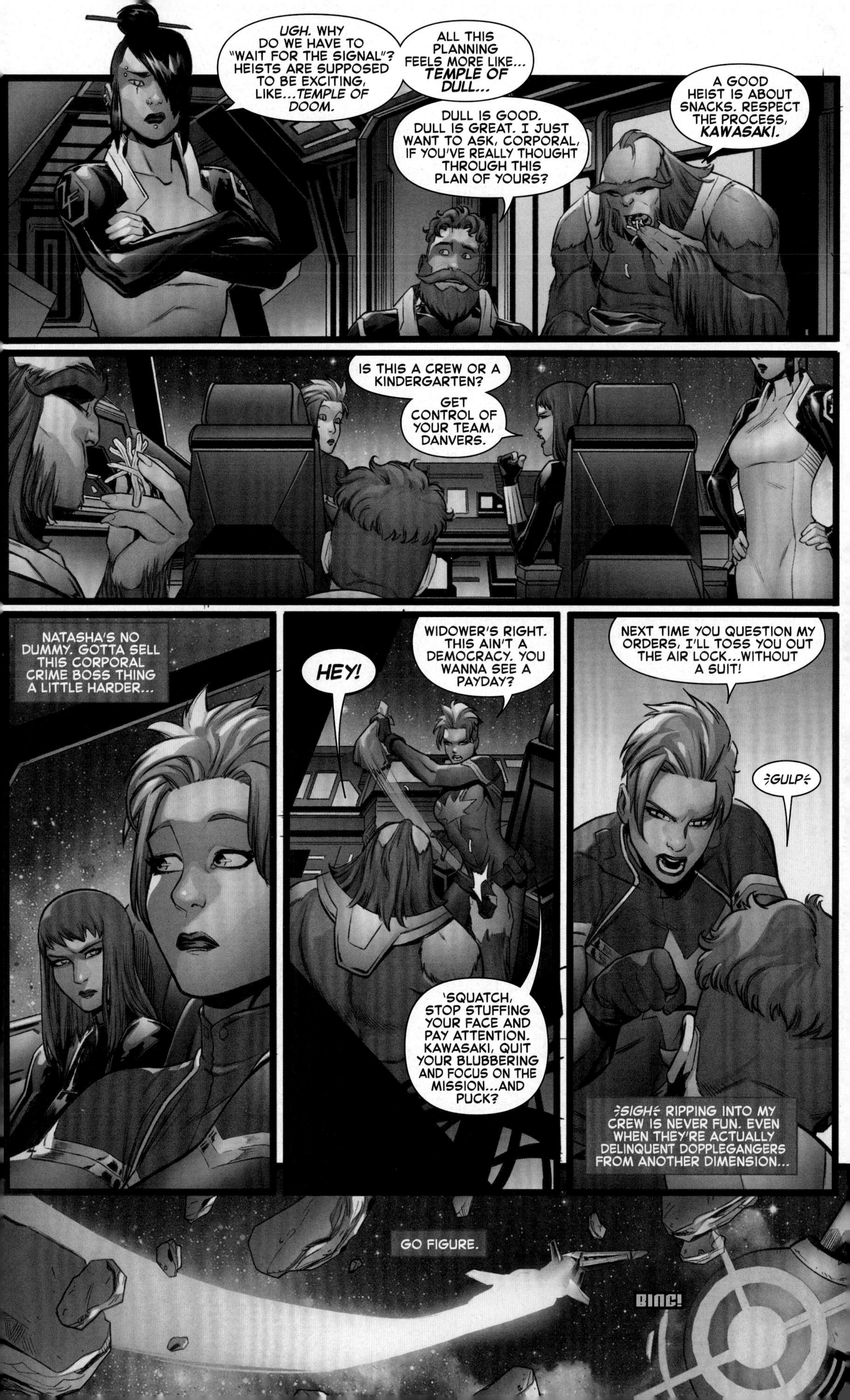
UGH. WHY DO WE HAVE TO "WAIT FOR THE SIGNAL"? HEISTS ARE SUPPOSED TO BE EXCITING, LIKE...TEMPLE OF DOOM.
ALL THIS PLANNING FEELS MORE LIKE... TEMPLE OF DULL...
DULL IS GOOD. DULL IS GREAT. I JUST WANT TO ASK, CORPORAL, IF YOU'VE REALLY THOUGHT THROUGH THIS PLAN OF YOURS?
A GOOD HEIST IS ABOUT SNACKS. RESPECT THE PROCESS, KAWASAKI.
IS THIS A CREW OR A KINDERGARTEN?
GET CONTROL OF YOUR TEAM, DANVERS.
NATASHA'S NO DUMMY. GOTTA SELL THIS CORPORAL CRIME BOSS THING A LITTLE HARDER...
HEY!
WIDOWER'S RIGHT. THIS AIN'T A DEMOCRACY. YOU WANNA SEE A PAYDAY?
'SQUATCH, STOP STUFFING YOUR FACE AND PAY ATTENTION. KAWASAKI, QUIT YOUR BLUBBERING AND FOCUS ON THE MISSION...AND PUCK?
NEXT TIME YOU QUESTION MY ORDERS, I'LL TOSS YOU OUT THE AIR LOCK...WITHOUT A SUIT!
GULP
SIGH RIPPING INTO MY CREW IS NEVER FUN. EVEN WHEN THEY'RE ACTUALLY DELINQUENT DOPPLEGANGERS FROM ANOTHER DIMENSION...
GO FIGURE.
BINC!

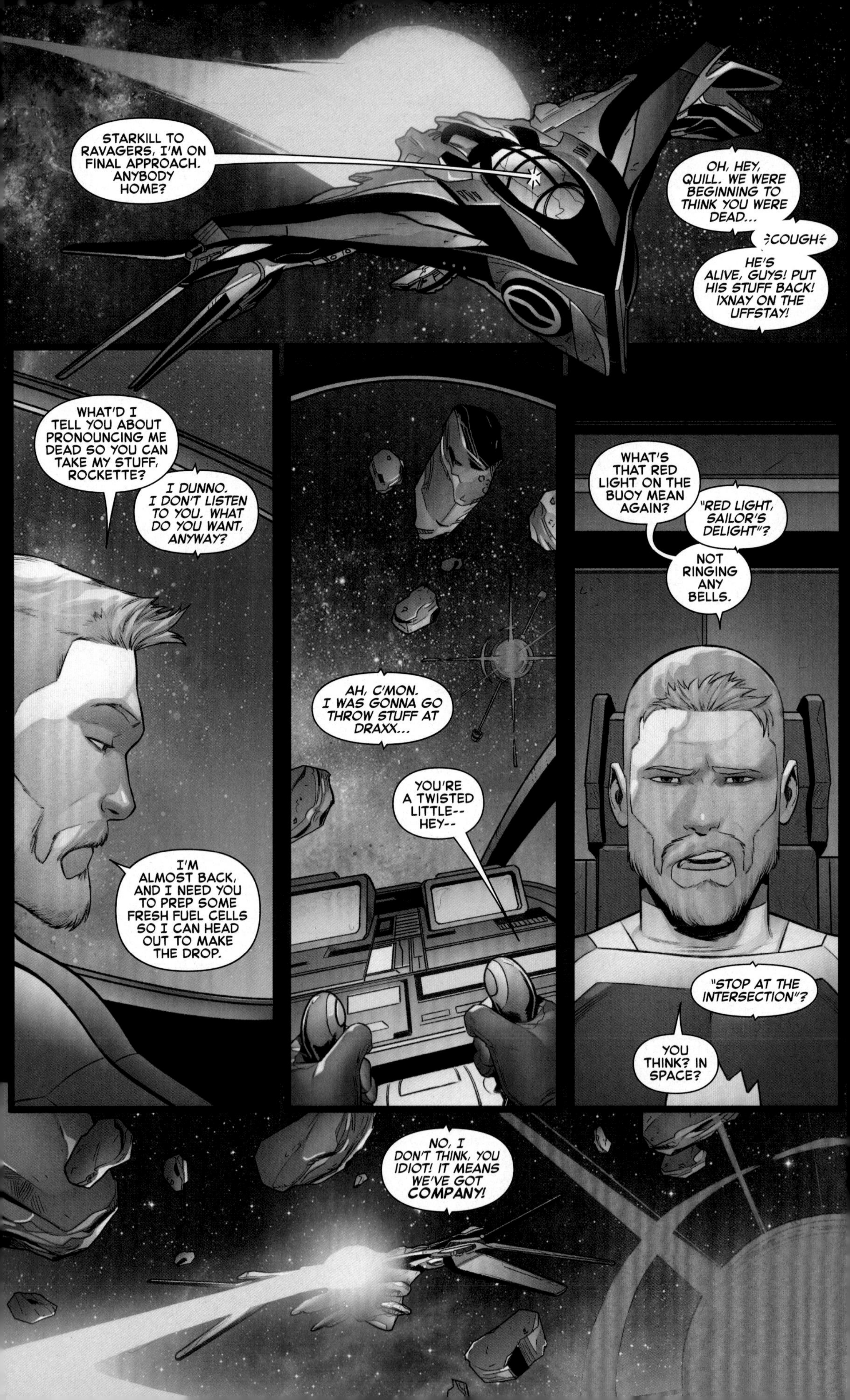
STARKILL TO RAVAGERS, I'M ON FINAL APPROACH. ANYBODY HOME?
OH, HEY, QUILL. WE WERE BEGINNING TO THINK YOU WERE DEAD...
COUGH
HE'S ALIVE, GUYS! PUT HIS STUFF BACK! IXNAY ON THE UFFSTAY!
WHAT'D I TELL YOU ABOUT PRONOUNCING ME DEAD SO YOU CAN TAKE MY STUFF, ROCKETTE?
I DUNNO. I DON'T LISTEN TO YOU. WHAT DO YOU WANT, ANYWAY?
I'M ALMOST BACK, AND I NEED YOU TO PREP SOME FRESH FUEL CELLS SO I CAN HEAD OUT TO MAKE THE DROP.
AH, C'MON. I WAS GONNA GO THROW STUFF AT DRAXX...
YOU'RE A TWISTED LITTLE-- HEY--
WHAT'S THAT RED LIGHT ON THE BUOY MEAN AGAIN?
"RED LIGHT, SAILOR'S DELIGHT"?
NOT RINGING ANY BELLS.
"STOP AT THE INTERSECTION"?
YOU THINK? IN SPACE?
NO, I DON'T THINK, YOU IDIOT! IT MEANS WE'VE GOT COMPANY!

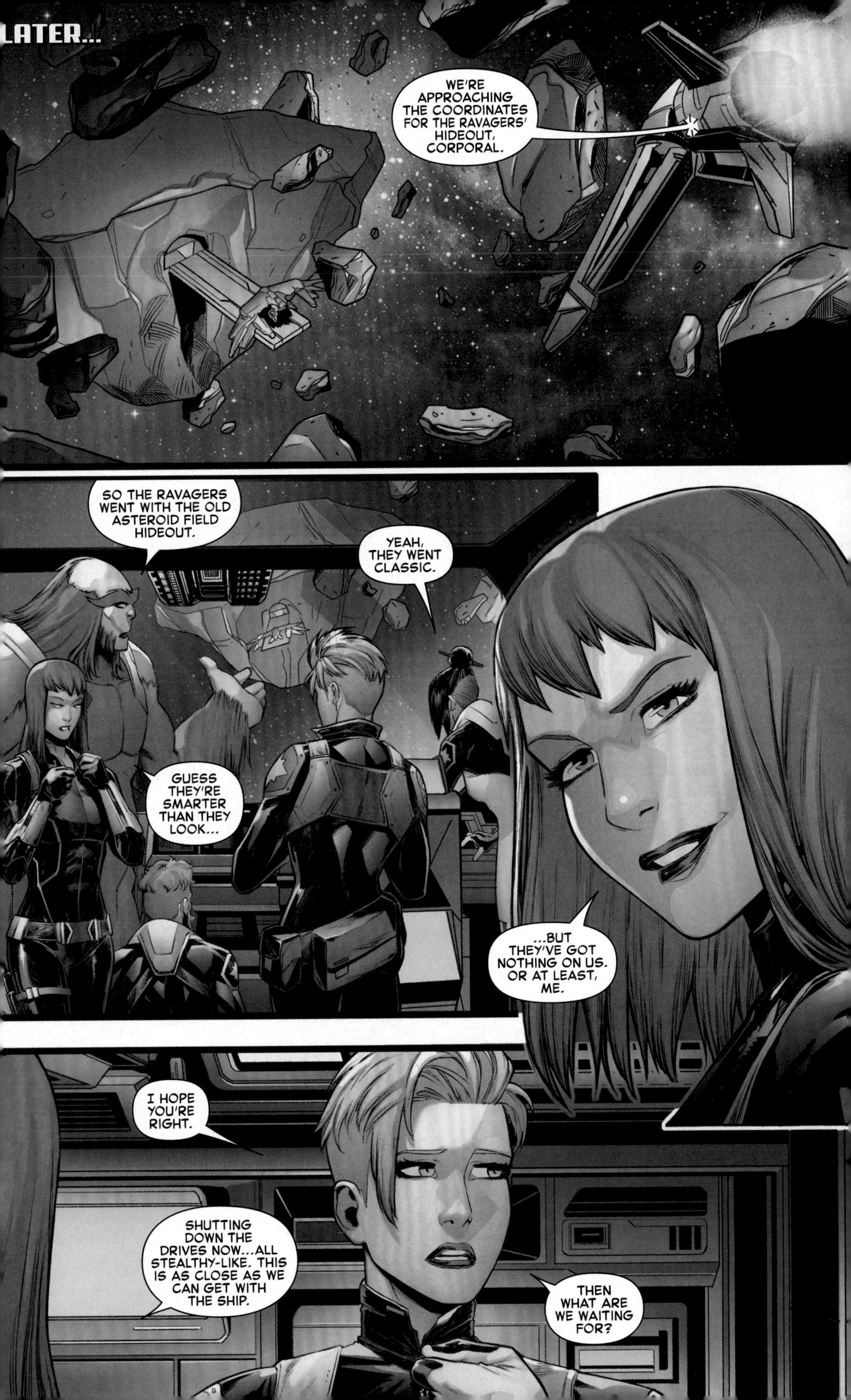
LATER...
WE'RE APPROACHING THE COORDINATES FOR THE RAVAGERS' HIDEOUT, CORPORAL.
SO THE RAVAGERS WENT WITH THE OLD ASTEROID FIELD HIDEOUT.
YEAH, THEY WENT CLASSIC.
GUESS THEY'RE SMARTER THAN THEY LOOK...
...BUT THEY'VE GOT NOTHING ON US. OR AT LEAST, ME.
I HOPE YOU'RE RIGHT.
SHUTTING DOWN THE DRIVES NOW...ALL STEALTHY-LIKE. THIS IS AS CLOSE AS WE CAN GET WITH THE SHIP.
THEN WHAT ARE WE WAITING FOR?

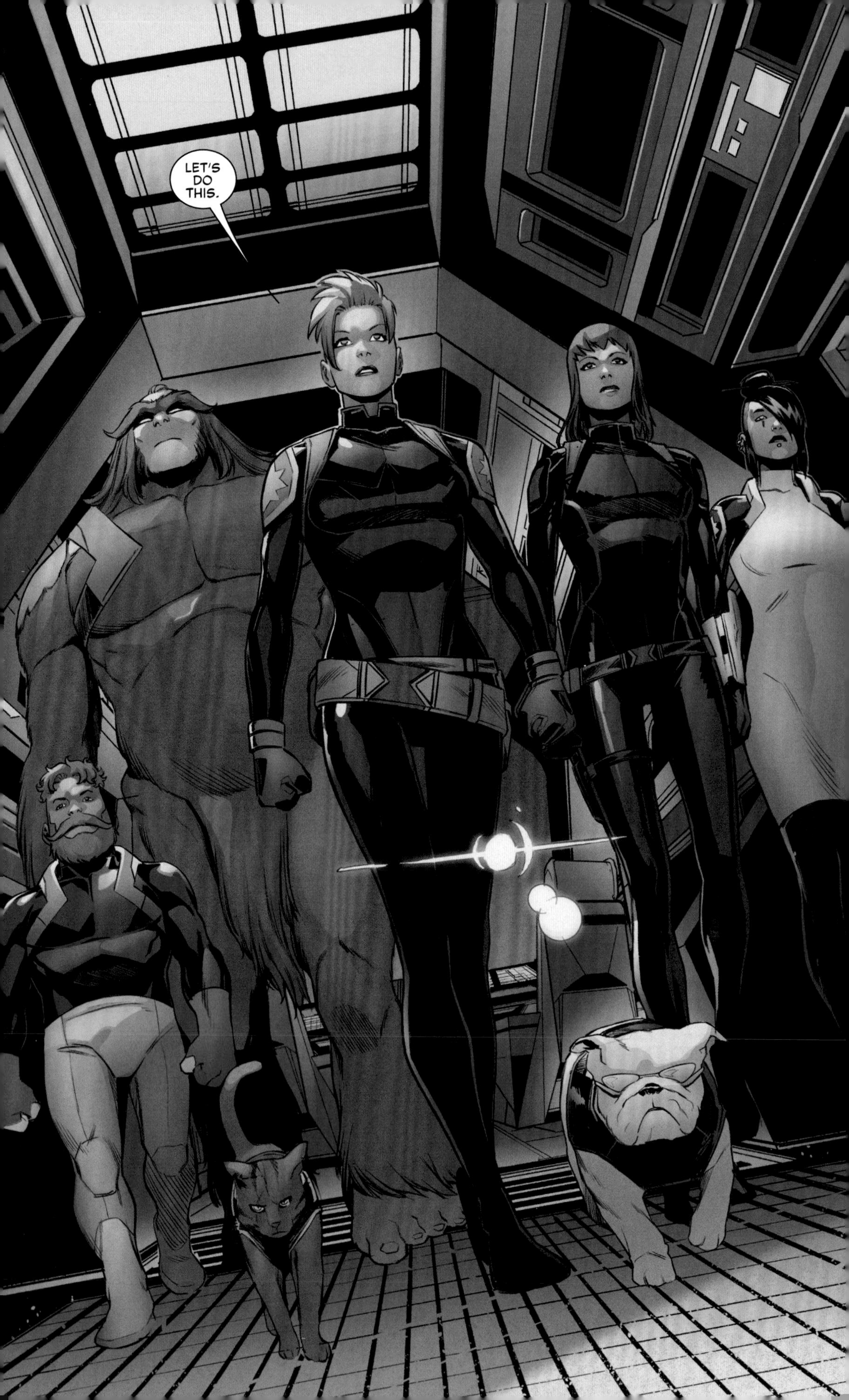
LET'S DO THIS.

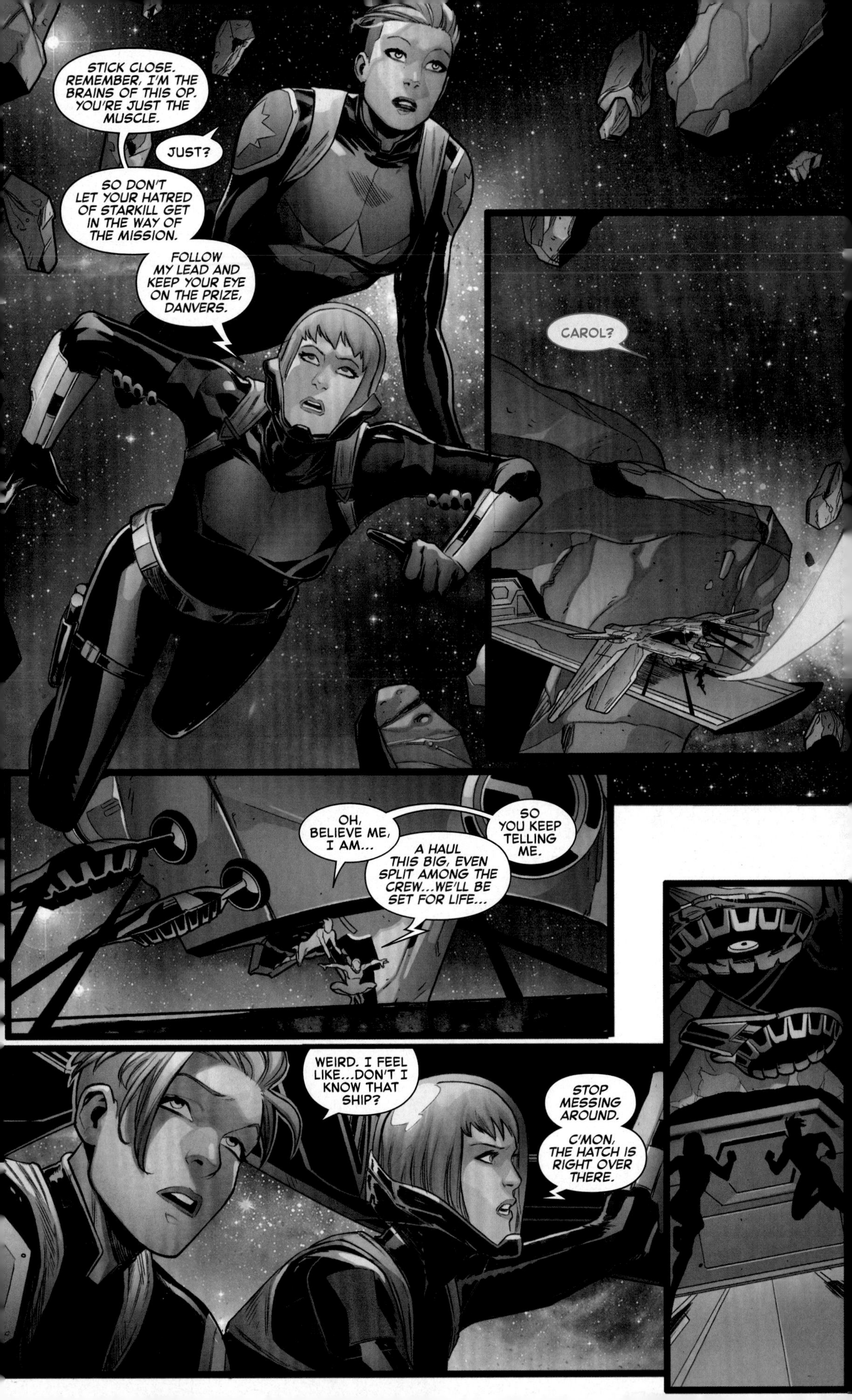
STICK CLOSE. REMEMBER, I'M THE BRAINS OF THIS OP. YOU'RE JUST THE MUSCLE.
JUST?
SO DON'T LET YOUR HATRED OF STARKILL GET IN THE WAY OF THE MISSION.
FOLLOW MY LEAD AND KEEP YOUR EYE ON THE PRIZE, DANVERS.
CAROL?
OH, BELIEVE ME, I AM...
SO YOU KEEP TELLING ME.
A HAUL THIS BIG, EVEN SPLIT AMONG THE CREW...WE'LL BE SET FOR LIFE...
WEIRD. I FEEL LIKE...DON'T I KNOW THAT SHIP?
STOP MESSING AROUND.
C'MON, THE HATCH IS RIGHT OVER THERE.

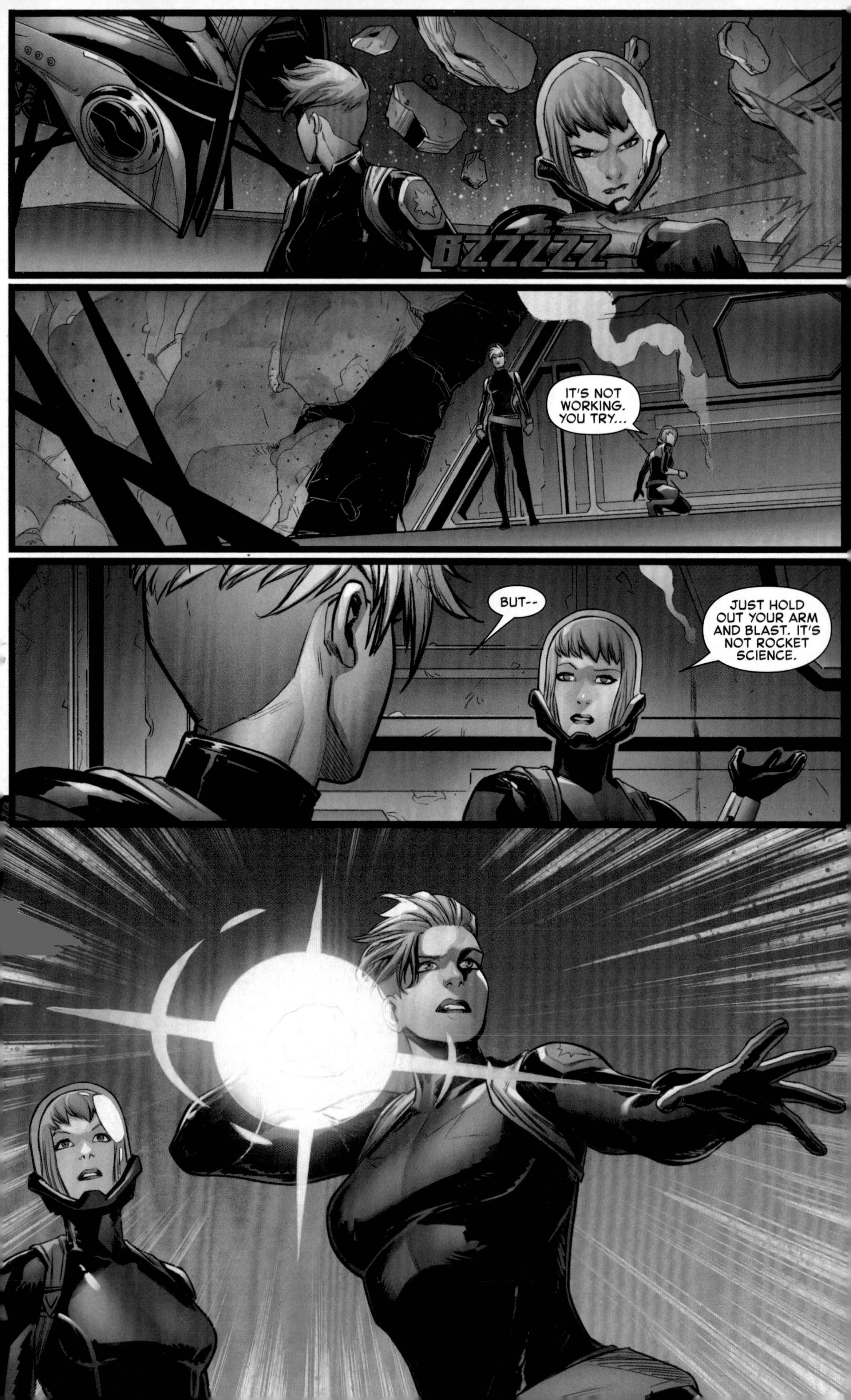
BZZZZZ
IT'S NOT WORKING. YOU TRY...
BUT--
JUST HOLD OUT YOUR ARM AND BLAST. IT'S NOT ROCKET SCIENCE.

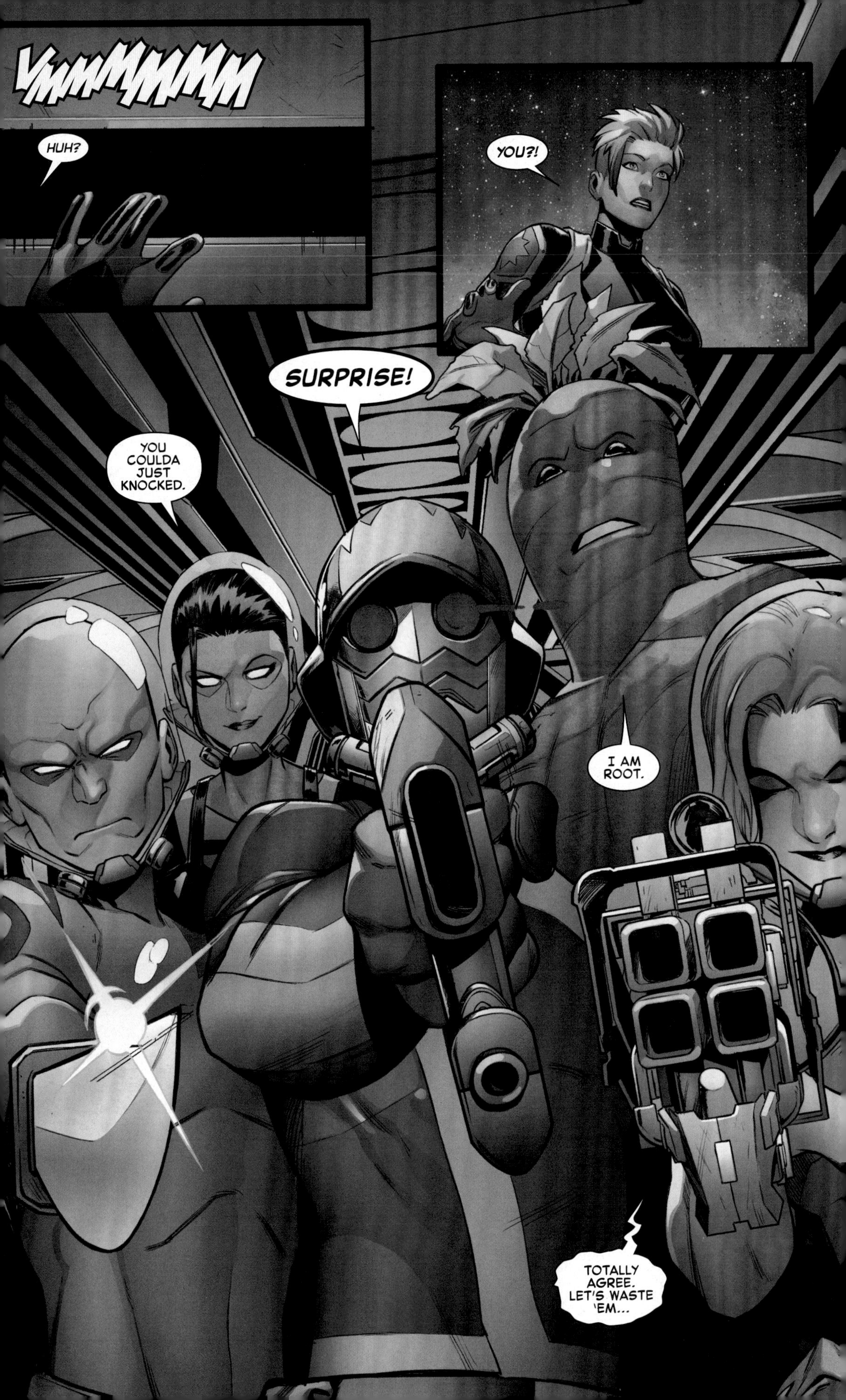
VMMMMMMM
HUH?
YOU?!
SURPRISE!
YOU COULDA JUST KNOCKED.
I AM ROOT.
TOTALLY AGREE. LET'S WASTE 'EM...

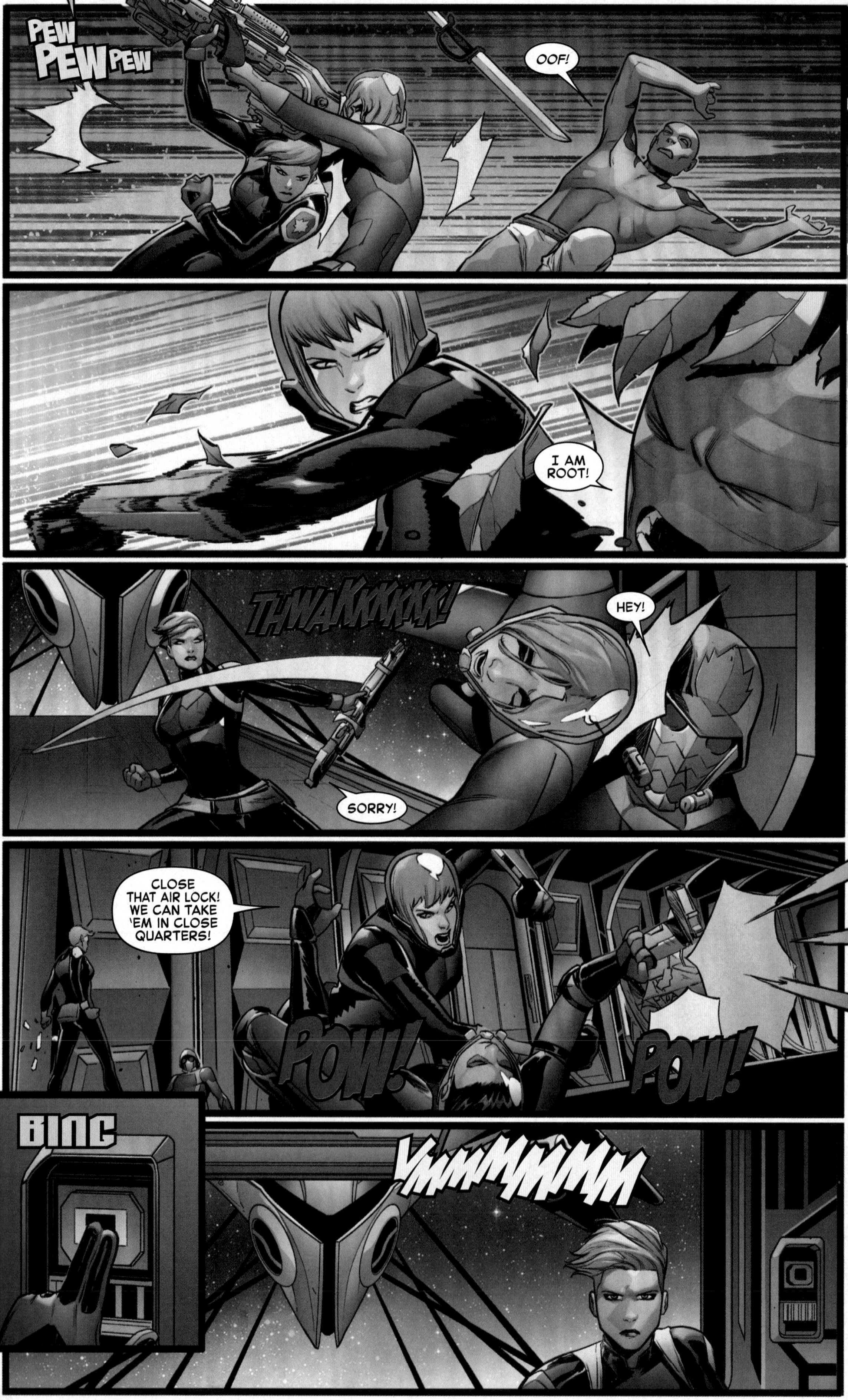
PEW PEW PEW
OOF!
I AM ROOT!
THWAKKKKKK!
HEY!
SORRY!
CLOSE THAT AIR LOCK! WE CAN TAKE 'EM IN CLOSE QUARTERS!
POW!
POW!
BING
VMMMMMM

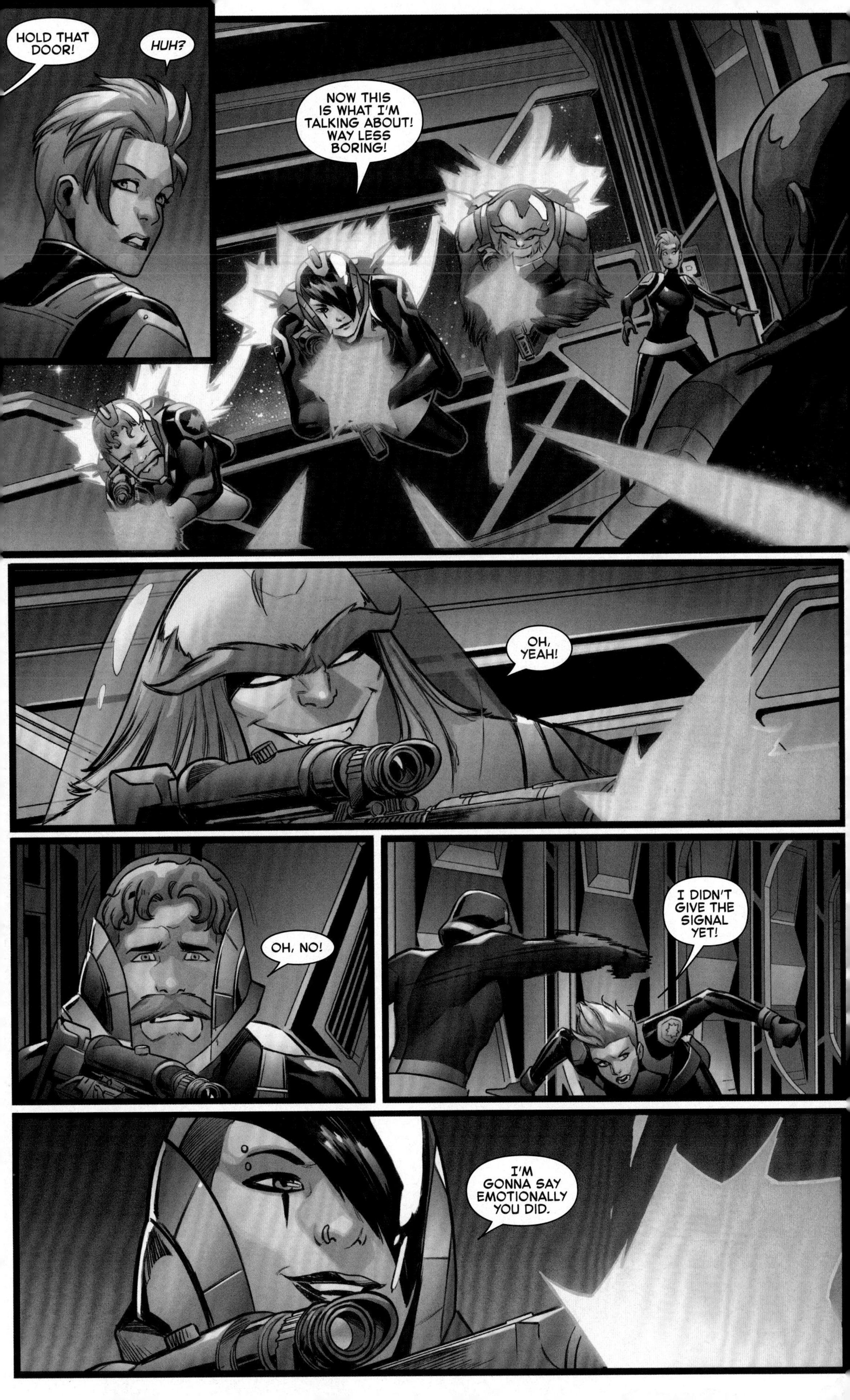
HOLD THAT DOOR!
HUH?
NOW THIS IS WHAT I'M TALKING ABOUT! WAY LESS BORING!
OH, YEAH!
OH, NO!
I DIDN'T GIVE THE SIGNAL YET!
I'M GONNA SAY EMOTIONALLY YOU DID.

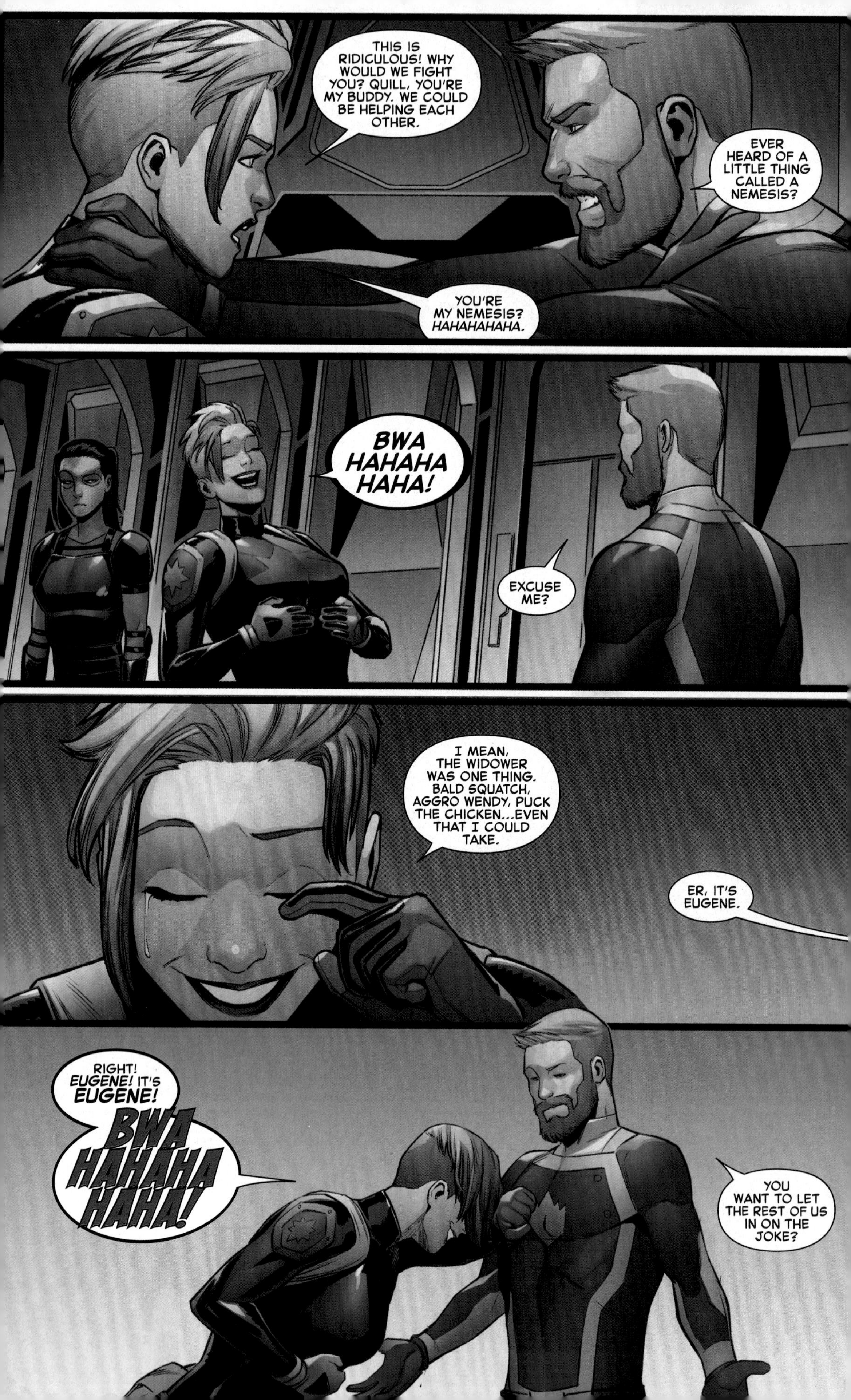
THIS IS RIDICULOUS! WHY WOULD WE FIGHT YOU? QUILL, YOU'RE MY BUDDY. WE COULD BE HELPING EACH OTHER.
EVER HEARD OF A LITTLE THING CALLED A NEMESIS?
YOU'RE MY NEMESIS? *HAHAHAHAHA.*
BWA HAHAHA HAHA!
EXCUSE ME?
I MEAN, THE WIDOWER WAS ONE THING. BALD SQUATCH, AGGRO WENDY, PUCK THE CHICKEN...EVEN THAT I COULD TAKE.
ER, IT'S EUGENE.
RIGHT! EUGENE! IT'S EUGENE!
BWA HAHAHA HAHA!
YOU WANT TO LET THE REST OF US IN ON THE JOKE?

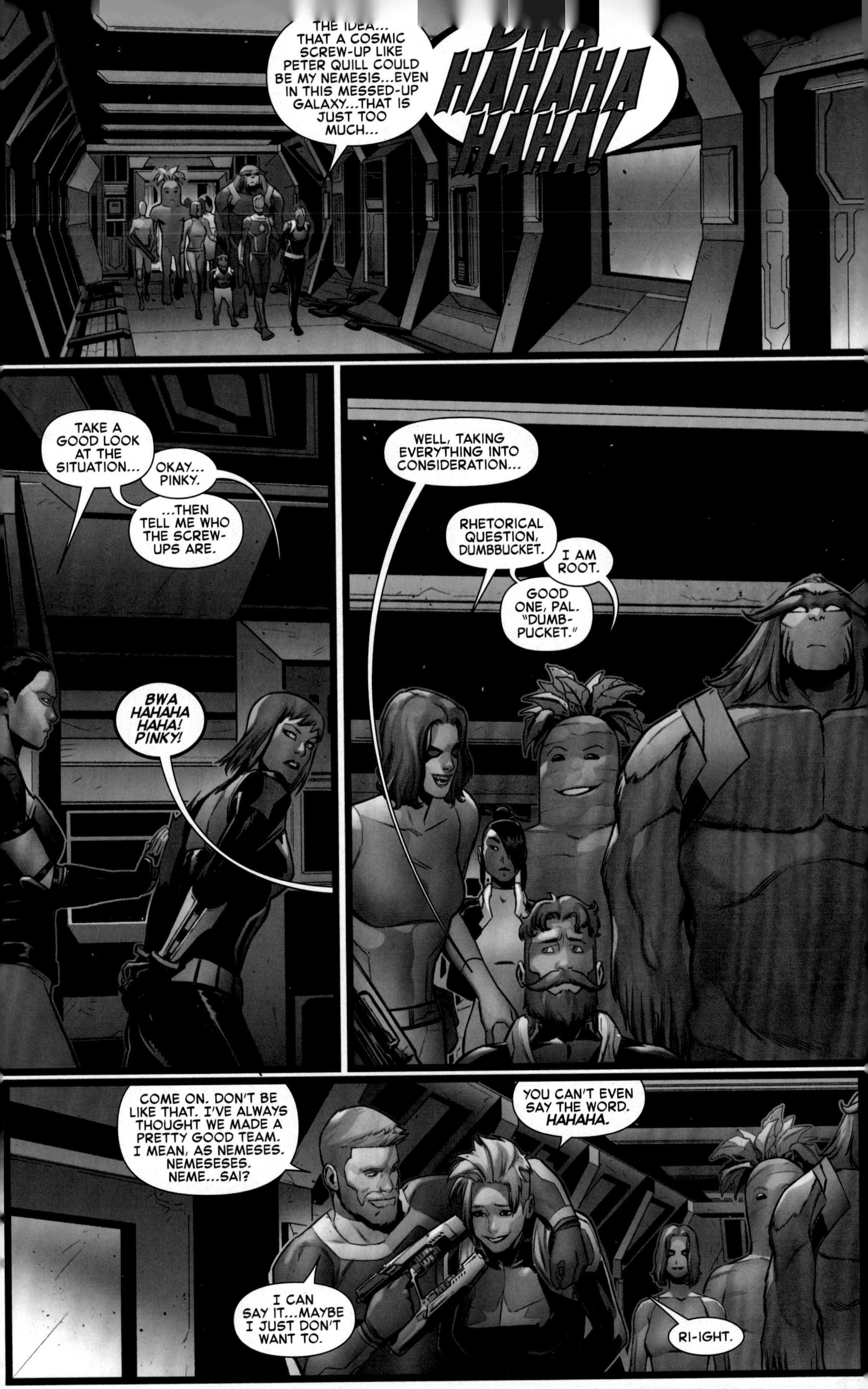
THE IDEA... THAT A COSMIC SCREW-UP LIKE PETER QUILL COULD BE MY NEMESIS...EVEN IN THIS MESSED-UP GALAXY...THAT IS JUST TOO MUCH...
HAHAHA HAHA!
TAKE A GOOD LOOK AT THE SITUATION...
OKAY... PINKY.
...THEN TELL ME WHO THE SCREW-UPS ARE.
BWA HAHAHA HAHA! PINKY!
WELL, TAKING EVERYTHING INTO CONSIDERATION...
RHETORICAL QUESTION, DUMBBUCKET.
I AM ROOT.
GOOD ONE, PAL. "DUMB-PUCKET."
COME ON. DON'T BE LIKE THAT. I'VE ALWAYS THOUGHT WE MADE A PRETTY GOOD TEAM. I MEAN, AS NEMESES. NEMESESES. NEME...SAI?
YOU CAN'T EVEN SAY THE WORD. HAHAHA.
I CAN SAY IT...MAYBE I JUST DON'T WANT TO.
RI-IGHT.

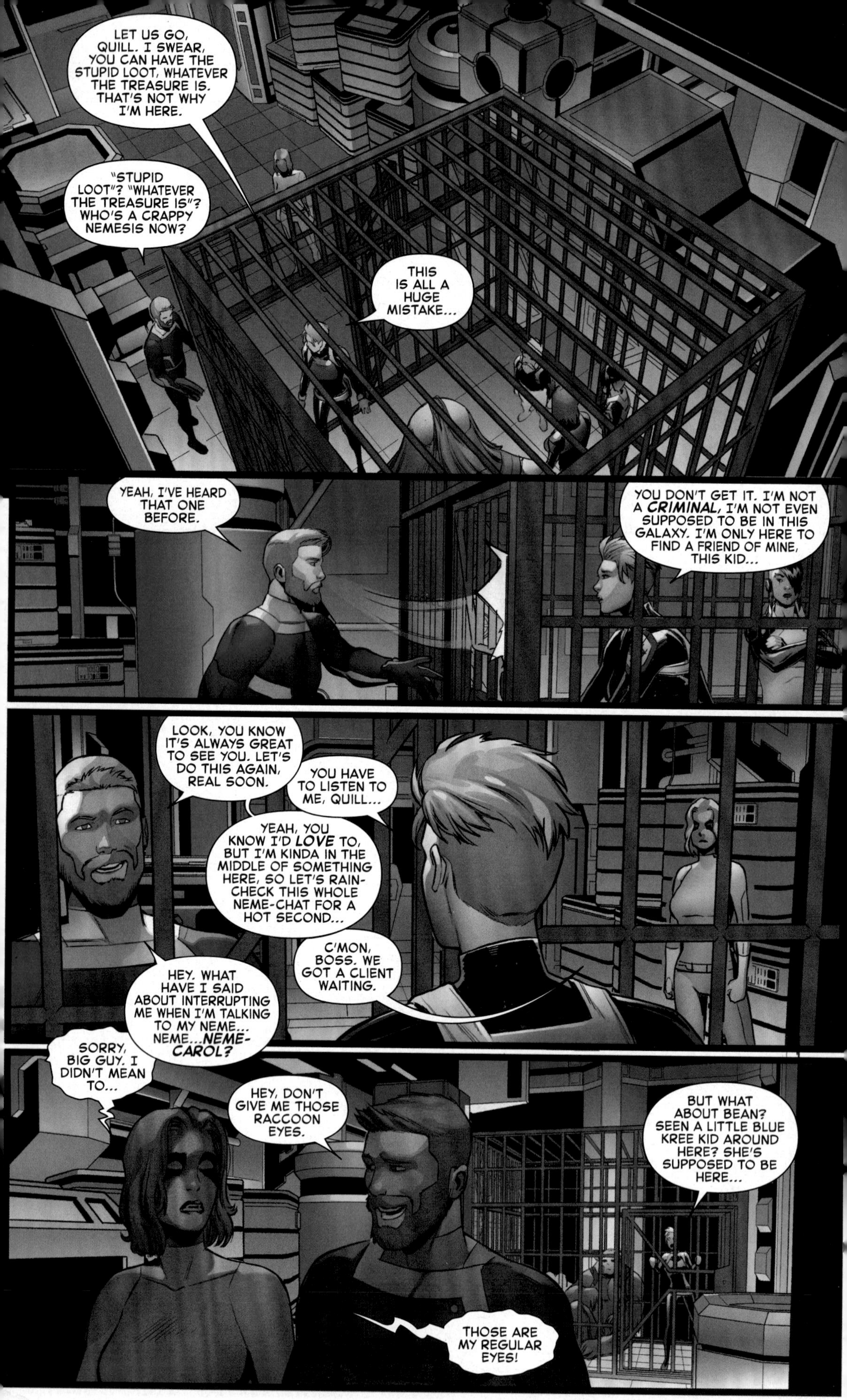
LET US GO, QUILL. I SWEAR, YOU CAN HAVE THE STUPID LOOT, WHATEVER THE TREASURE IS. THAT'S NOT WHY I'M HERE.
"STUPID LOOT"? "WHATEVER THE TREASURE IS"? WHO'S A CRAPPY NEMESIS NOW?
THIS IS ALL A HUGE MISTAKE...
YEAH, I'VE HEARD THAT ONE BEFORE.
YOU DON'T GET IT. I'M NOT A CRIMINAL, I'M NOT EVEN SUPPOSED TO BE IN THIS GALAXY. I'M ONLY HERE TO FIND A FRIEND OF MINE, THIS KID...
LOOK, YOU KNOW IT'S ALWAYS GREAT TO SEE YOU. LET'S DO THIS AGAIN, REAL SOON.
YOU HAVE TO LISTEN TO ME, QUILL...
YEAH, YOU KNOW I'D LOVE TO, BUT I'M KINDA IN THE MIDDLE OF SOMETHING HERE, SO LET'S RAIN-CHECK THIS WHOLE NEME-CHAT FOR A HOT SECOND...
C'MON, BOSS. WE GOT A CLIENT WAITING.
HEY. WHAT HAVE I SAID ABOUT INTERRUPTING ME WHEN I'M TALKING TO MY NEME... NEME...NEME-CAROL?
SORRY, BIG GUY. I DIDN'T MEAN TO...
HEY, DON'T GIVE ME THOSE RACCOON EYES.
THOSE ARE MY REGULAR EYES!
BUT WHAT ABOUT BEAN? SEEN A LITTLE BLUE KREE KID AROUND HERE? SHE'S SUPPOSED TO BE HERE...

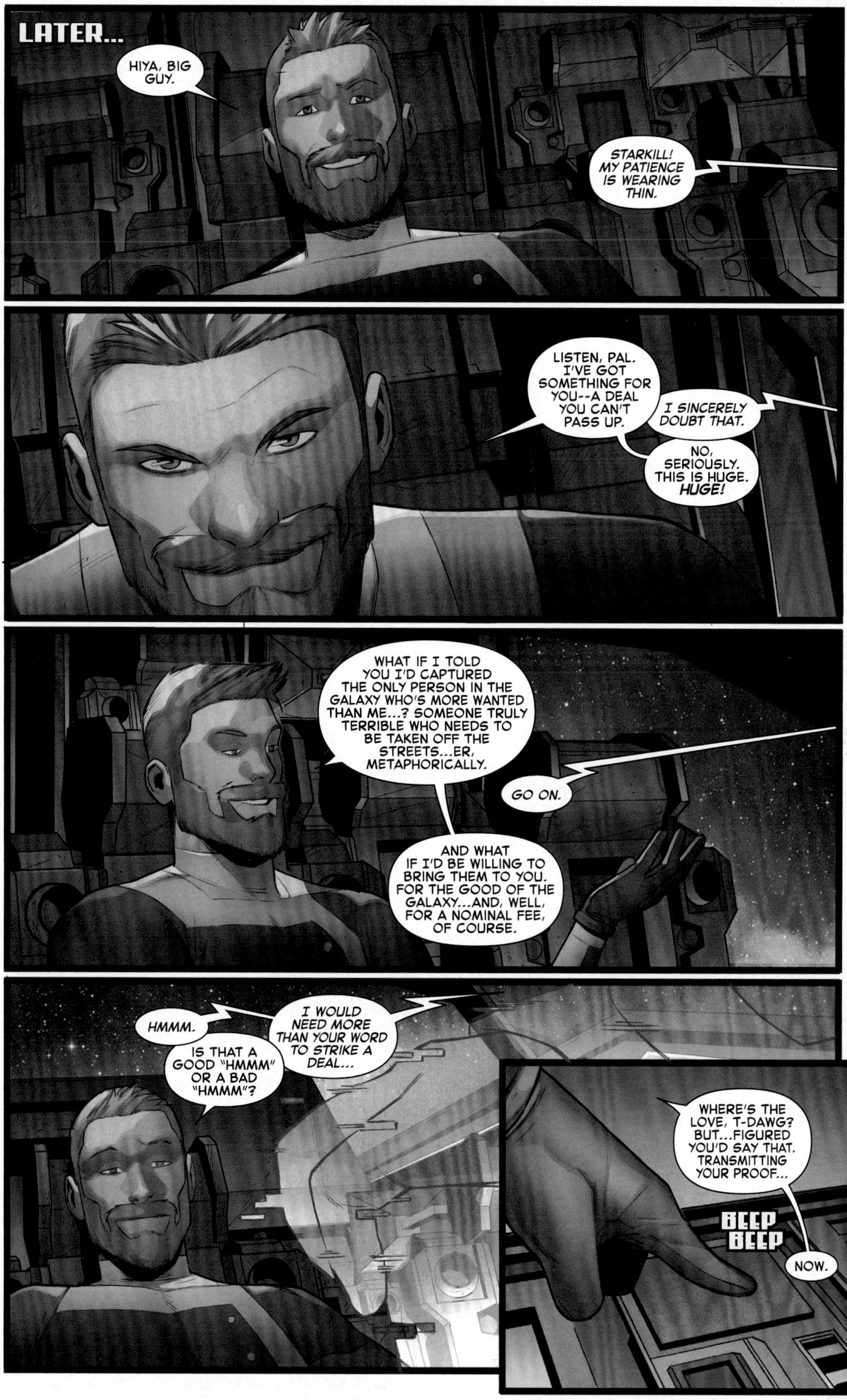
LATER...
HIYA, BIG GUY.
STARKILL! MY PATIENCE IS WEARING THIN.
LISTEN, PAL. I'VE GOT SOMETHING FOR YOU--A DEAL YOU CAN'T PASS UP.
I SINCERELY DOUBT THAT.
NO, SERIOUSLY. THIS IS HUGE. HUGE!
WHAT IF I TOLD YOU I'D CAPTURED THE ONLY PERSON IN THE GALAXY WHO'S MORE WANTED THAN ME...? SOMEONE TRULY TERRIBLE WHO NEEDS TO BE TAKEN OFF THE STREETS...ER, METAPHORICALLY.
GO ON.
AND WHAT IF I'D BE WILLING TO BRING THEM TO YOU. FOR THE GOOD OF THE GALAXY...AND, WELL, FOR A NOMINAL FEE, OF COURSE.
HMMM.
IS THAT A GOOD "HMMM" OR A BAD "HMMM"?
I WOULD NEED MORE THAN YOUR WORD TO STRIKE A DEAL...
WHERE'S THE LOVE, T-DAWG? BUT...FIGURED YOU'D SAY THAT. TRANSMITTING YOUR PROOF...
BEEP BEEP
NOW.

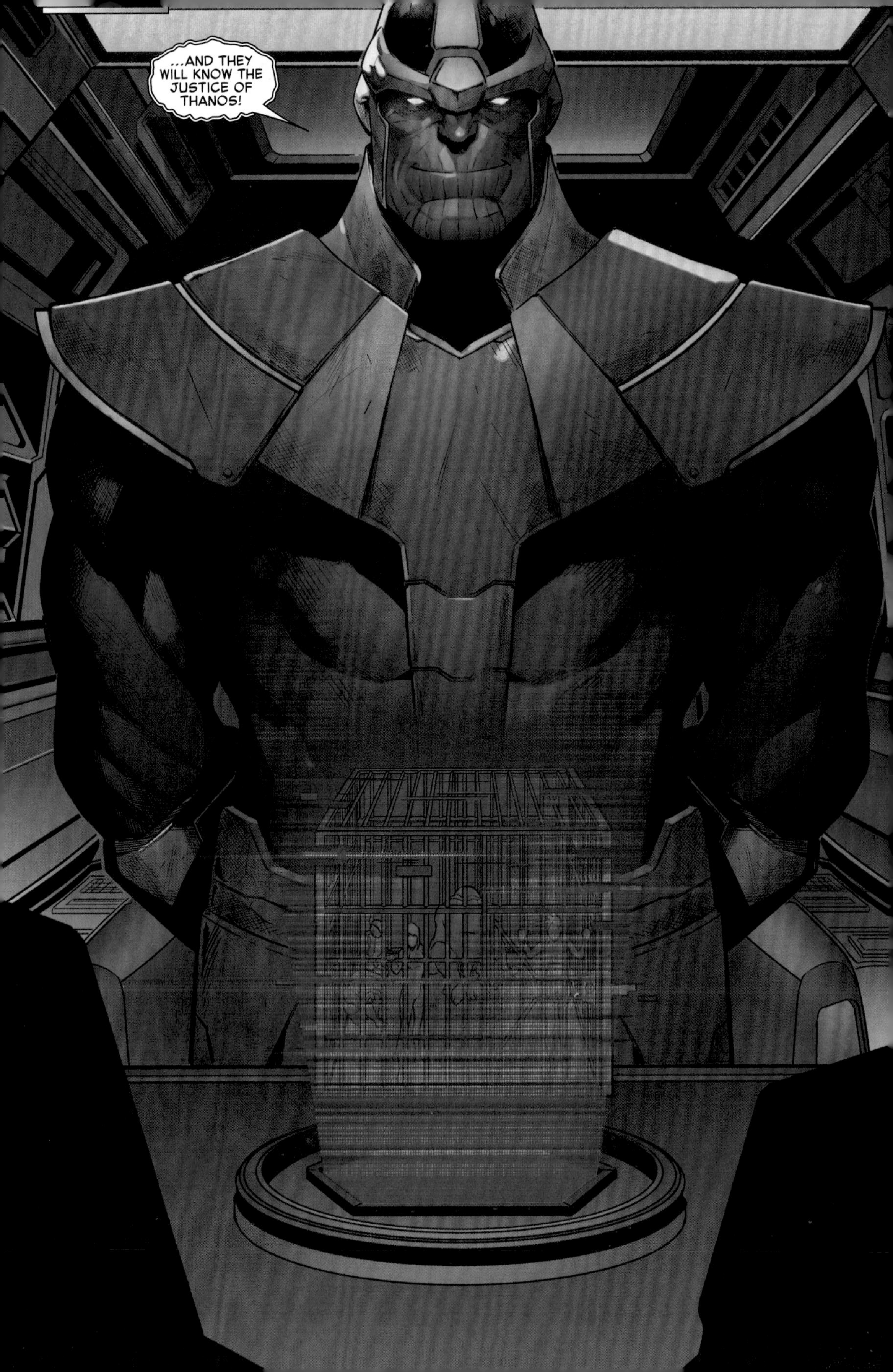
...AND THEY WILL KNOW THE JUSTICE OF THANOS!

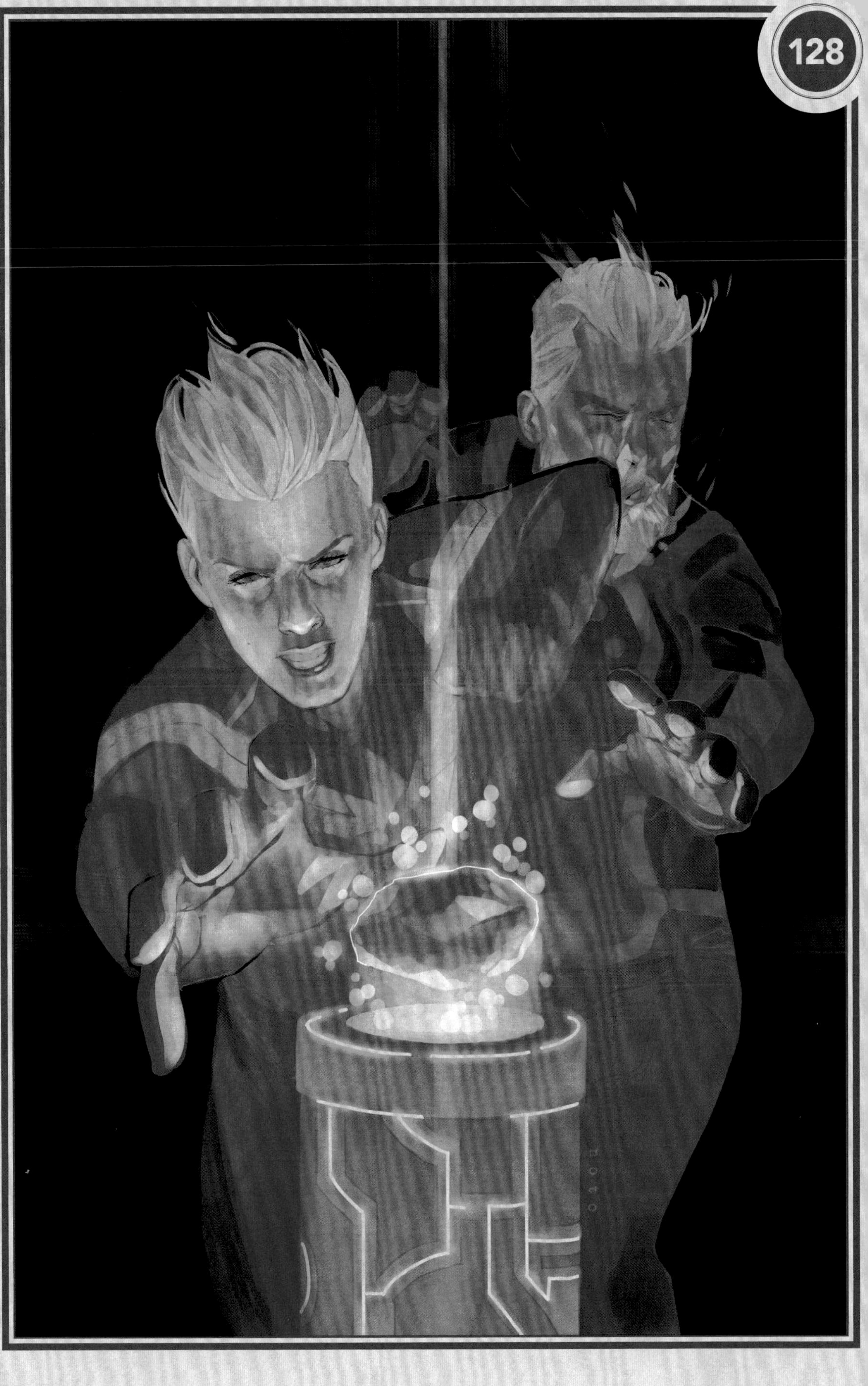
128

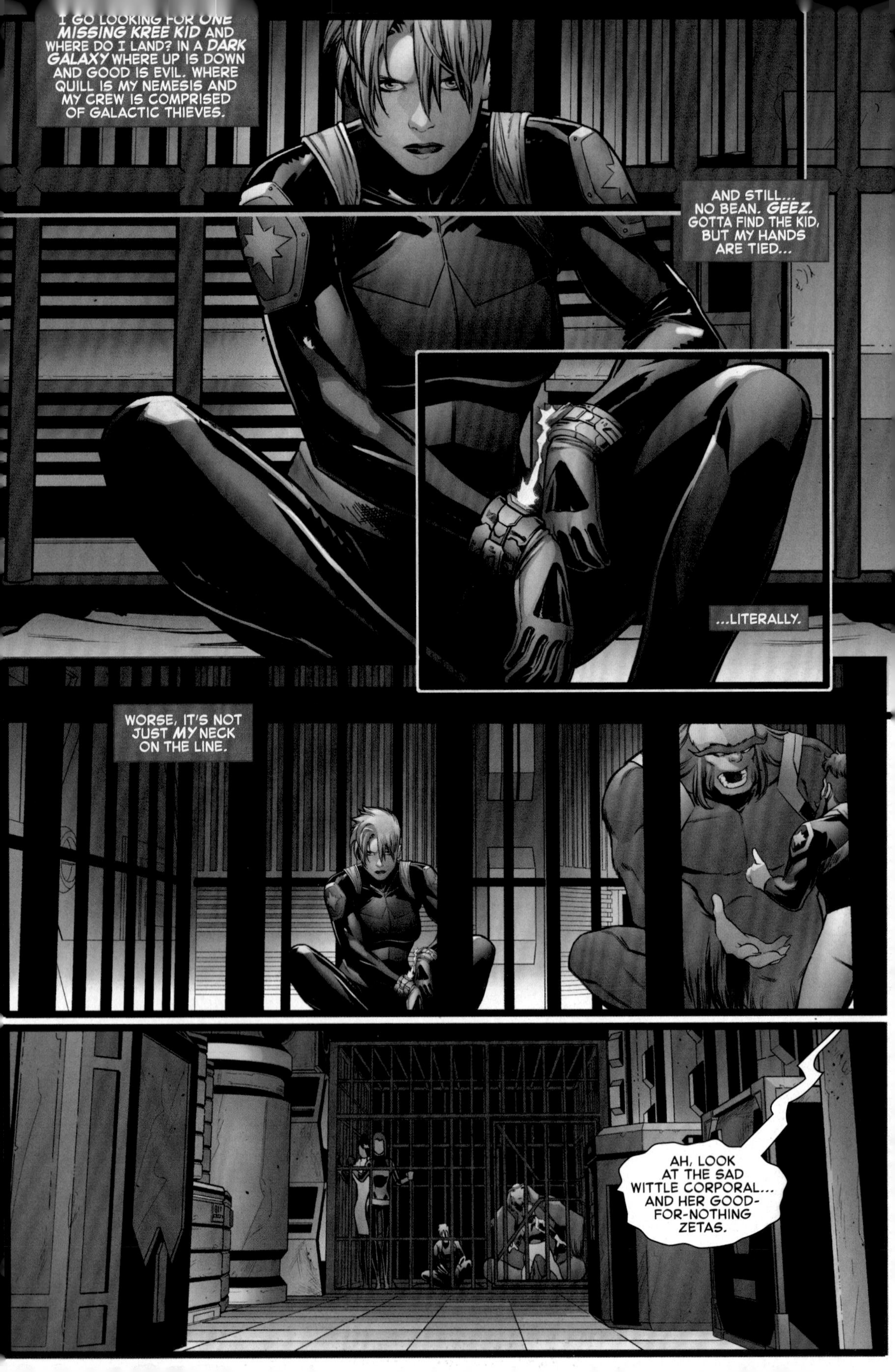
I GO LOOKING FOR ONE MISSING KREE KID AND WHERE DO I LAND? IN A DARK GALAXY WHERE UP IS DOWN AND GOOD IS EVIL. WHERE QUILL IS MY NEMESIS AND MY CREW IS COMPRISED OF GALACTIC THIEVES.
AND STILL... NO BEAN. GEEZ. GOTTA FIND THE KID, BUT MY HANDS ARE TIED...
...LITERALLY.
WORSE, IT'S NOT JUST MY NECK ON THE LINE.
AH, LOOK AT THE SAD WITTLE CORPORAL... AND HER GOOD-FOR-NOTHING ZETAS.

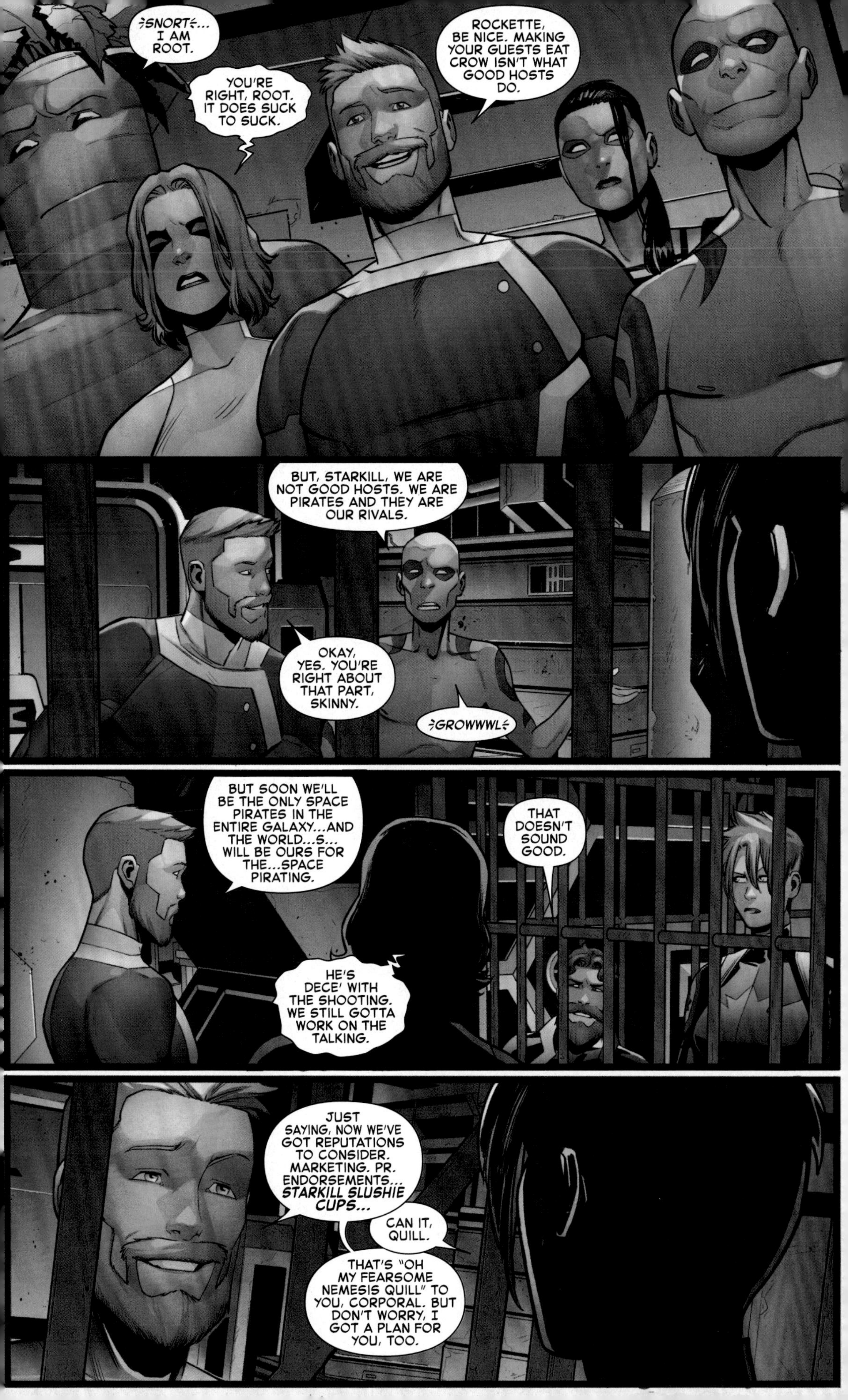

⚡SNORT⚡... I AM ROOT.
YOU'RE RIGHT, ROOT. IT DOES SUCK TO SUCK.
ROCKETTE, BE NICE. MAKING YOUR GUESTS EAT CROW ISN'T WHAT GOOD HOSTS DO.
BUT, STARKILL, WE ARE NOT GOOD HOSTS. WE ARE PIRATES AND THEY ARE OUR RIVALS.
OKAY, YES. YOU'RE RIGHT ABOUT THAT PART, SKINNY.
⚡GROWWWL⚡
BUT SOON WE'LL BE THE ONLY SPACE PIRATES IN THE ENTIRE GALAXY...AND THE WORLD...S... WILL BE OURS FOR THE...SPACE PIRATING.
THAT DOESN'T SOUND GOOD.
HE'S DECE' WITH THE SHOOTING. WE STILL GOTTA WORK ON THE TALKING.
JUST SAYING, NOW WE'VE GOT REPUTATIONS TO CONSIDER. MARKETING. PR. ENDORSEMENTS... STARKILL SLUSHIE CUPS...
CAN IT, QUILL.
THAT'S "OH MY FEARSOME NEMESIS QUILL" TO YOU, CORPORAL. BUT DON'T WORRY, I GOT A PLAN FOR YOU, TOO.

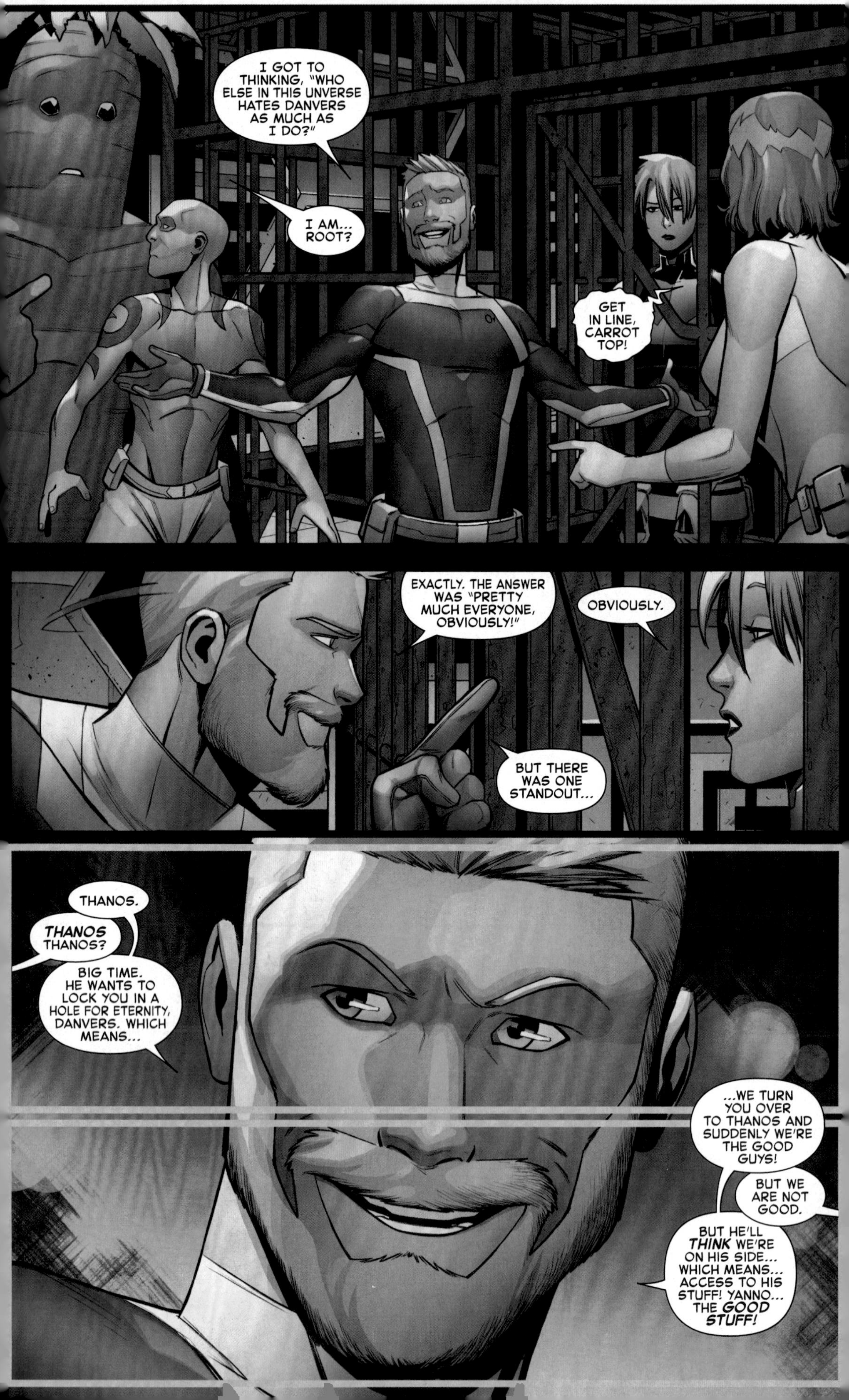
I GOT TO THINKING, "WHO ELSE IN THIS UNVERSE HATES DANVERS AS MUCH AS I DO?"
I AM... ROOT?
GET IN LINE, CARROT TOP!
EXACTLY. THE ANSWER WAS "PRETTY MUCH EVERYONE, OBVIOUSLY!"
OBVIOUSLY.
BUT THERE WAS ONE STANDOUT...
THANOS.
THANOS THANOS?
BIG TIME. HE WANTS TO LOCK YOU IN A HOLE FOR ETERNITY, DANVERS. WHICH MEANS...
...WE TURN YOU OVER TO THANOS AND SUDDENLY WE'RE THE GOOD GUYS!
BUT WE ARE NOT GOOD.
BUT HE'LL *THINK* WE'RE ON HIS SIDE... WHICH MEANS... ACCESS TO HIS STUFF! YANNO... THE *GOOD STUFF!*

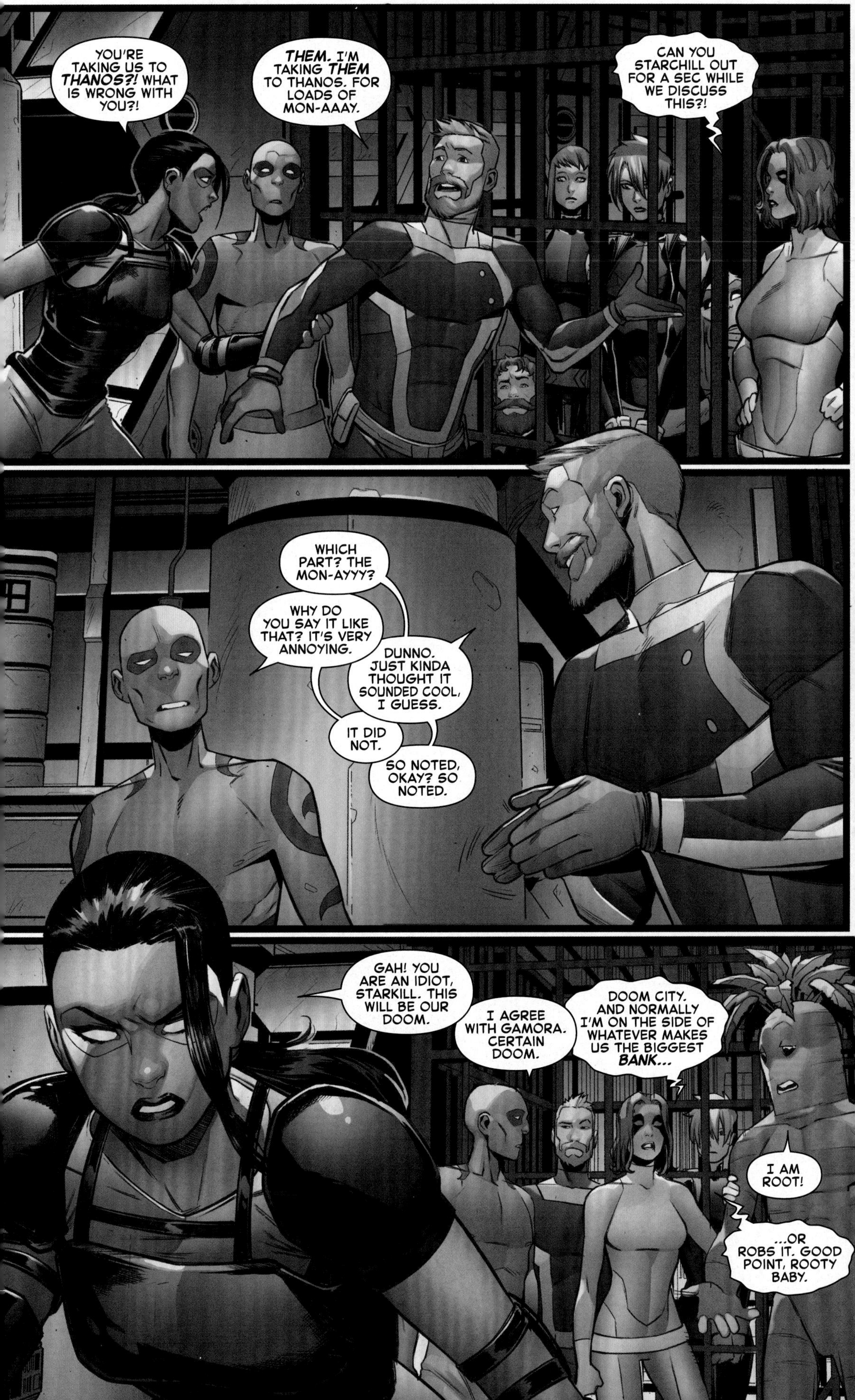
YOU'RE TAKING US TO *THANOS?!* WHAT IS WRONG WITH YOU?!
THEM. I'M TAKING *THEM* TO THANOS. FOR LOADS OF MON-AAAY.
CAN YOU STARCHILL OUT FOR A SEC WHILE WE DISCUSS THIS?!
WHICH PART? THE MON-AYYY?
WHY DO YOU SAY IT LIKE THAT? IT'S VERY ANNOYING.
DUNNO. JUST KINDA THOUGHT IT SOUNDED COOL, I GUESS.
IT DID NOT.
SO NOTED, OKAY? SO NOTED.
GAH! YOU ARE AN IDIOT, STARKILL. THIS WILL BE OUR DOOM.
I AGREE WITH GAMORA. CERTAIN DOOM.
DOOM CITY. AND NORMALLY I'M ON THE SIDE OF WHATEVER MAKES US THE BIGGEST *BANK...*
I AM ROOT!
...OR ROBS IT. GOOD POINT, ROOTY BABY.

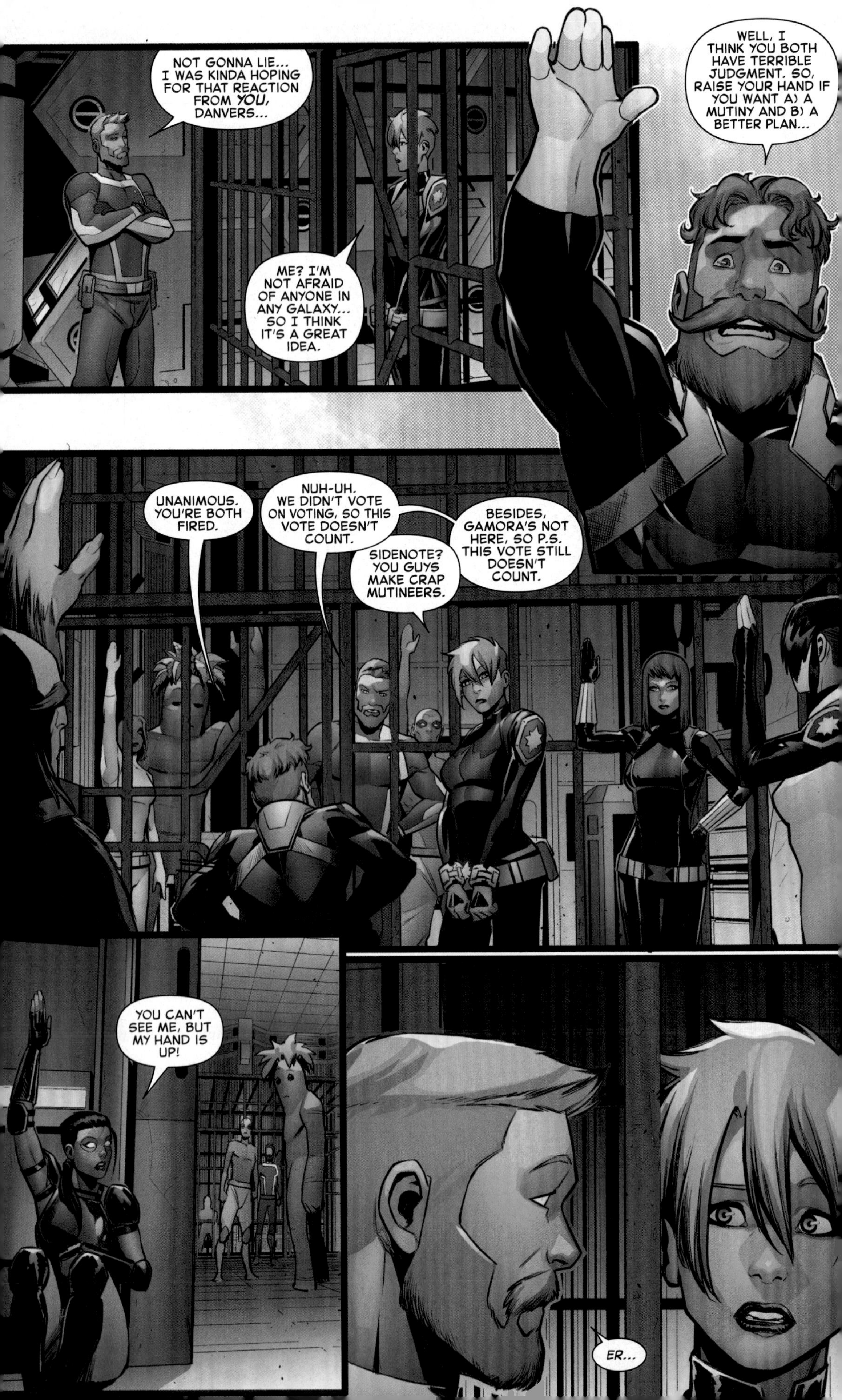
NOT GONNA LIE... I WAS KINDA HOPING FOR THAT REACTION FROM YOU, DANVERS...
ME? I'M NOT AFRAID OF ANYONE IN ANY GALAXY... SO I THINK IT'S A GREAT IDEA.
WELL, I THINK YOU BOTH HAVE TERRIBLE JUDGMENT. SO, RAISE YOUR HAND IF YOU WANT A) A MUTINY AND B) A BETTER PLAN...
UNANIMOUS. YOU'RE BOTH FIRED.
NUH-UH. WE DIDN'T VOTE ON VOTING, SO THIS VOTE DOESN'T COUNT.
BESIDES, GAMORA'S NOT HERE, SO P.S. THIS VOTE STILL DOESN'T COUNT.
SIDENOTE? YOU GUYS MAKE CRAP MUTINEERS.
YOU CAN'T SEE ME, BUT MY HAND IS UP!
ER...

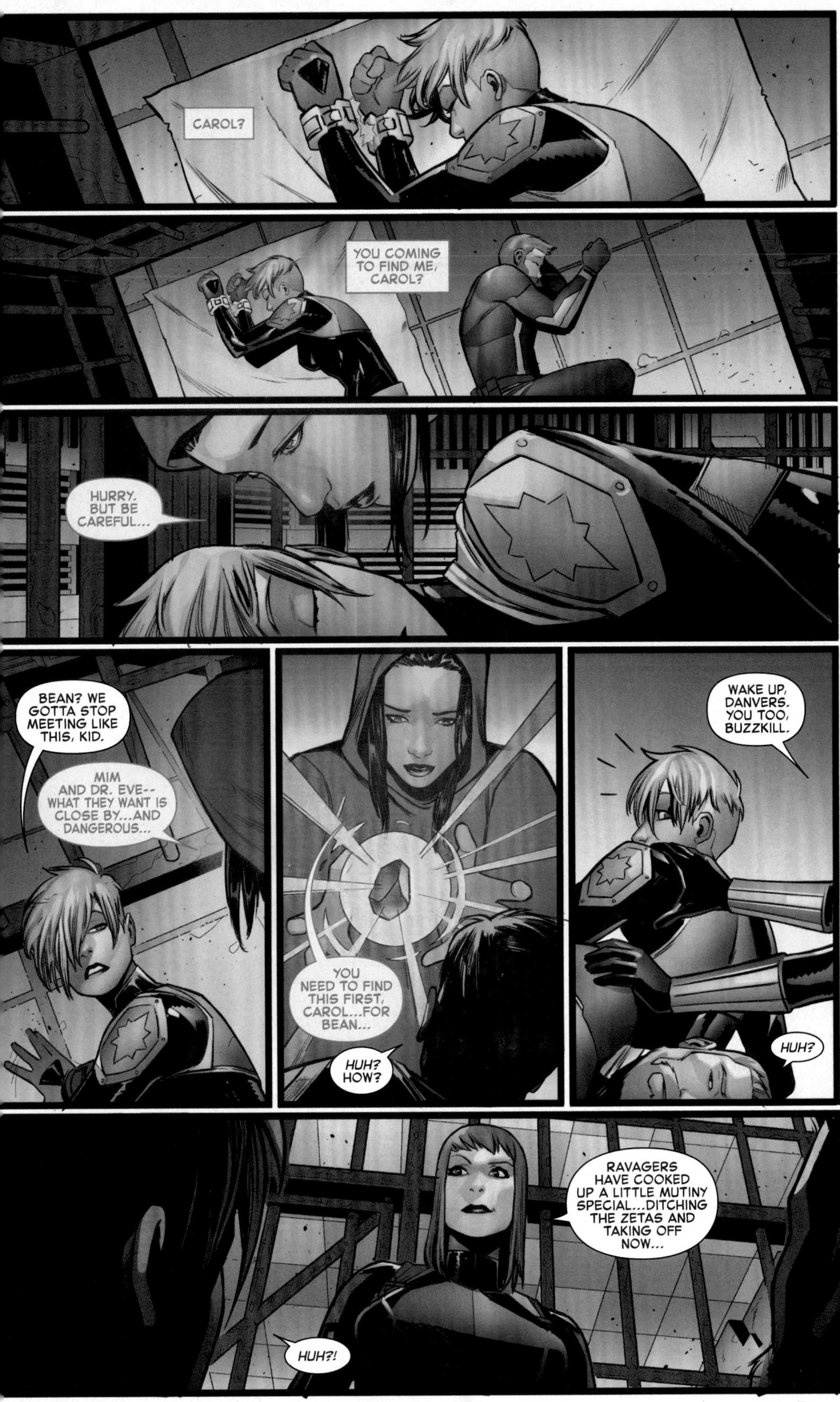
CAROL?
YOU COMING TO FIND ME, CAROL?
HURRY. BUT BE CAREFUL...
BEAN? WE GOTTA STOP MEETING LIKE THIS, KID.
MIM AND DR. EVE--WHAT THEY WANT IS CLOSE BY...AND DANGEROUS...
YOU NEED TO FIND THIS FIRST, CAROL...FOR BEAN...
HUH? HOW?
WAKE UP, DANVERS. YOU TOO, BUZZKILL.
HUH?
RAVAGERS HAVE COOKED UP A LITTLE MUTINY SPECIAL...DITCHING THE ZETAS AND TAKING OFF NOW...
HUH?!

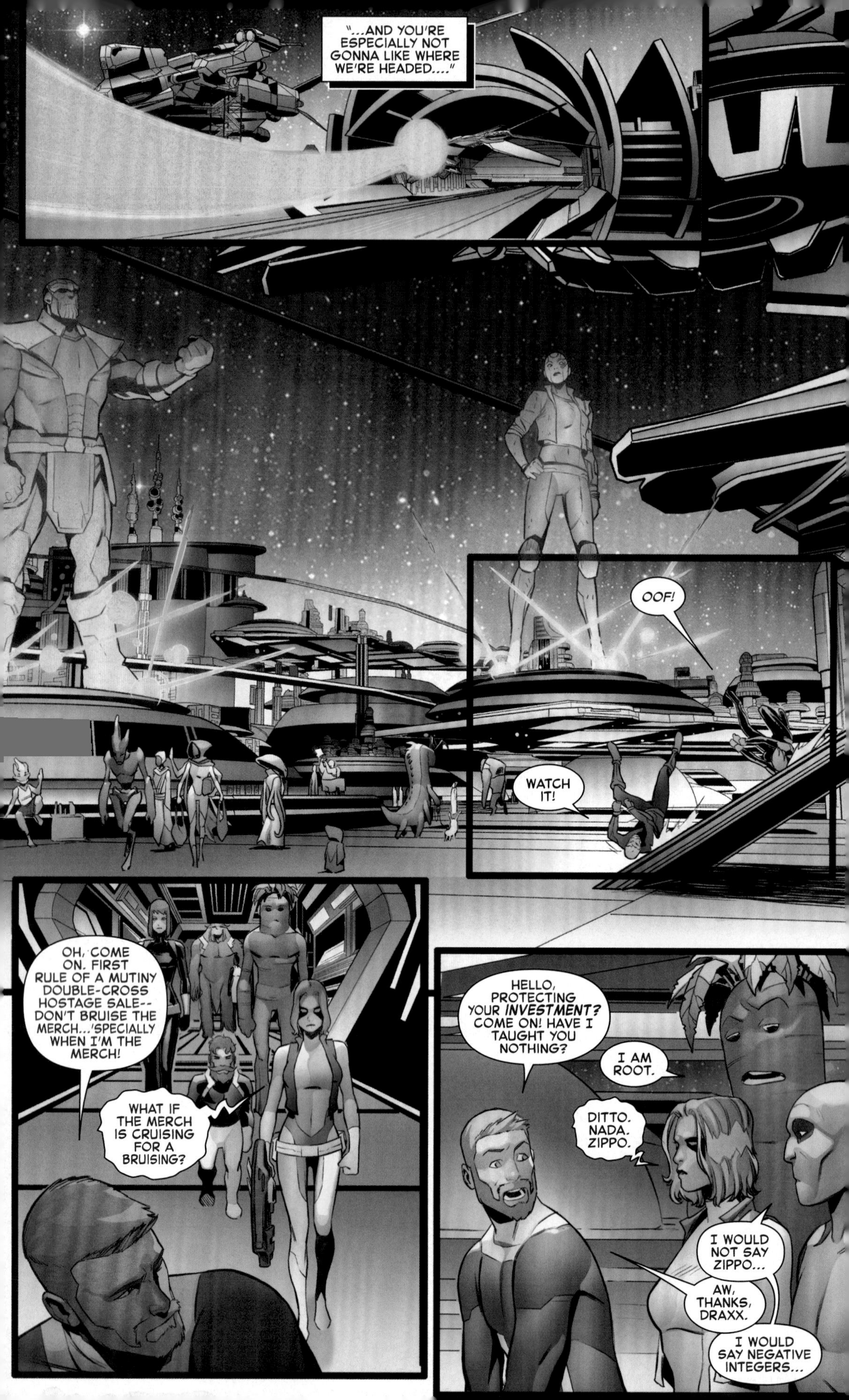
"...AND YOU'RE ESPECIALLY NOT GONNA LIKE WHERE WE'RE HEADED...."
OOF!
WATCH IT!
OH, COME ON. FIRST RULE OF A MUTINY DOUBLE-CROSS HOSTAGE SALE--DON'T BRUISE THE MERCH...'SPECIALLY WHEN I'M THE MERCH!
WHAT IF THE MERCH IS CRUISING FOR A BRUISING?
HELLO, PROTECTING YOUR INVESTMENT? COME ON! HAVE I TAUGHT YOU NOTHING?
I AM ROOT.
DITTO. NADA. ZIPPO.
I WOULD NOT SAY ZIPPO...
AW, THANKS, DRAXX.
I WOULD SAY NEGATIVE INTEGERS...

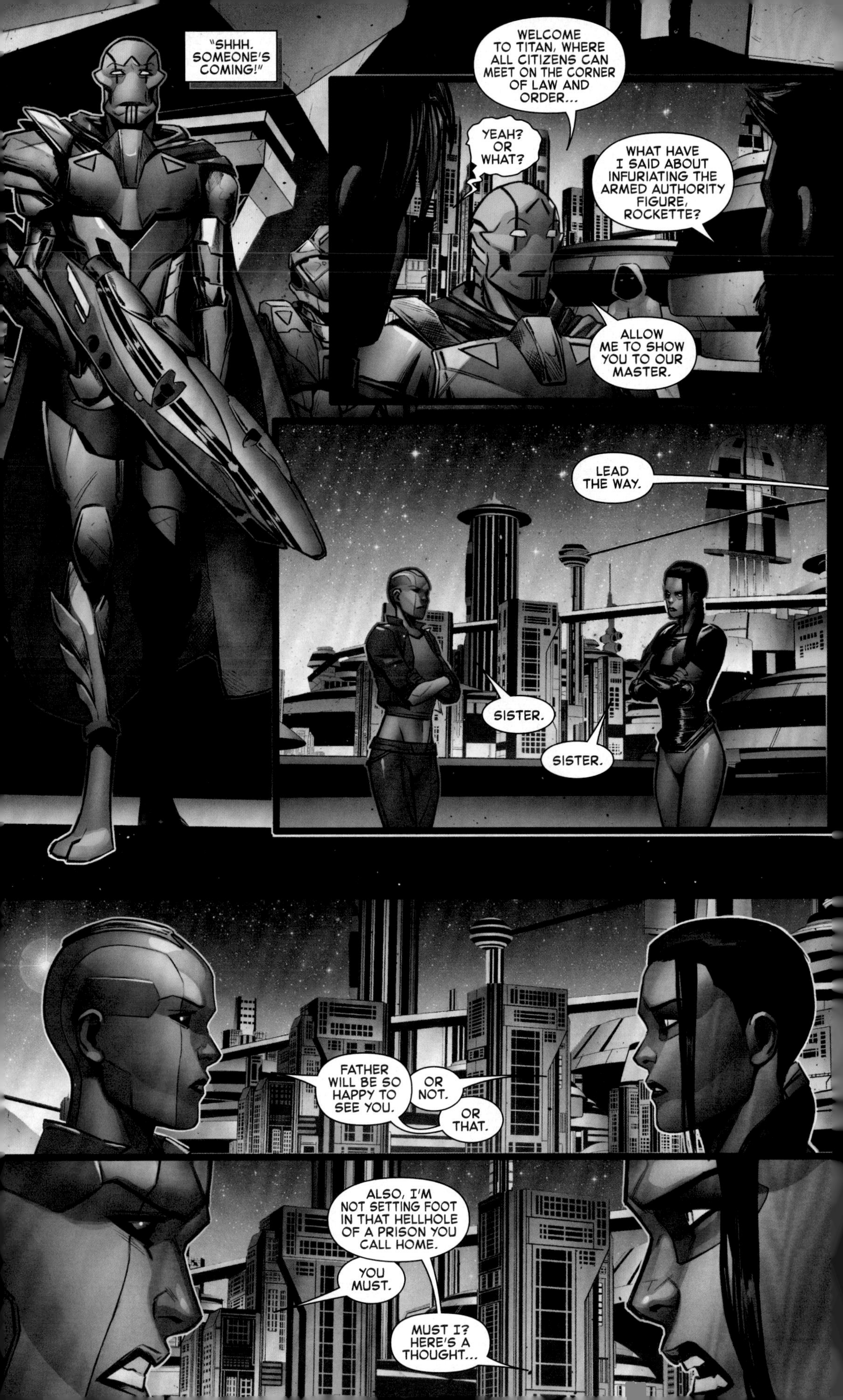
"SHHH. SOMEONE'S COMING!"
WELCOME TO TITAN, WHERE ALL CITIZENS CAN MEET ON THE CORNER OF LAW AND ORDER...
YEAH? OR WHAT?
WHAT HAVE I SAID ABOUT INFURIATING THE ARMED AUTHORITY FIGURE, ROCKETTE?
ALLOW ME TO SHOW YOU TO OUR MASTER.
LEAD THE WAY.
SISTER.
SISTER.
FATHER WILL BE SO HAPPY TO SEE YOU.
OR NOT.
OR THAT.
ALSO, I'M NOT SETTING FOOT IN THAT HELLHOLE OF A PRISON YOU CALL HOME.
YOU MUST.
MUST I? HERE'S A THOUGHT...

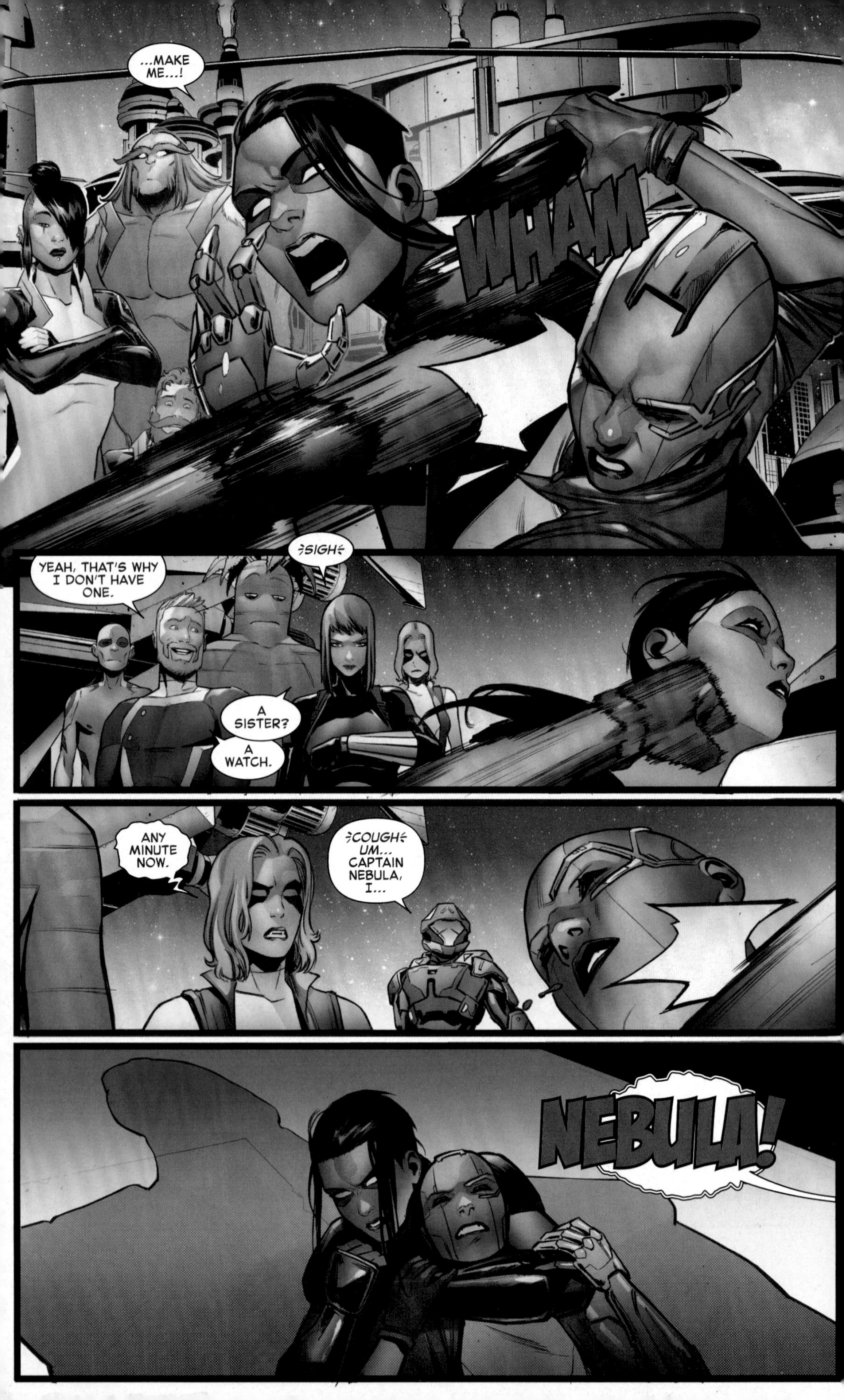
...MAKE ME...!
WHAM
YEAH, THAT'S WHY I DON'T HAVE ONE.
⸗SIGH⸗
A SISTER?
A WATCH.
ANY MINUTE NOW.
⸗COUGH⸗ UM... CAPTAIN NEBULA, I...
NEBULA!

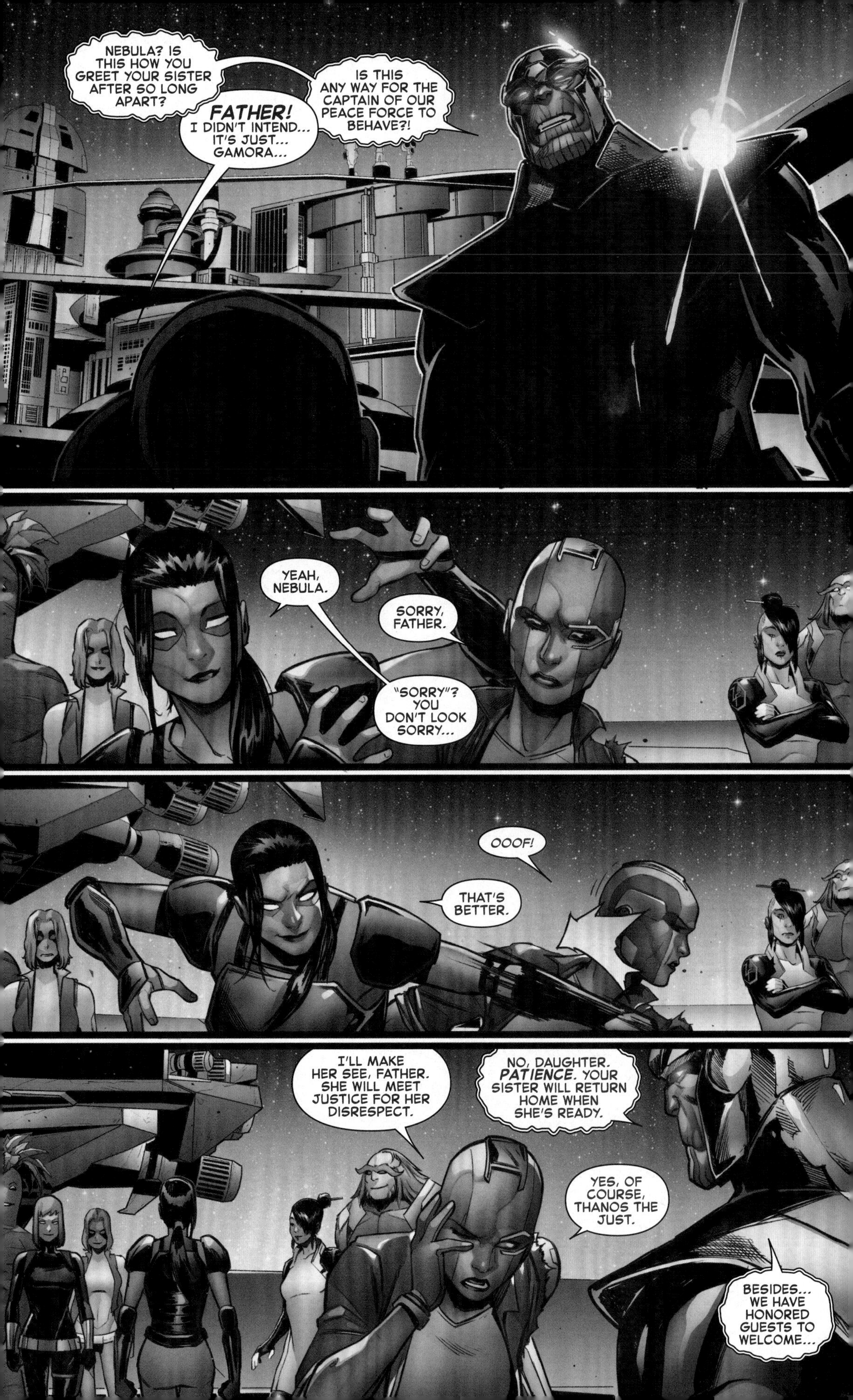

NEBULA? IS THIS HOW YOU GREET YOUR SISTER AFTER SO LONG APART?
IS THIS ANY WAY FOR THE CAPTAIN OF OUR PEACE FORCE TO BEHAVE?!
FATHER! I DIDN'T INTEND... IT'S JUST... GAMORA...
YEAH, NEBULA.
SORRY, FATHER.
"SORRY"? YOU DON'T LOOK SORRY...
OOOF!
THAT'S BETTER.
I'LL MAKE HER SEE, FATHER. SHE WILL MEET JUSTICE FOR HER DISRESPECT.
NO, DAUGHTER. PATIENCE. YOUR SISTER WILL RETURN HOME WHEN SHE'S READY.
YES, OF COURSE, THANOS THE JUST.
BESIDES... WE HAVE HONORED GUESTS TO WELCOME...

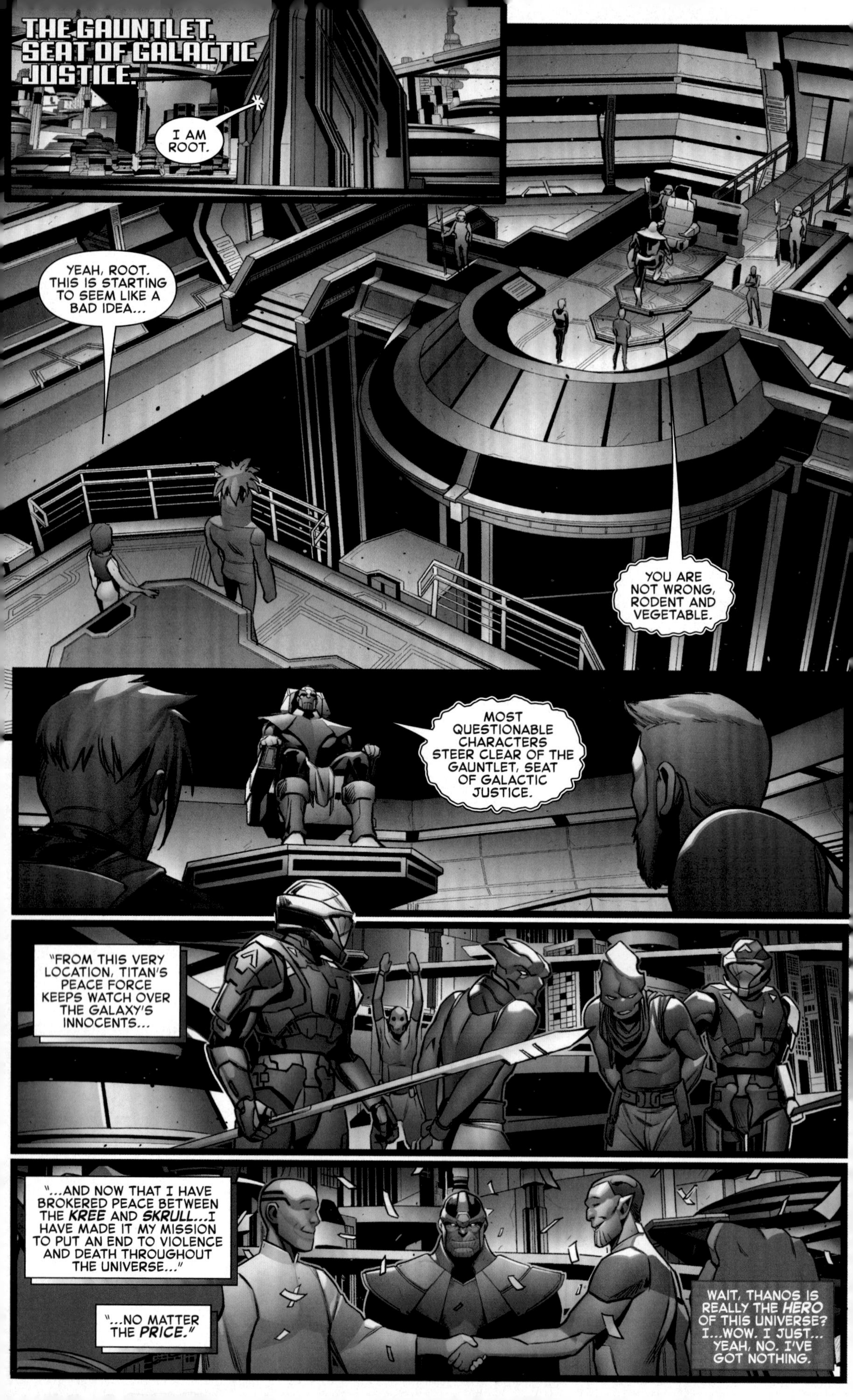
THE GAUNTLET. SEAT OF GALACTIC JUSTICE.
I AM ROOT.
YEAH, ROOT. THIS IS STARTING TO SEEM LIKE A BAD IDEA...
YOU ARE NOT WRONG, RODENT AND VEGETABLE.
MOST QUESTIONABLE CHARACTERS STEER CLEAR OF THE GAUNTLET, SEAT OF GALACTIC JUSTICE.
"FROM THIS VERY LOCATION, TITAN'S PEACE FORCE KEEPS WATCH OVER THE GALAXY'S INNOCENTS...
"...AND NOW THAT I HAVE BROKERED PEACE BETWEEN THE KREE AND SKRULL...I HAVE MADE IT MY MISSION TO PUT AN END TO VIOLENCE AND DEATH THROUGHOUT THE UNIVERSE..."
"...NO MATTER THE PRICE."
WAIT, THANOS IS REALLY THE HERO OF THIS UNIVERSE? I...WOW. I JUST... YEAH, NO. I'VE GOT NOTHING.

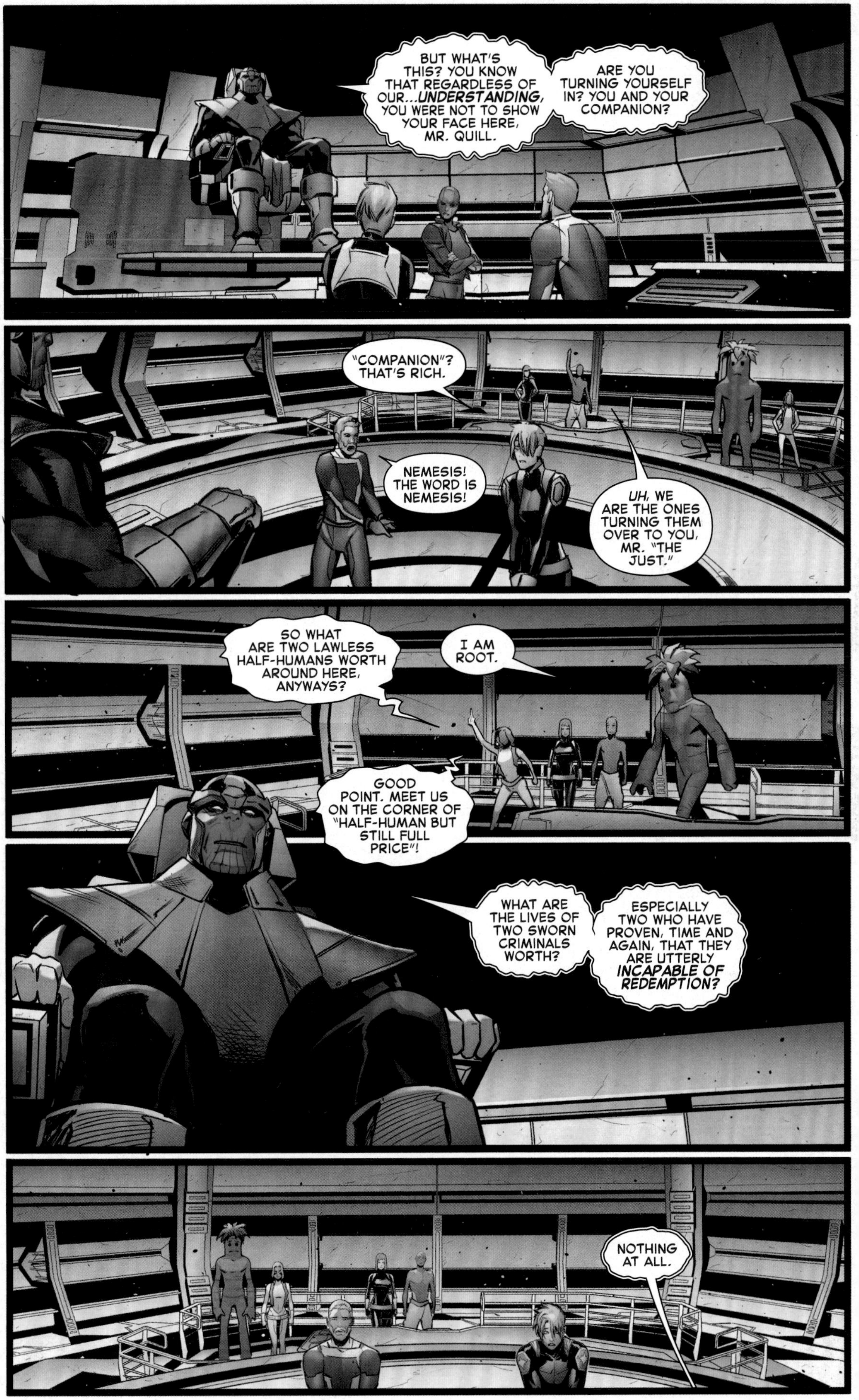
BUT WHAT'S THIS? YOU KNOW THAT REGARDLESS OF OUR...UNDERSTANDING, YOU WERE NOT TO SHOW YOUR FACE HERE, MR. QUILL.
ARE YOU TURNING YOURSELF IN? YOU AND YOUR COMPANION?
"COMPANION"? THAT'S RICH.
NEMESIS! THE WORD IS NEMESIS!
UH, WE ARE THE ONES TURNING THEM OVER TO YOU, MR. "THE JUST."
SO WHAT ARE TWO LAWLESS HALF-HUMANS WORTH AROUND HERE, ANYWAYS?
I AM ROOT.
GOOD POINT. MEET US ON THE CORNER OF "HALF-HUMAN BUT STILL FULL PRICE"!
WHAT ARE THE LIVES OF TWO SWORN CRIMINALS WORTH?
ESPECIALLY TWO WHO HAVE PROVEN, TIME AND AGAIN, THAT THEY ARE UTTERLY INCAPABLE OF REDEMPTION?
NOTHING AT ALL.

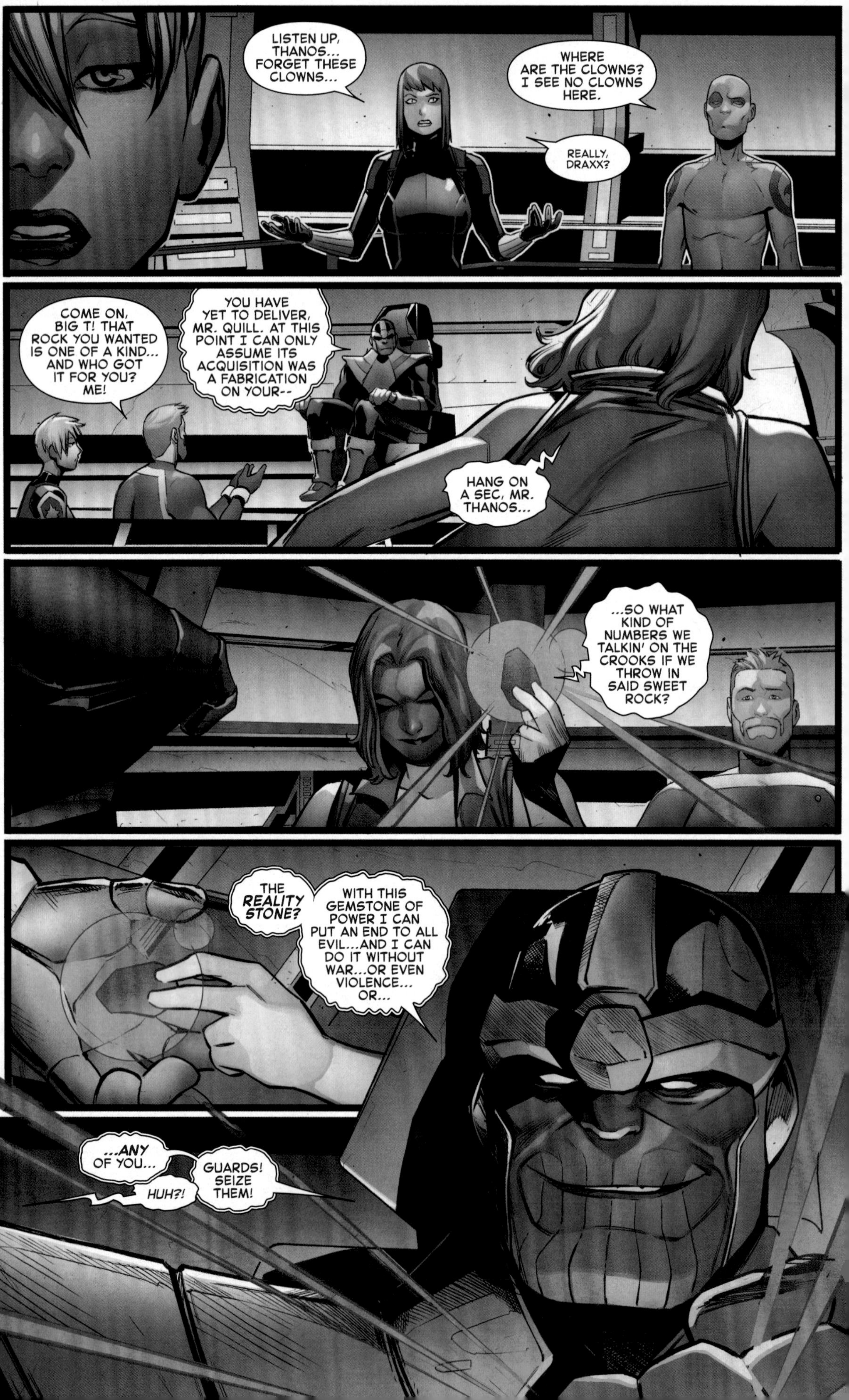
LISTEN UP, THANOS... FORGET THESE CLOWNS...
WHERE ARE THE CLOWNS? I SEE NO CLOWNS HERE.
REALLY, DRAXX?
COME ON, BIG T! THAT ROCK YOU WANTED IS ONE OF A KIND... AND WHO GOT IT FOR YOU? ME!
YOU HAVE YET TO DELIVER, MR. QUILL. AT THIS POINT I CAN ONLY ASSUME ITS ACQUISITION WAS A FABRICATION ON YOUR--
HANG ON A SEC, MR. THANOS...
...SO WHAT KIND OF NUMBERS WE TALKIN' ON THE CROOKS IF WE THROW IN SAID SWEET ROCK?
THE *REALITY STONE?*
WITH THIS GEMSTONE OF POWER I CAN PUT AN END TO ALL EVIL...AND I CAN DO IT WITHOUT WAR...OR EVEN VIOLENCE... OR...
...ANY OF YOU...
HUH?!
GUARDS! SEIZE THEM!

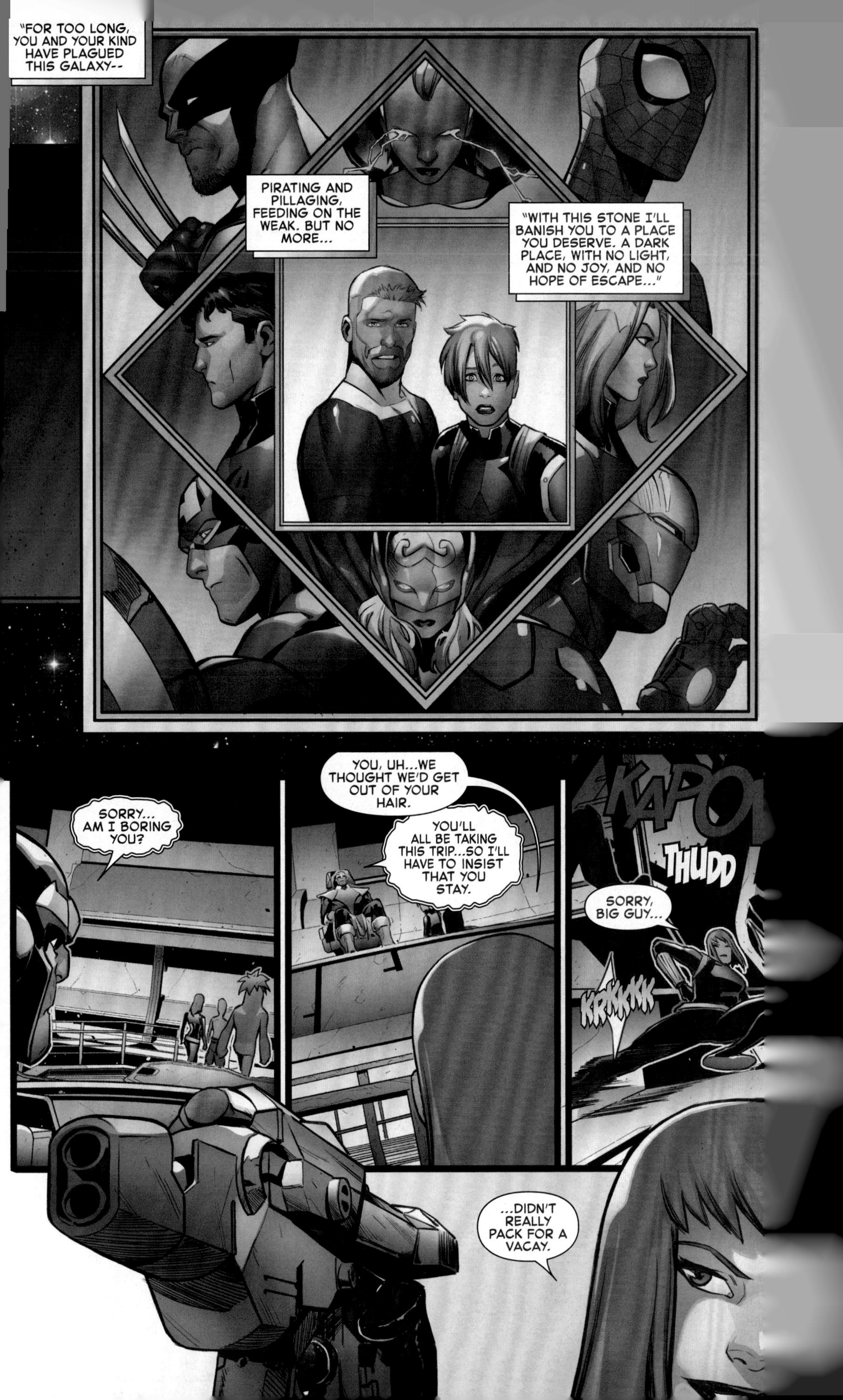
"FOR TOO LONG, YOU AND YOUR KIND HAVE PLAGUED THIS GALAXY--
PIRATING AND PILLAGING, FEEDING ON THE WEAK. BUT NO MORE...
"WITH THIS STONE I'LL BANISH YOU TO A PLACE YOU DESERVE. A DARK PLACE, WITH NO LIGHT, AND NO JOY, AND NO HOPE OF ESCAPE..."
SORRY... AM I BORING YOU?
YOU, UH...WE THOUGHT WE'D GET OUT OF YOUR HAIR.
YOU'LL ALL BE TAKING THIS TRIP...SO I'LL HAVE TO INSIST THAT YOU STAY.
THUDD
SORRY, BIG GUY...
KRKKKK
...DIDN'T REALLY PACK FOR A VACAY.

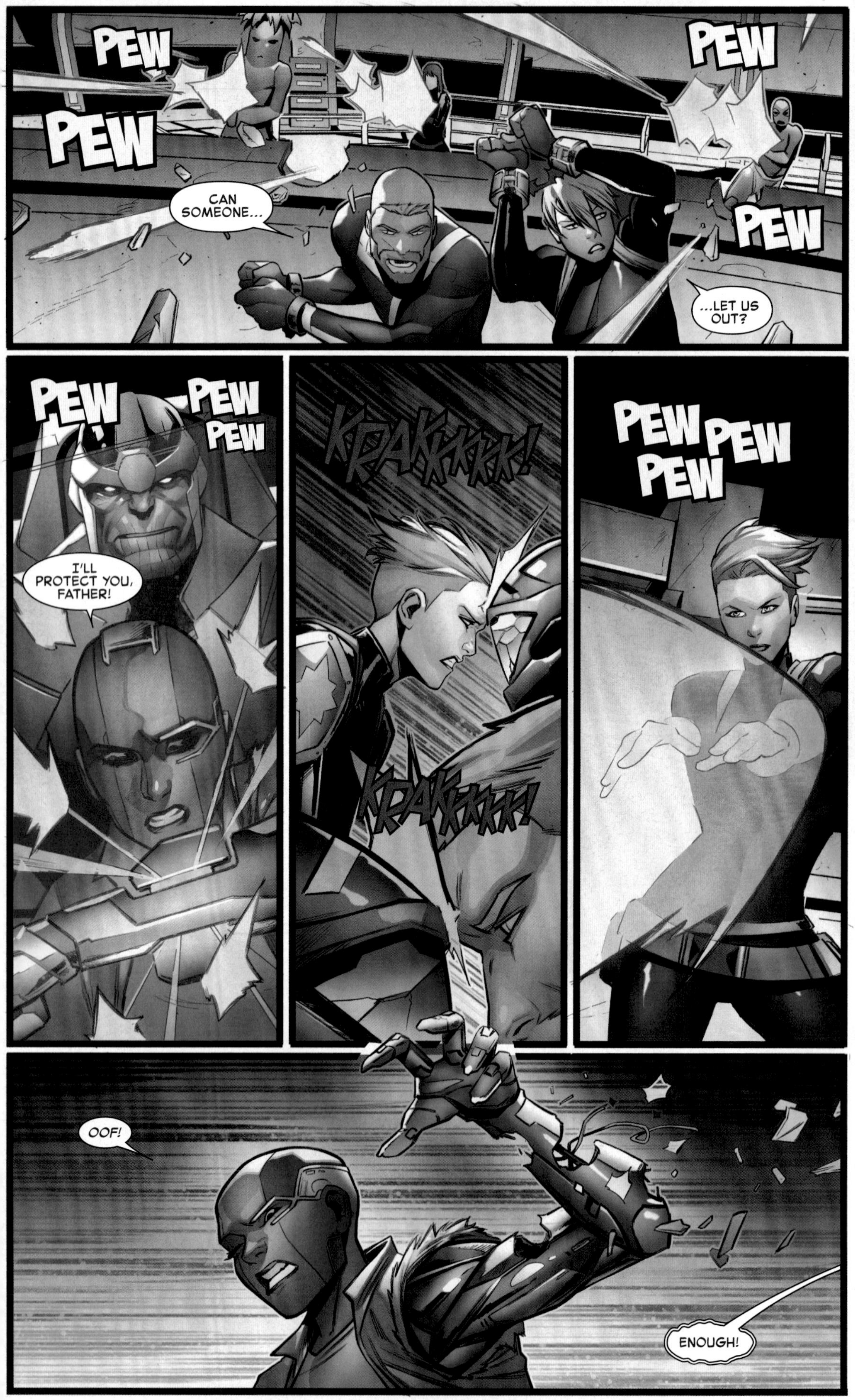
PEW
PEW
CAN SOMEONE...
PEW
PEW
...LET US OUT?
PEW PEW PEW
I'LL PROTECT YOU, FATHER!
KRAKKKKK!
KRAKKKKK!
PEW PEW PEW
OOF!
ENOUGH!

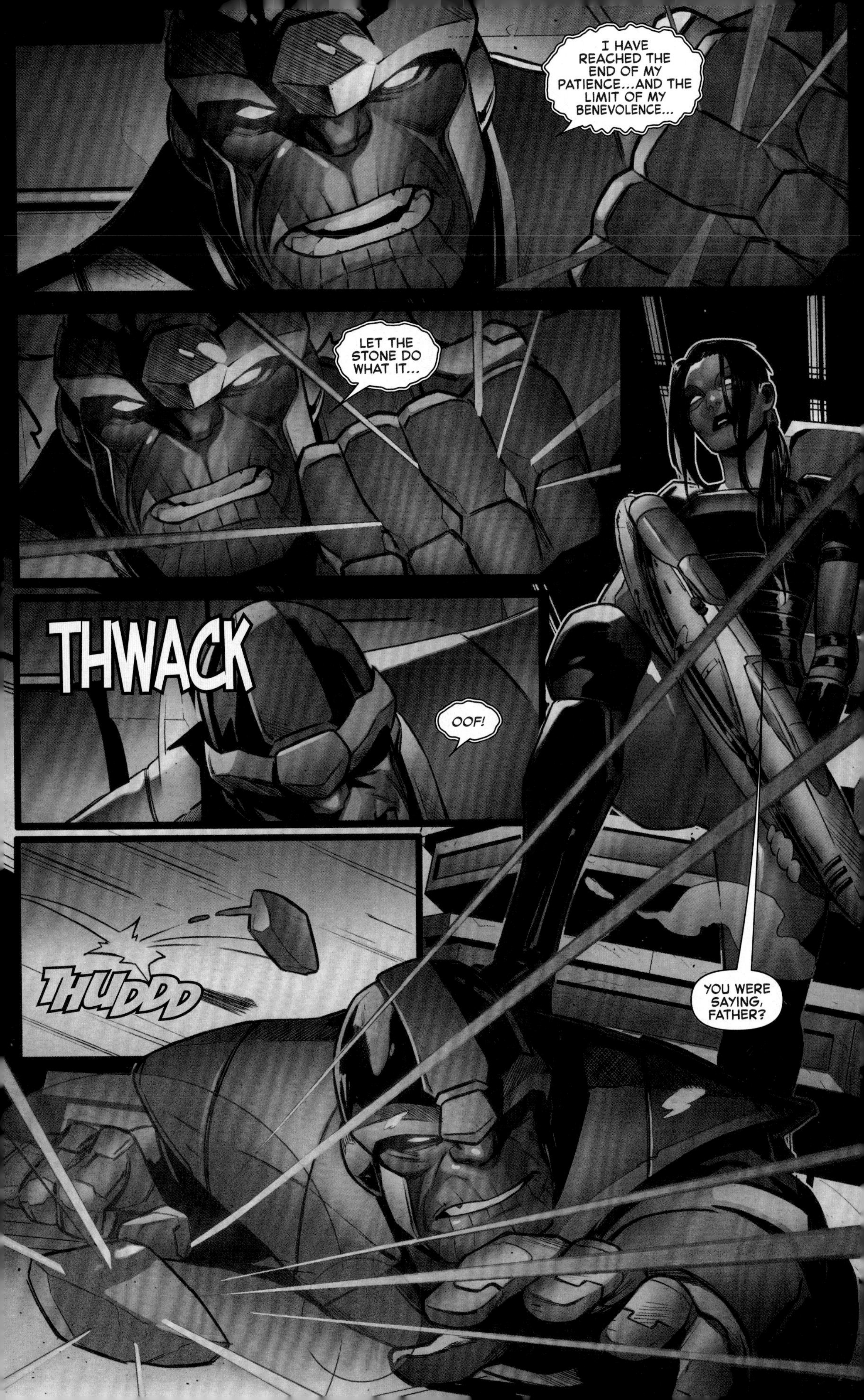
I HAVE REACHED THE END OF MY PATIENCE...AND THE LIMIT OF MY BENEVOLENCE...
LET THE STONE DO WHAT IT...
THWACK
OOF!
THUDDD
YOU WERE SAYING, FATHER?

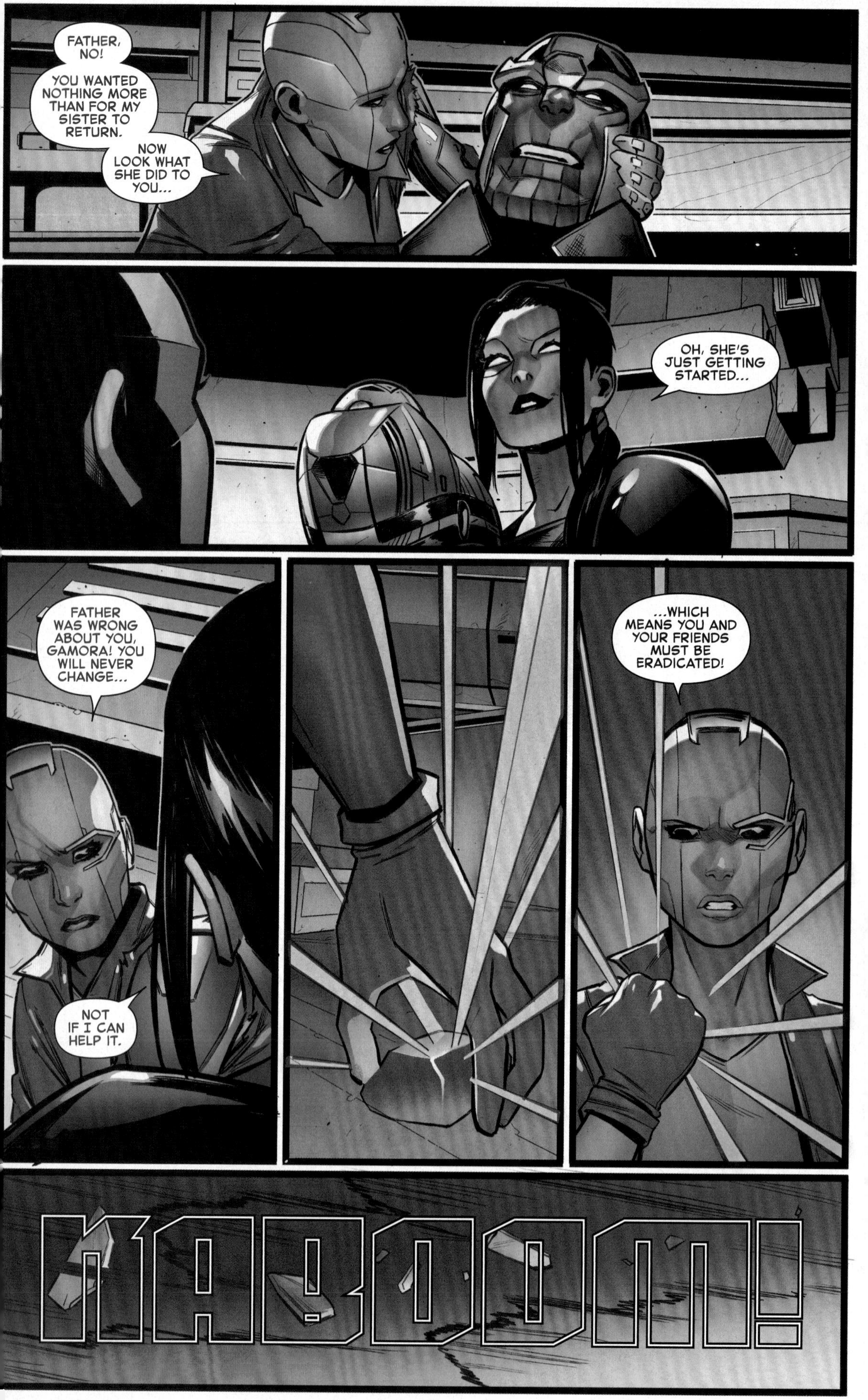
FATHER, NO!
YOU WANTED NOTHING MORE THAN FOR MY SISTER TO RETURN.
NOW LOOK WHAT SHE DID TO YOU...
OH, SHE'S JUST GETTING STARTED...
FATHER WAS WRONG ABOUT YOU, GAMORA! YOU WILL NEVER CHANGE...
NOT IF I CAN HELP IT.
...WHICH MEANS YOU AND YOUR FRIENDS MUST BE ERADICATED!
KABOOM!

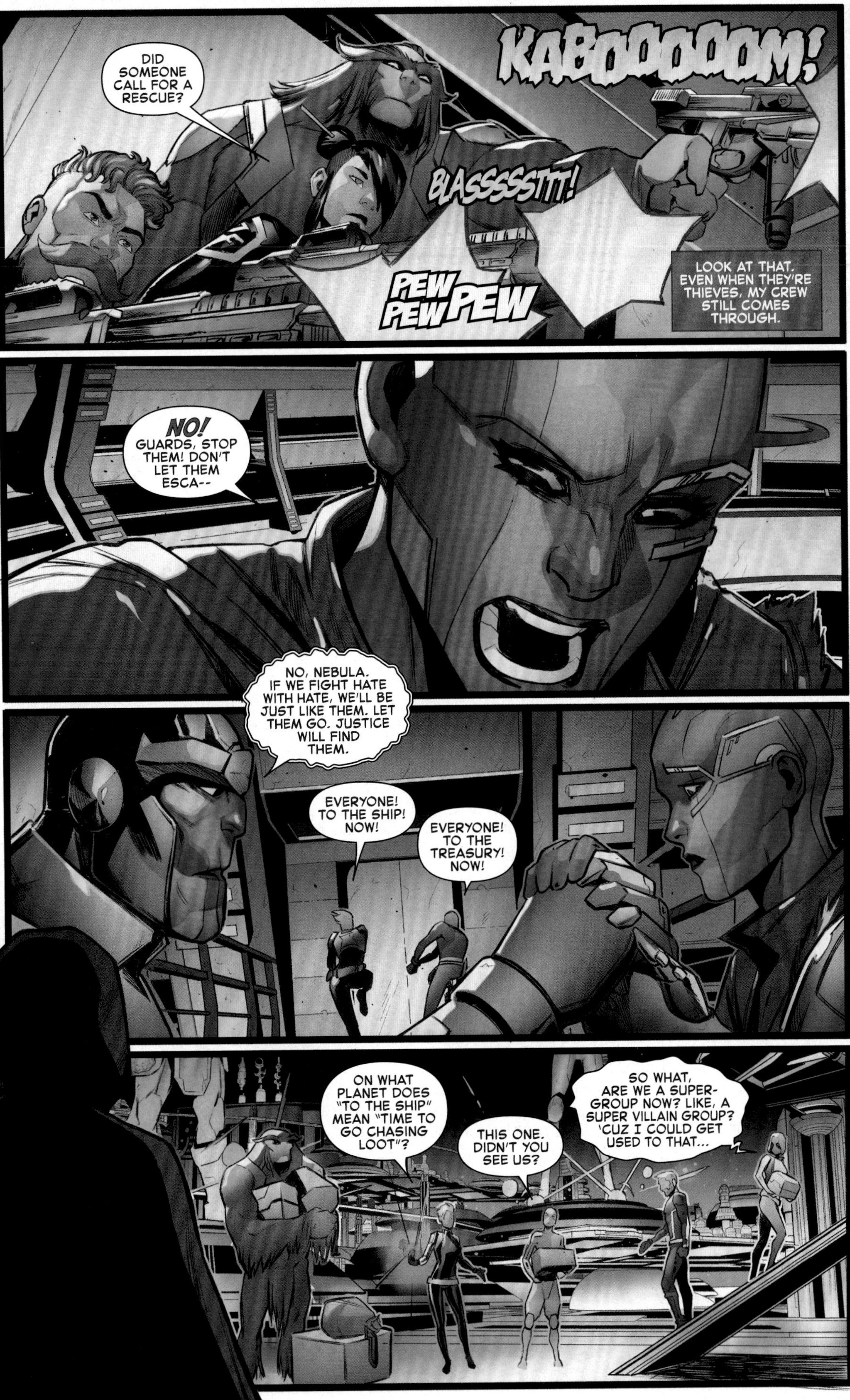
KABOOOOOOM!
DID SOMEONE CALL FOR A RESCUE?
BLASSSSSTTT!
PEW PEW PEW
LOOK AT THAT. EVEN WHEN THEY'RE THIEVES, MY CREW STILL COMES THROUGH.
NO! GUARDS, STOP THEM! DON'T LET THEM ESCA--
NO, NEBULA. IF WE FIGHT HATE WITH HATE, WE'LL BE JUST LIKE THEM. LET THEM GO. JUSTICE WILL FIND THEM.
EVERYONE! TO THE SHIP! NOW!
EVERYONE! TO THE TREASURY! NOW!
ON WHAT PLANET DOES "TO THE SHIP" MEAN "TIME TO GO CHASING LOOT"?
THIS ONE. DIDN'T YOU SEE US?
SO WHAT, ARE WE A SUPER-GROUP NOW? LIKE, A SUPER VILLAIN GROUP? 'CUZ I COULD GET USED TO THAT...

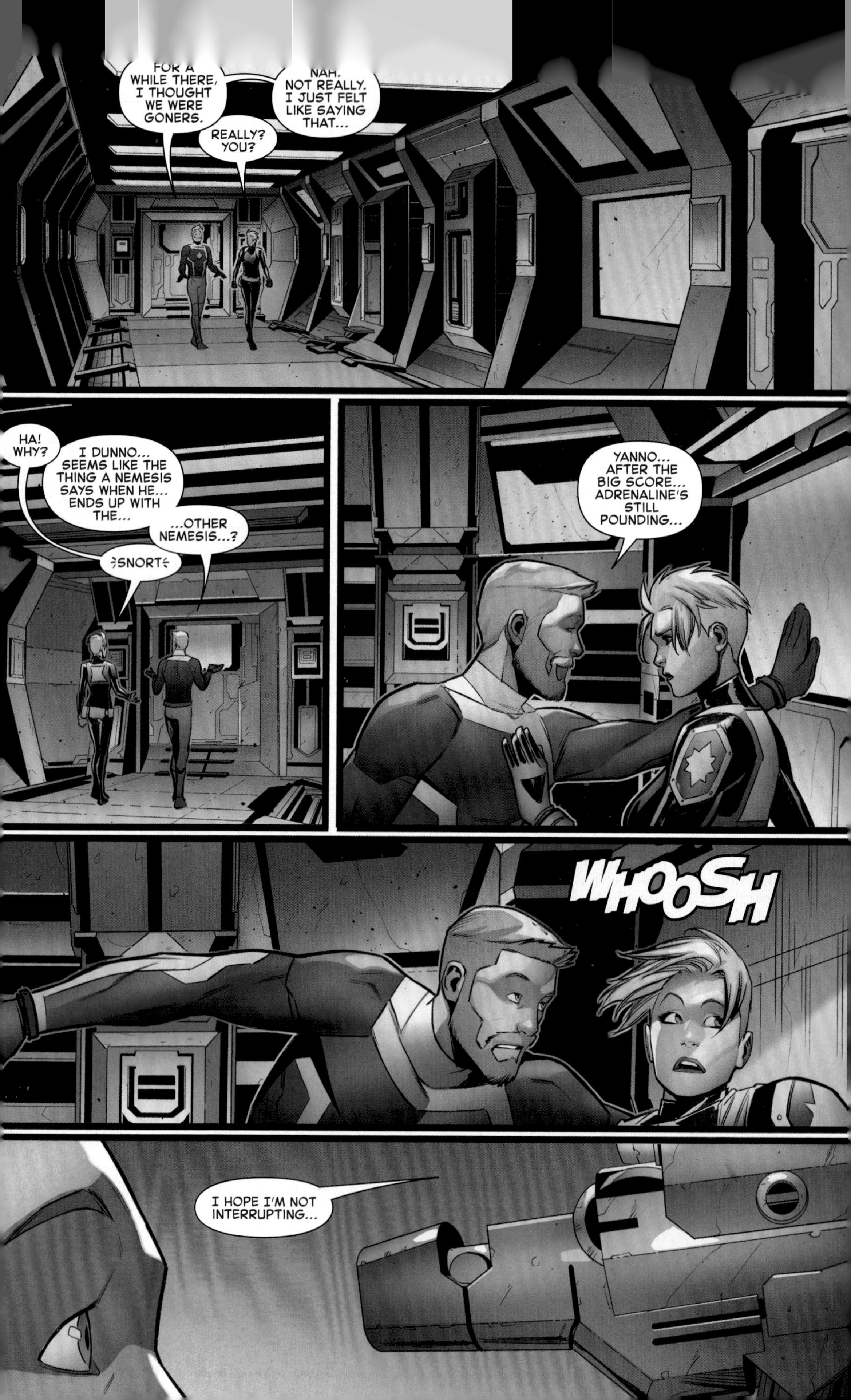
FOR A WHILE THERE, I THOUGHT WE WERE GONERS.
REALLY? YOU?
NAH. NOT REALLY. I JUST FELT LIKE SAYING THAT...
I DUNNO... SEEMS LIKE THE THING A NEMESIS SAYS WHEN HE... ENDS UP WITH THE...
...OTHER NEMESIS...?
HA! WHY?
SNORT
YANNO... AFTER THE BIG SCORE... ADRENALINE'S STILL POUNDING...
WHOOSH
I HOPE I'M NOT INTERRUPTING...

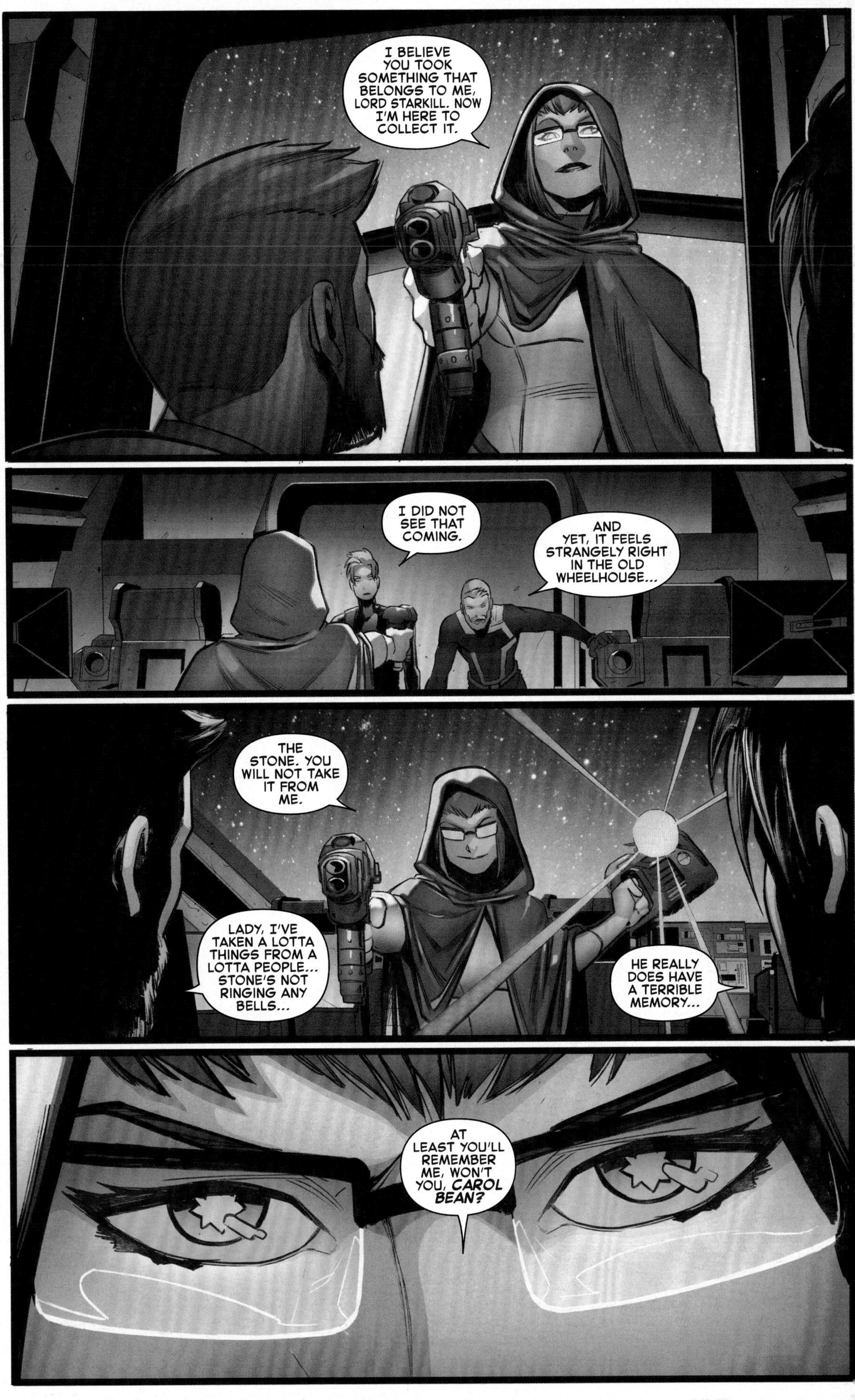
I BELIEVE YOU TOOK SOMETHING THAT BELONGS TO ME, LORD STARKILL. NOW I'M HERE TO COLLECT IT.
I DID NOT SEE THAT COMING.
AND YET, IT FEELS STRANGELY RIGHT IN THE OLD WHEELHOUSE...
THE STONE. YOU WILL NOT TAKE IT FROM ME.
LADY, I'VE TAKEN A LOTTA THINGS FROM A LOTTA PEOPLE... STONE'S NOT RINGING ANY BELLS...
HE REALLY DOES HAVE A TERRIBLE MEMORY...
AT LEAST YOU'LL REMEMBER ME, WON'T YOU, CAROL BEAN?

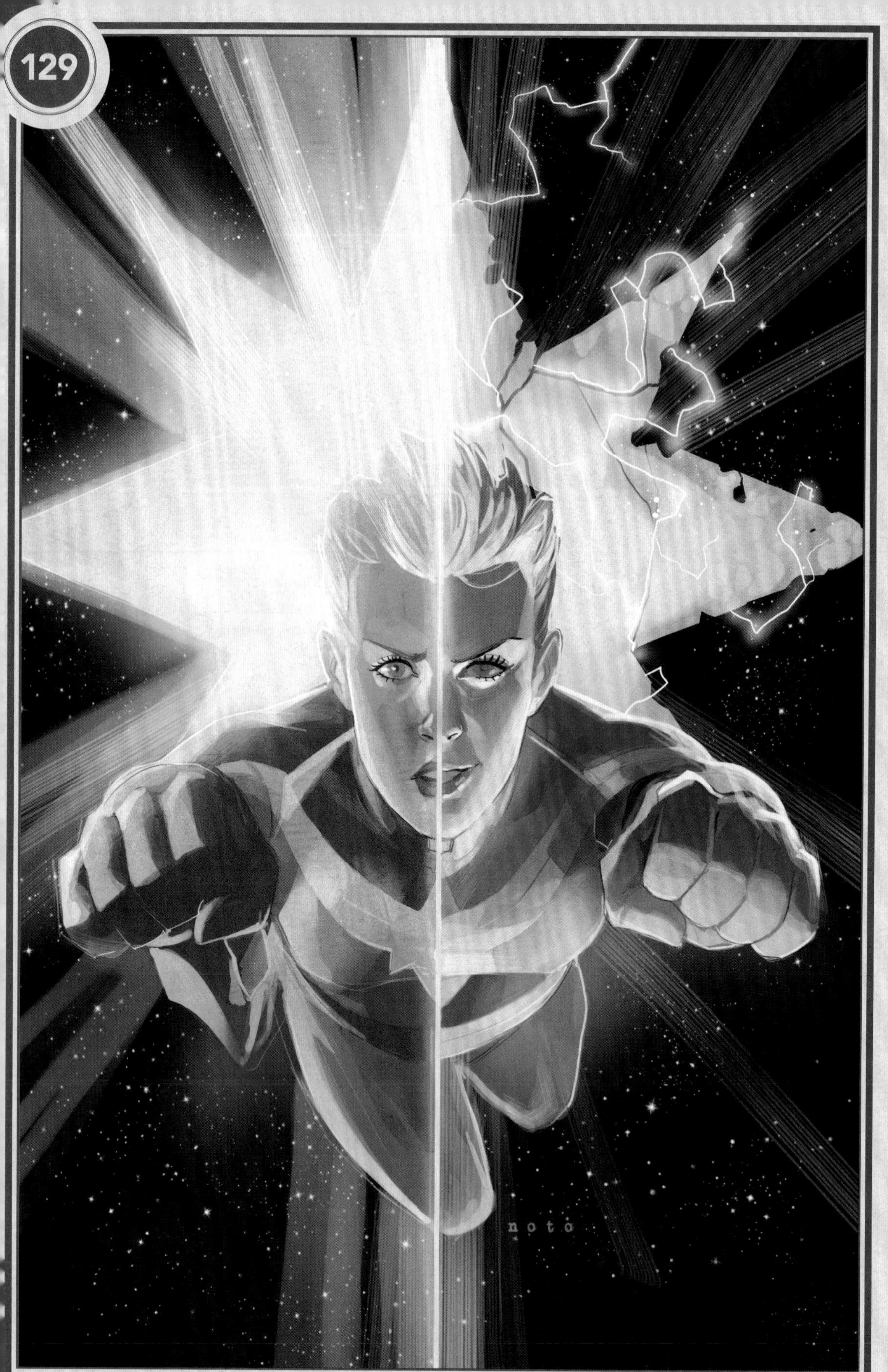
129
noto

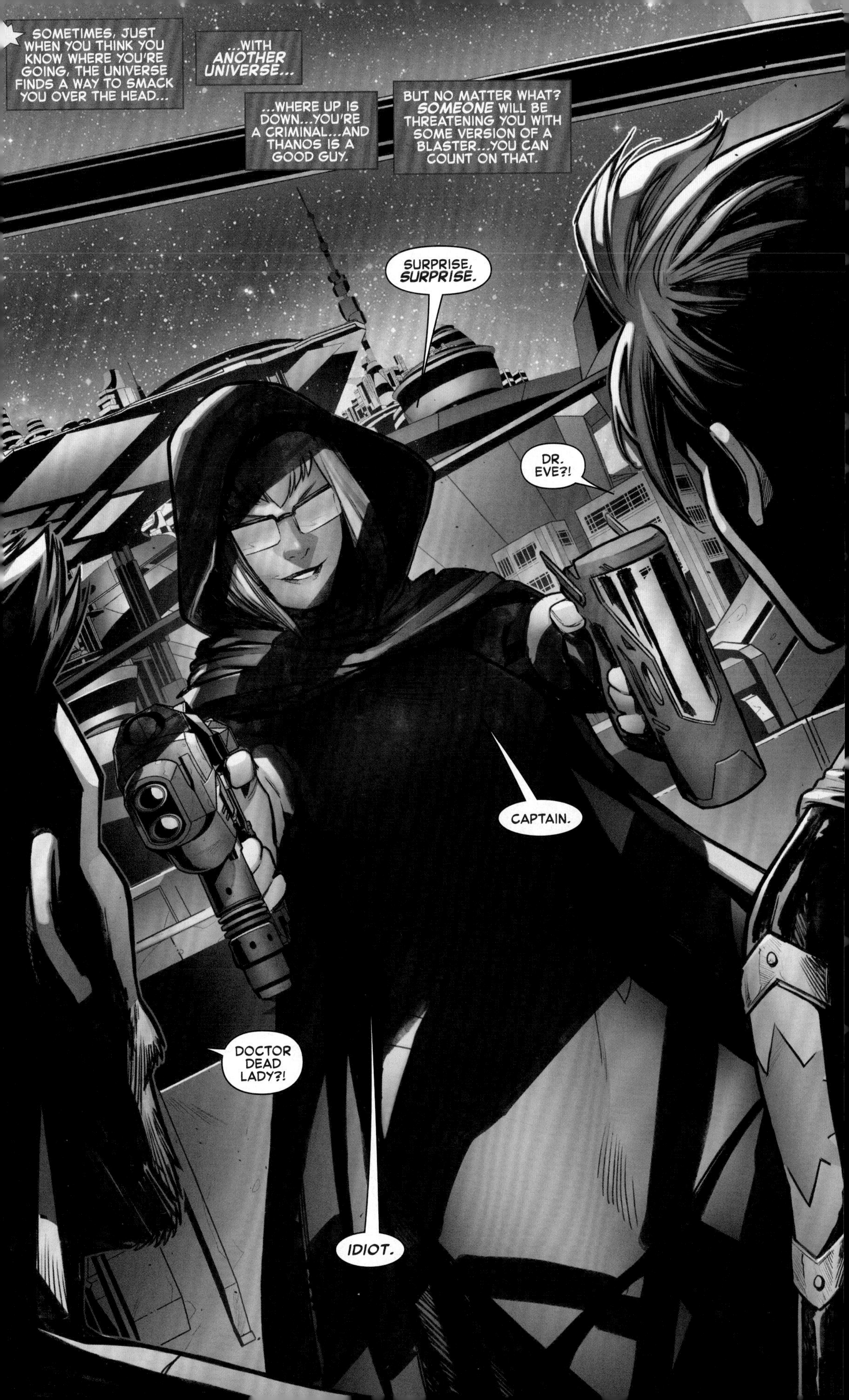
SOMETIMES, JUST WHEN YOU THINK YOU KNOW WHERE YOU'RE GOING, THE UNIVERSE FINDS A WAY TO SMACK YOU OVER THE HEAD...
...WITH ANOTHER UNIVERSE...
...WHERE UP IS DOWN...YOU'RE A CRIMINAL...AND THANOS IS A GOOD GUY.
BUT NO MATTER WHAT? SOMEONE WILL BE THREATENING YOU WITH SOME VERSION OF A BLASTER...YOU CAN COUNT ON THAT.
SURPRISE, SURPRISE.
DR. EVE?!
CAPTAIN.
DOCTOR DEAD LADY?!
IDIOT.

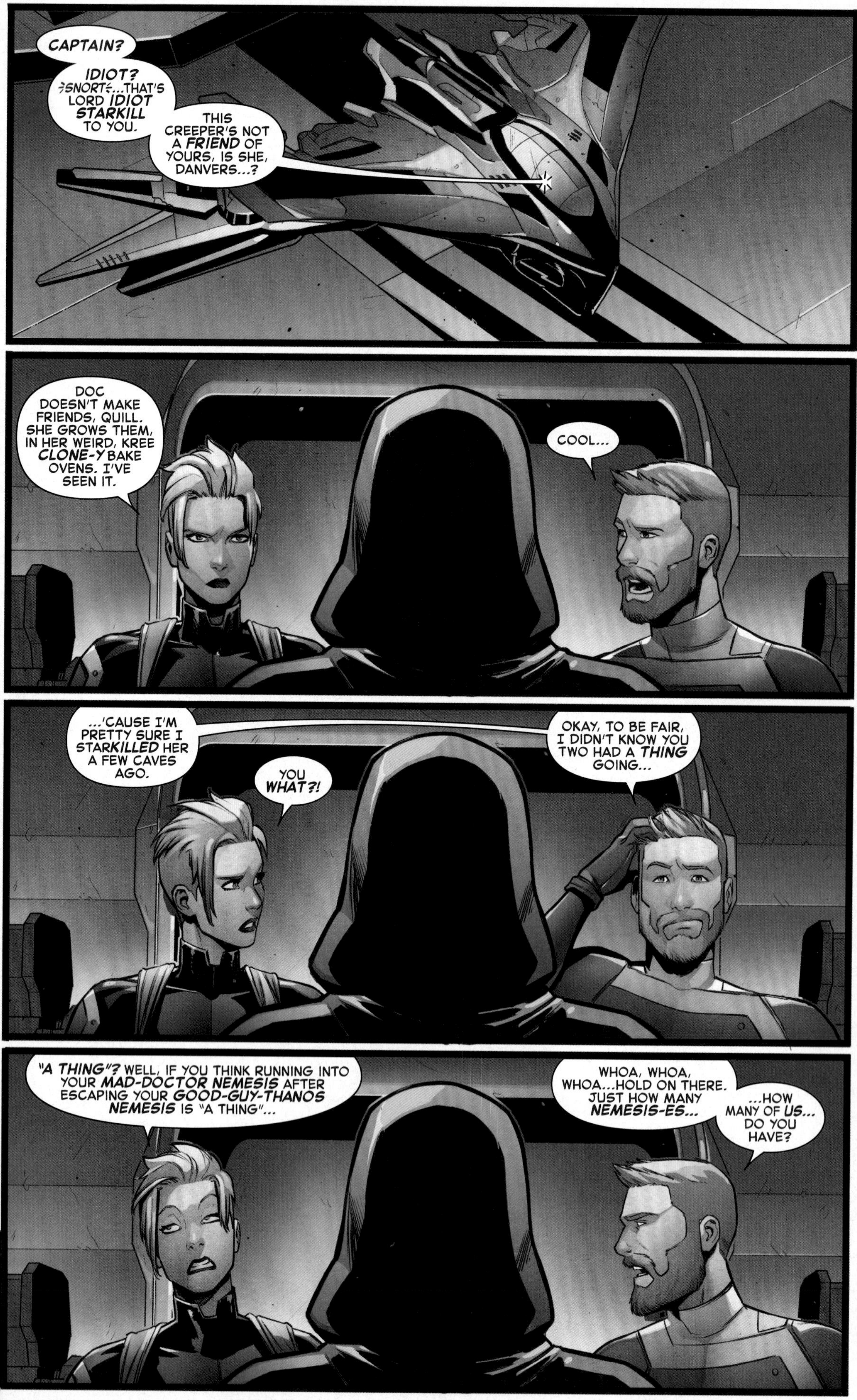
CAPTAIN?
IDIOT? ⸗SNORT⸗...THAT'S LORD IDIOT STARKILL TO YOU.
THIS CREEPER'S NOT A FRIEND OF YOURS, IS SHE, DANVERS...?
DOC DOESN'T MAKE FRIENDS, QUILL. SHE GROWS THEM, IN HER WEIRD, KREE CLONE-Y BAKE OVENS. I'VE SEEN IT.
COOL...
...'CAUSE I'M PRETTY SURE I STARKILLED HER A FEW CAVES AGO.
OKAY, TO BE FAIR, I DIDN'T KNOW YOU TWO HAD A THING GOING...
YOU WHAT?!
"A THING"? WELL, IF YOU THINK RUNNING INTO YOUR MAD-DOCTOR NEMESIS AFTER ESCAPING YOUR GOOD-GUY-THANOS NEMESIS IS "A THING"...
WHOA, WHOA, WHOA...HOLD ON THERE. JUST HOW MANY NEMESIS-ES...
...HOW MANY OF US... DO YOU HAVE?

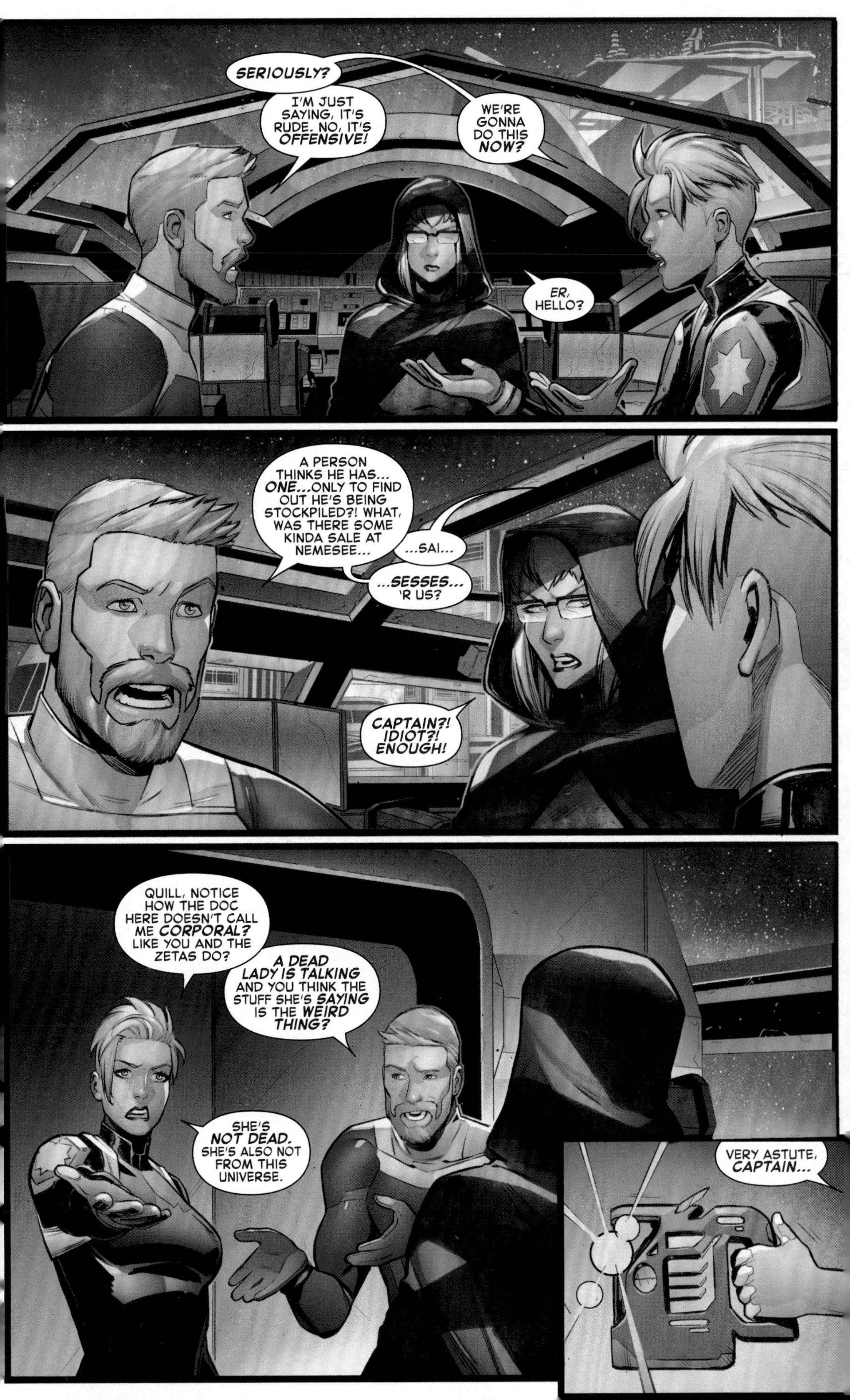
SERIOUSLY?
I'M JUST SAYING, IT'S RUDE. NO, IT'S OFFENSIVE!
WE'RE GONNA DO THIS NOW?
ER, HELLO?
A PERSON THINKS HE HAS... ONE...ONLY TO FIND OUT HE'S BEING STOCKPILED?! WHAT, WAS THERE SOME KINDA SALE AT NEMESEE...
...SAI...
...SESSES... 'R US?
CAPTAIN?! IDIOT?! ENOUGH!
QUILL, NOTICE HOW THE DOC HERE DOESN'T CALL ME CORPORAL? LIKE YOU AND THE ZETAS DO?
A DEAD LADY IS TALKING AND YOU THINK THE STUFF SHE'S SAYING IS THE WEIRD THING?
SHE'S NOT DEAD. SHE'S ALSO NOT FROM THIS UNIVERSE.
VERY ASTUTE, CAPTAIN...

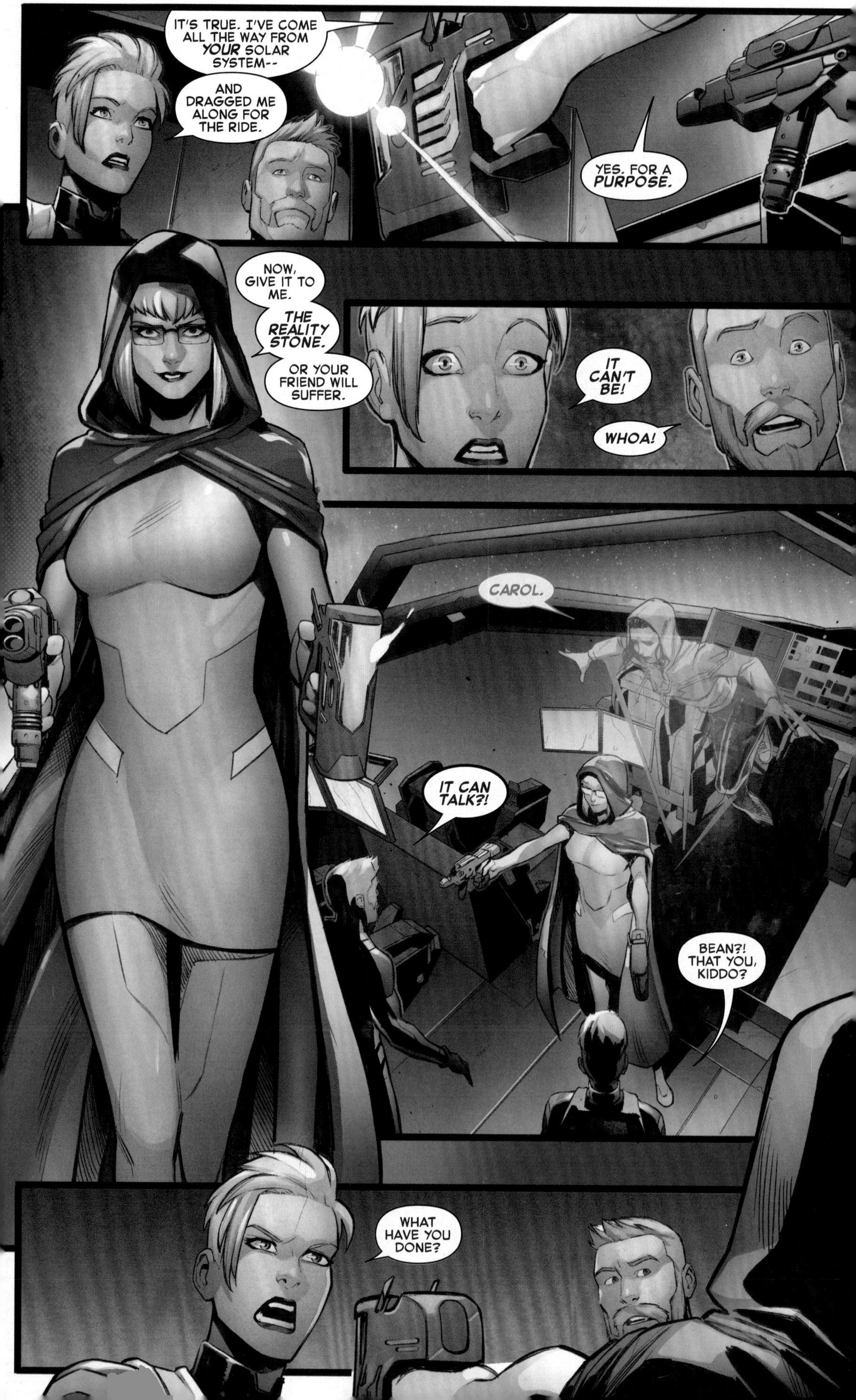
IT'S TRUE. I'VE COME ALL THE WAY FROM YOUR SOLAR SYSTEM--
AND DRAGGED ME ALONG FOR THE RIDE.
YES. FOR A PURPOSE.
NOW, GIVE IT TO ME.
THE REALITY STONE.
OR YOUR FRIEND WILL SUFFER.
IT CAN'T BE!
WHOA!
CAROL.
IT CAN TALK?!
BEAN?! THAT YOU, KIDDO?
WHAT HAVE YOU DONE?

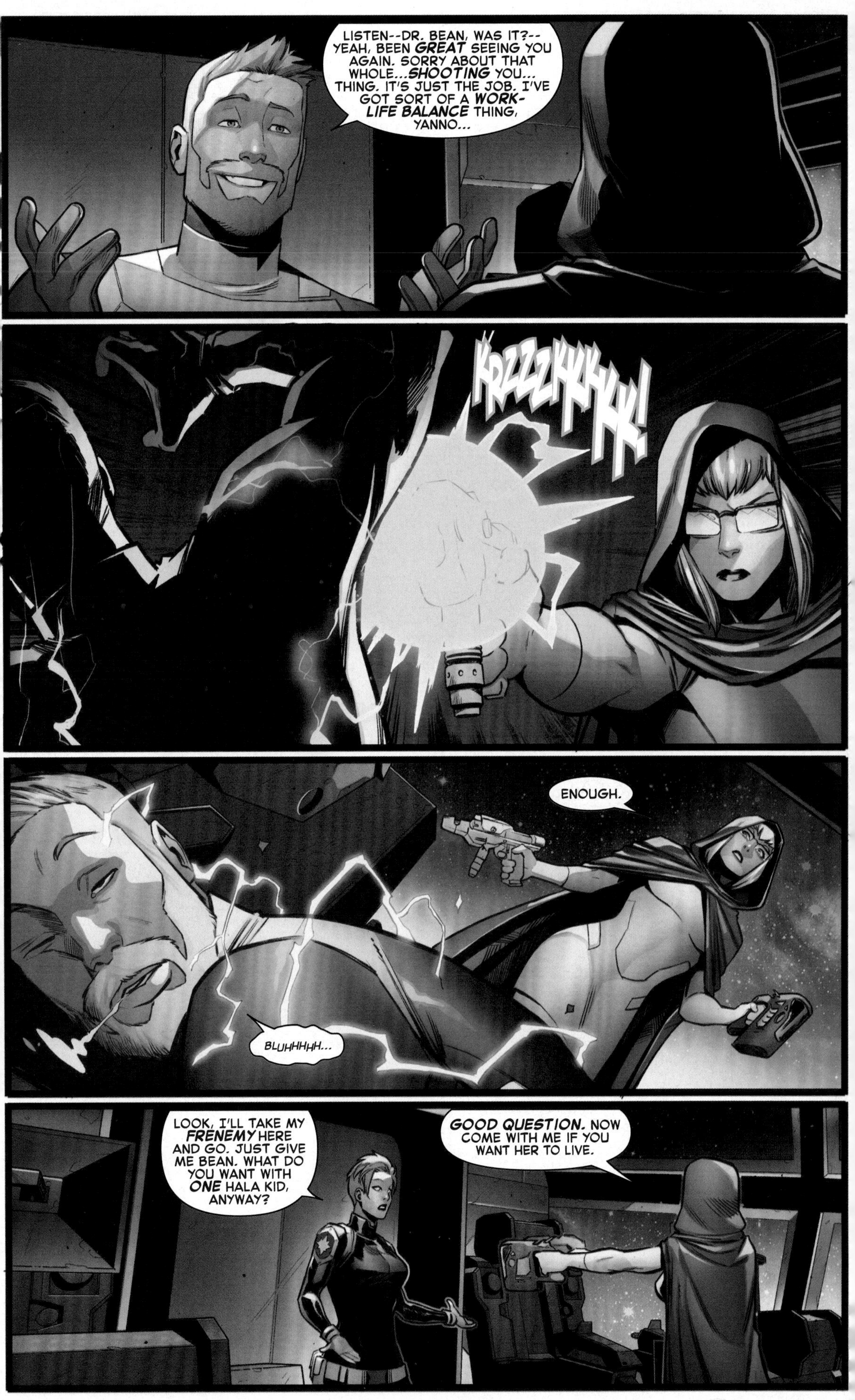
LISTEN--DR. BEAN, WAS IT?-- YEAH, BEEN GREAT SEEING YOU AGAIN. SORRY ABOUT THAT WHOLE...SHOOTING YOU... THING. IT'S JUST THE JOB. I'VE GOT SORT OF A WORK-LIFE BALANCE THING, YANNO...
KRZZZKKKKK!
ENOUGH.
BLUHHHHH...
LOOK, I'LL TAKE MY FRENEMY HERE AND GO. JUST GIVE ME BEAN. WHAT DO YOU WANT WITH ONE HALA KID, ANYWAY?
GOOD QUESTION. NOW COME WITH ME IF YOU WANT HER TO LIVE.

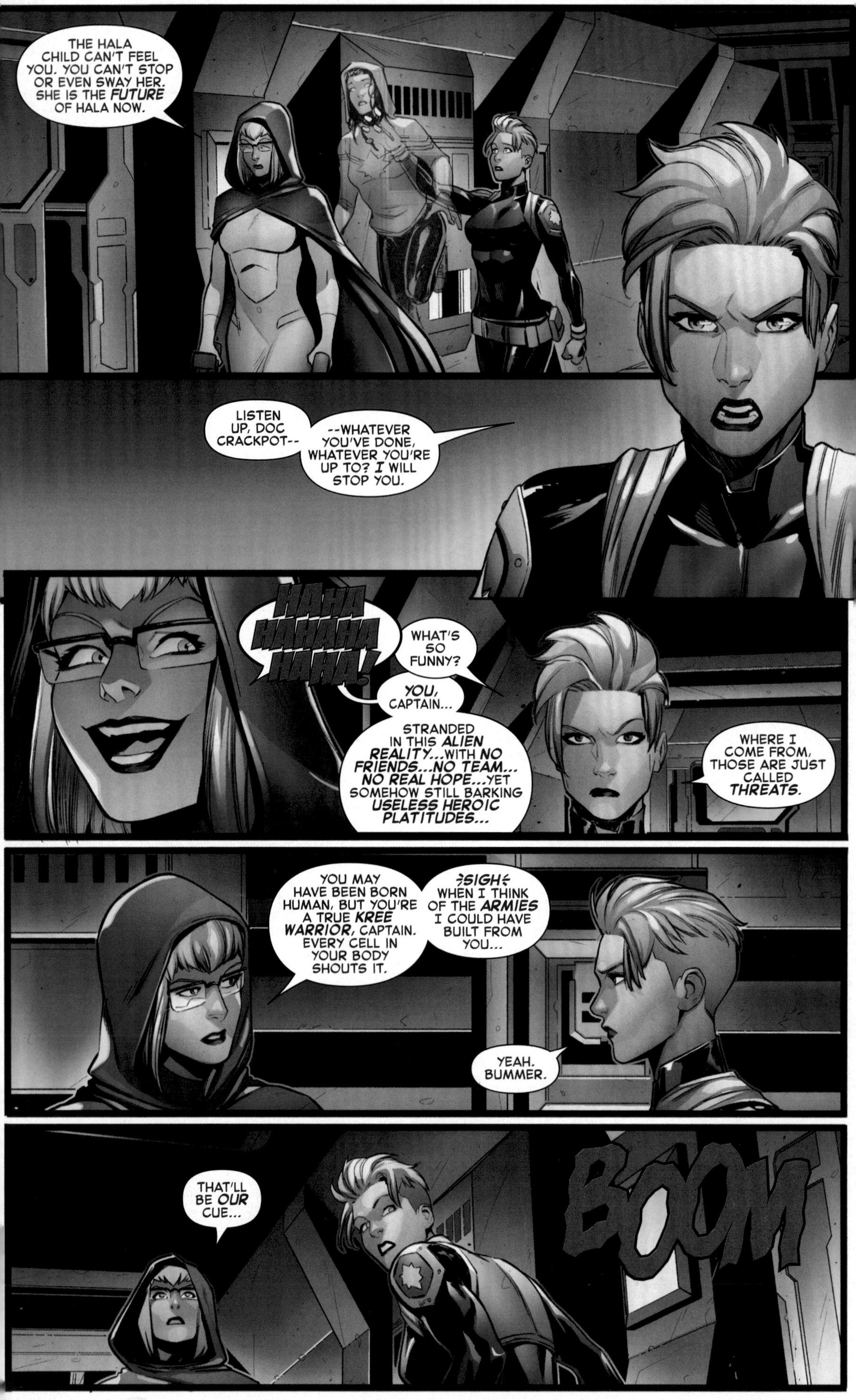
THE HALA CHILD CAN'T FEEL YOU. YOU CAN'T STOP OR EVEN SWAY HER. SHE IS THE FUTURE OF HALA NOW.
LISTEN UP, DOC CRACKPOT--
--WHATEVER YOU'VE DONE, WHATEVER YOU'RE UP TO? I WILL STOP YOU.
HAHA HAHAHA HAHA!
WHAT'S SO FUNNY?
YOU, CAPTAIN...
STRANDED IN THIS ALIEN REALITY...WITH NO FRIENDS...NO TEAM... NO REAL HOPE...YET SOMEHOW STILL BARKING USELESS HEROIC PLATITUDES...
WHERE I COME FROM, THOSE ARE JUST CALLED THREATS.
YOU MAY HAVE BEEN BORN HUMAN, BUT YOU'RE A TRUE KREE WARRIOR, CAPTAIN. EVERY CELL IN YOUR BODY SHOUTS IT.
SIGH WHEN I THINK OF THE ARMIES I COULD HAVE BUILT FROM YOU...
YEAH. BUMMER.
THAT'LL BE OUR CUE...
BOOM

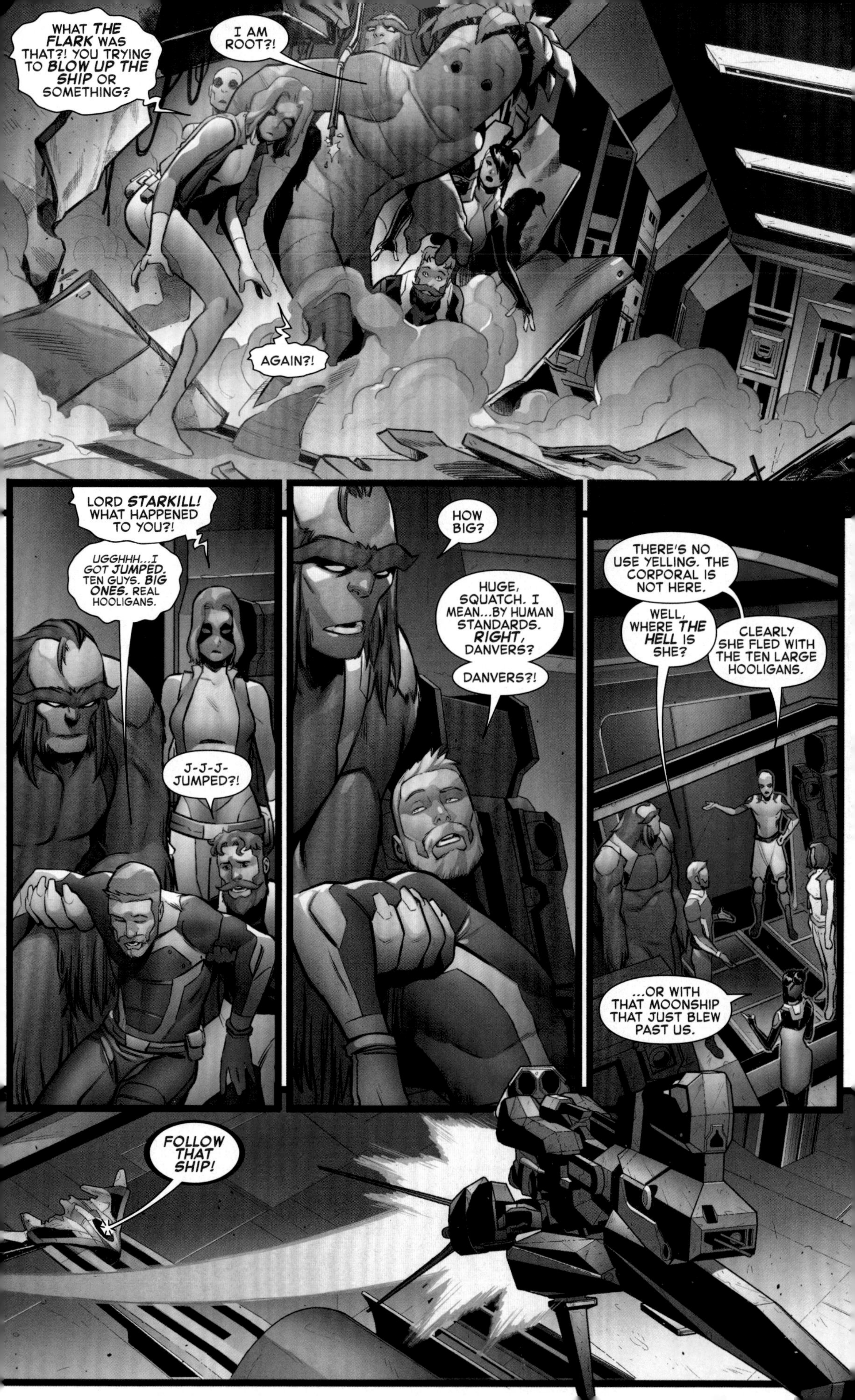
WHAT THE FLARK WAS THAT?! YOU TRYING TO BLOW UP THE SHIP OR SOMETHING?
I AM ROOT?!
AGAIN?!
LORD STARKILL! WHAT HAPPENED TO YOU?!
UGGHHH...I GOT JUMPED. TEN GUYS. BIG ONES. REAL HOOLIGANS.
J-J-J-JUMPED?!
HOW BIG?
HUGE, SQUATCH. I MEAN...BY HUMAN STANDARDS. RIGHT, DANVERS?
DANVERS?!
THERE'S NO USE YELLING. THE CORPORAL IS NOT HERE.
WELL, WHERE THE HELL IS SHE?
CLEARLY SHE FLED WITH THE TEN LARGE HOOLIGANS.
...OR WITH THAT MOONSHIP THAT JUST BLEW PAST US.
FOLLOW THAT SHIP!

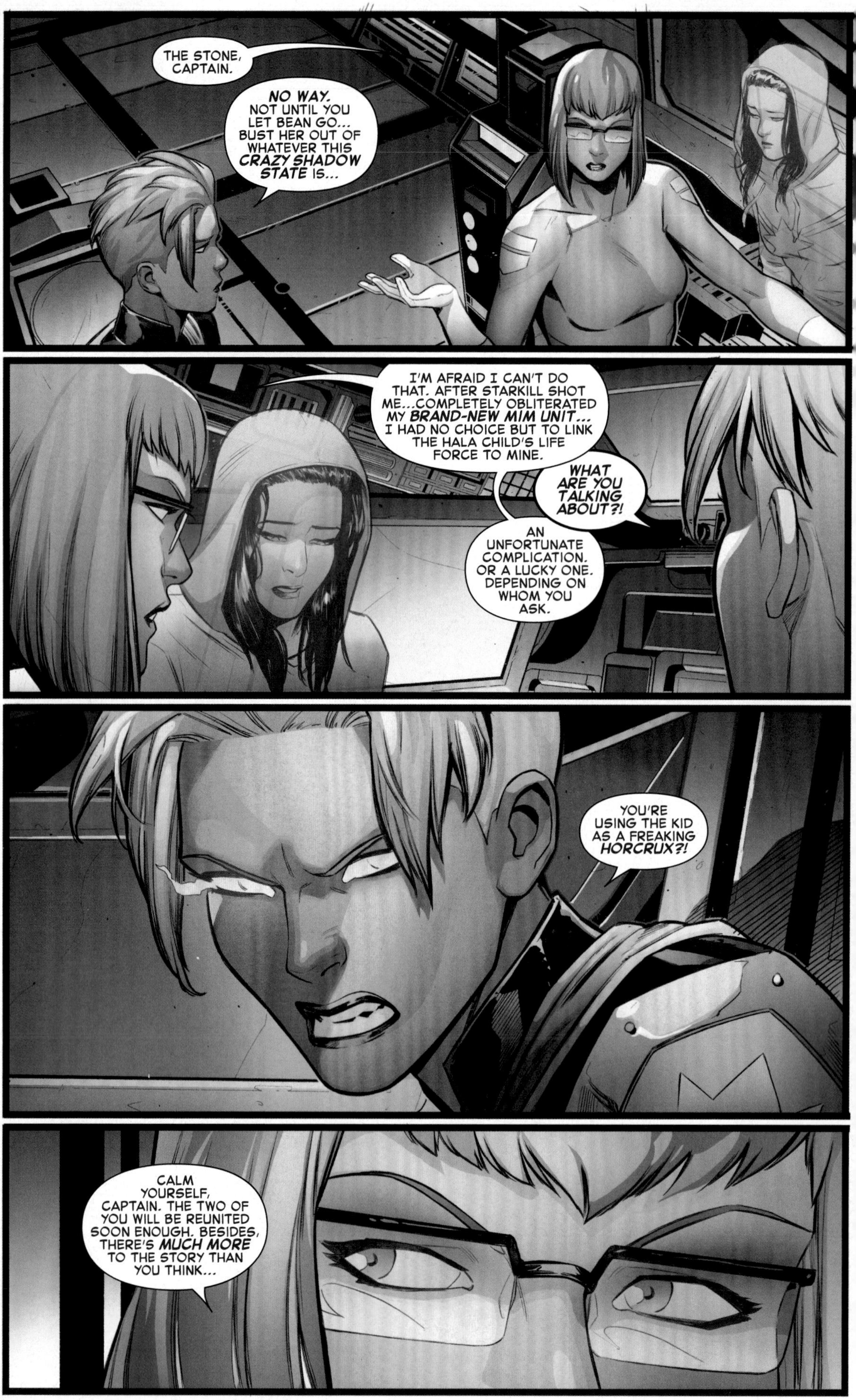

THE STONE, CAPTAIN.
NO WAY. NOT UNTIL YOU LET BEAN GO... BUST HER OUT OF WHATEVER THIS CRAZY SHADOW STATE IS...
I'M AFRAID I CAN'T DO THAT. AFTER STARKILL SHOT ME...COMPLETELY OBLITERATED MY BRAND-NEW MIM UNIT... I HAD NO CHOICE BUT TO LINK THE HALA CHILD'S LIFE FORCE TO MINE.
WHAT ARE YOU TALKING ABOUT?!
AN UNFORTUNATE COMPLICATION. OR A LUCKY ONE. DEPENDING ON WHOM YOU ASK.
YOU'RE USING THE KID AS A FREAKING HORCRUX?!
CALM YOURSELF, CAPTAIN. THE TWO OF YOU WILL BE REUNITED SOON ENOUGH. BESIDES, THERE'S MUCH MORE TO THE STORY THAN YOU THINK...

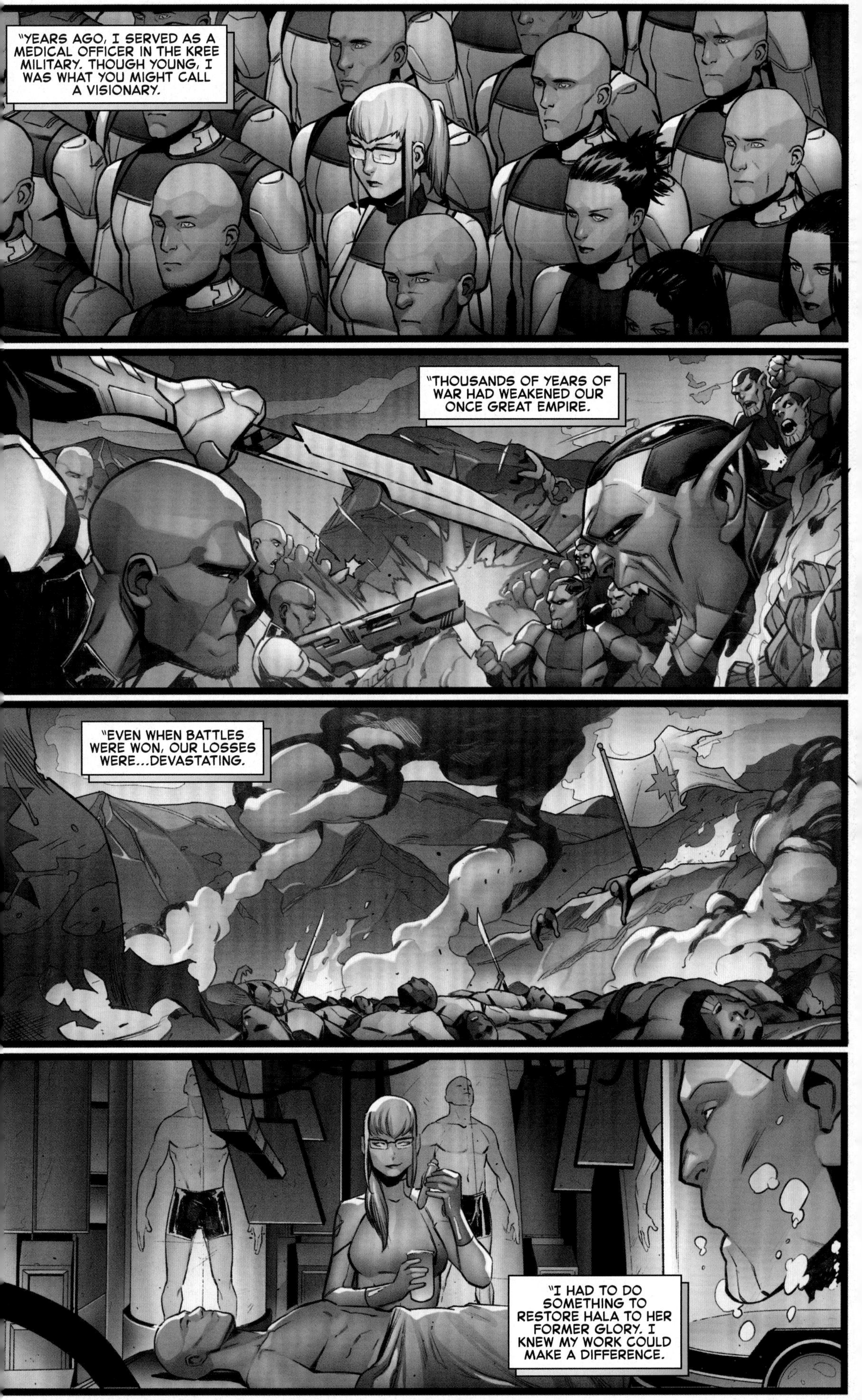
"YEARS AGO, I SERVED AS A MEDICAL OFFICER IN THE KREE MILITARY. THOUGH YOUNG, I WAS WHAT YOU MIGHT CALL A VISIONARY.
"THOUSANDS OF YEARS OF WAR HAD WEAKENED OUR ONCE GREAT EMPIRE.
"EVEN WHEN BATTLES WERE WON, OUR LOSSES WERE...DEVASTATING.
"I HAD TO DO SOMETHING TO RESTORE HALA TO HER FORMER GLORY. I KNEW MY WORK COULD MAKE A DIFFERENCE.

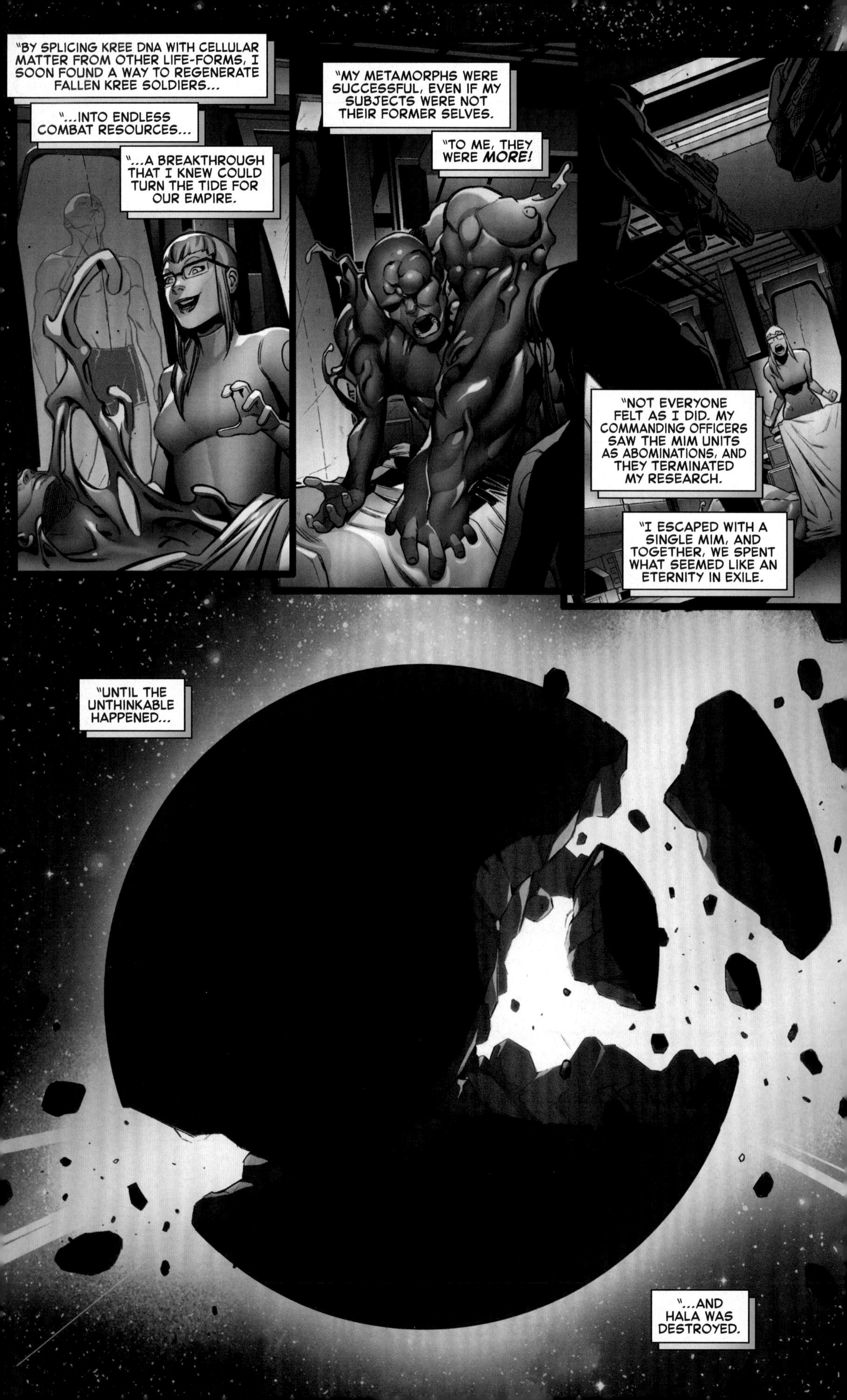
"BY SPLICING KREE DNA WITH CELLULAR MATTER FROM OTHER LIFE-FORMS, I SOON FOUND A WAY TO REGENERATE FALLEN KREE SOLDIERS...
"...INTO ENDLESS COMBAT RESOURCES...
"...A BREAKTHROUGH THAT I KNEW COULD TURN THE TIDE FOR OUR EMPIRE.
"MY METAMORPHS WERE SUCCESSFUL, EVEN IF MY SUBJECTS WERE NOT THEIR FORMER SELVES.
"TO ME, THEY WERE *MORE!*
"NOT EVERYONE FELT AS I DID. MY COMMANDING OFFICERS SAW THE MIM UNITS AS ABOMINATIONS, AND THEY TERMINATED MY RESEARCH.
"I ESCAPED WITH A SINGLE MIM, AND TOGETHER, WE SPENT WHAT SEEMED LIKE AN ETERNITY IN EXILE.
"UNTIL THE UNTHINKABLE HAPPENED...
"...AND HALA WAS DESTROYED.

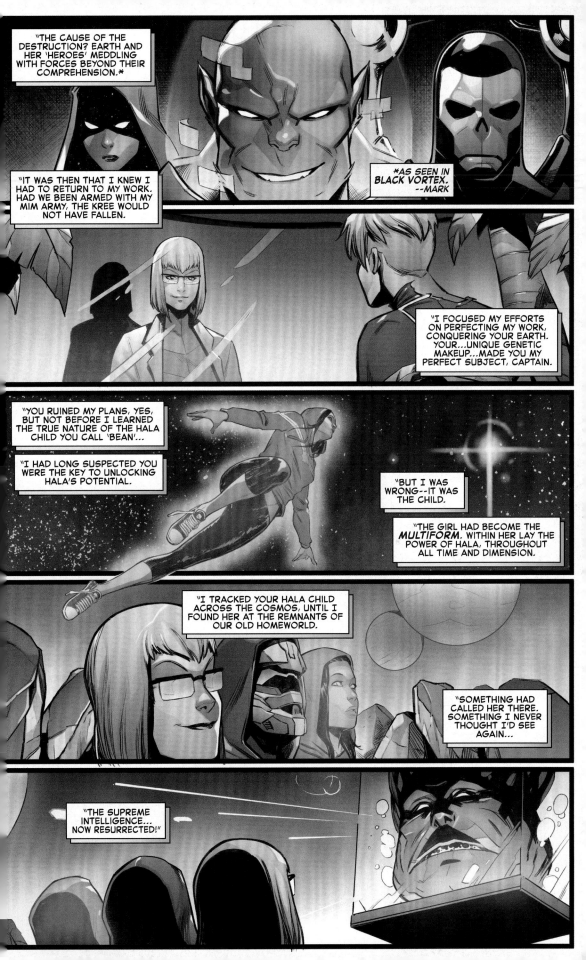

"THE CAUSE OF THE DESTRUCTION? EARTH AND HER 'HEROES' MEDDLING WITH FORCES BEYOND THEIR COMPREHENSION.*

"IT WAS THEN THAT I KNEW I HAD TO RETURN TO MY WORK. HAD WE BEEN ARMED WITH MY MIM ARMY, THE KREE WOULD NOT HAVE FALLEN.

*AS SEEN IN BLACK VORTEX. --MARK

"I FOCUSED MY EFFORTS ON PERFECTING MY WORK, CONQUERING YOUR EARTH. YOUR...UNIQUE GENETIC MAKEUP...MADE YOU MY PERFECT SUBJECT, CAPTAIN.

"YOU RUINED MY PLANS, YES, BUT NOT BEFORE I LEARNED THE TRUE NATURE OF THE HALA CHILD YOU CALL 'BEAN'...

"I HAD LONG SUSPECTED YOU WERE THE KEY TO UNLOCKING HALA'S POTENTIAL.

"BUT I WAS WRONG--IT WAS THE CHILD.

"THE GIRL HAD BECOME THE MULTIFORM. WITHIN HER LAY THE POWER OF HALA, THROUGHOUT ALL TIME AND DIMENSION.

"I TRACKED YOUR HALA CHILD ACROSS THE COSMOS, UNTIL I FOUND HER AT THE REMNANTS OF OUR OLD HOMEWORLD.

"SOMETHING HAD CALLED HER THERE. SOMETHING I NEVER THOUGHT I'D SEE AGAIN...

"THE SUPREME INTELLIGENCE... NOW RESURRECTED!"

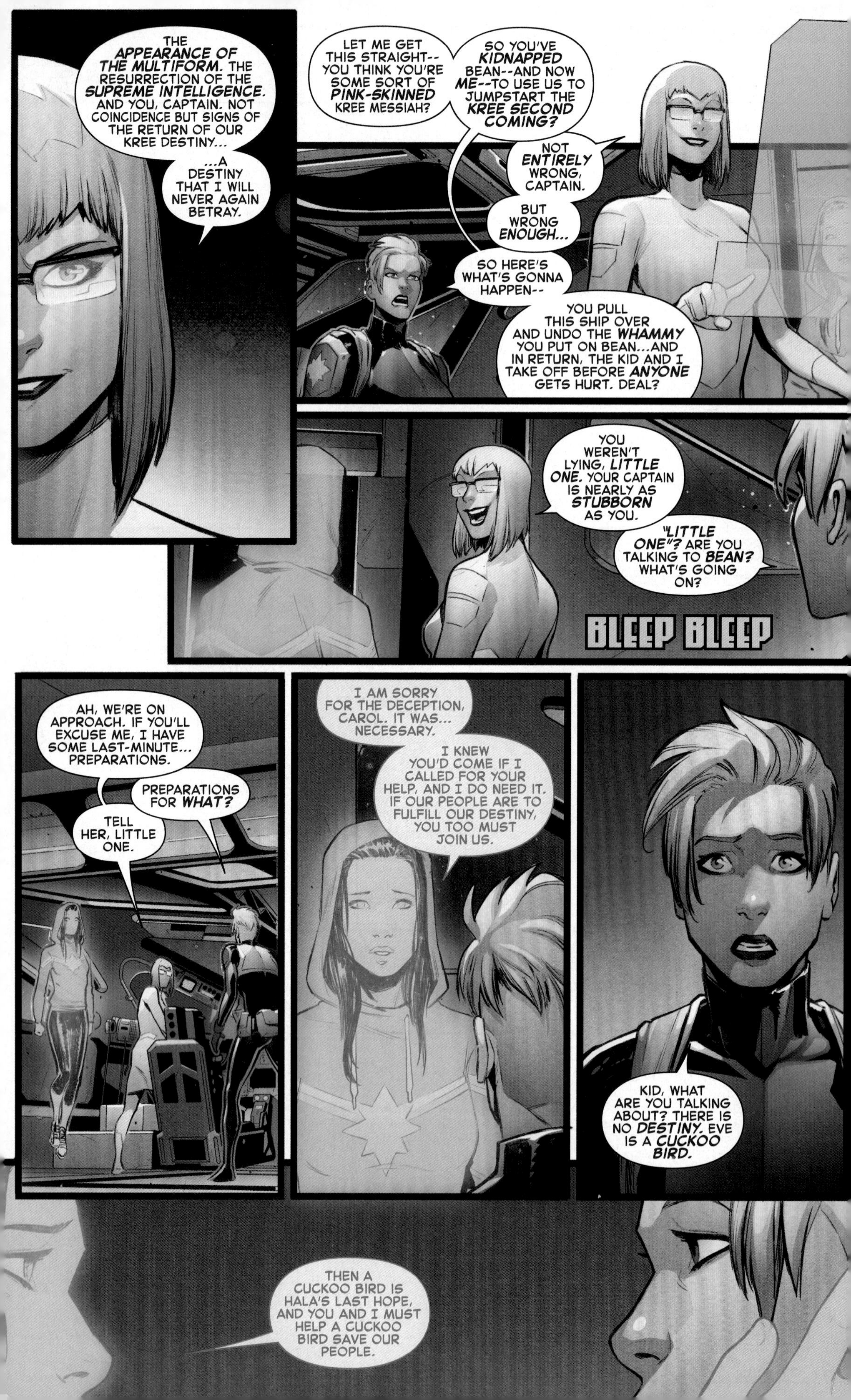
THE APPEARANCE OF THE MULTIFORM. THE RESURRECTION OF THE SUPREME INTELLIGENCE. AND YOU, CAPTAIN. NOT COINCIDENCE BUT SIGNS OF THE RETURN OF OUR KREE DESTINY...
...A DESTINY THAT I WILL NEVER AGAIN BETRAY.
LET ME GET THIS STRAIGHT-- YOU THINK YOU'RE SOME SORT OF PINK-SKINNED KREE MESSIAH?
SO YOU'VE KIDNAPPED BEAN--AND NOW ME--TO USE US TO JUMPSTART THE KREE SECOND COMING?
NOT ENTIRELY WRONG, CAPTAIN.
BUT WRONG ENOUGH...
SO HERE'S WHAT'S GONNA HAPPEN--
YOU PULL THIS SHIP OVER AND UNDO THE WHAMMY YOU PUT ON BEAN...AND IN RETURN, THE KID AND I TAKE OFF BEFORE ANYONE GETS HURT. DEAL?
YOU WEREN'T LYING, LITTLE ONE. YOUR CAPTAIN IS NEARLY AS STUBBORN AS YOU.
"LITTLE ONE"? ARE YOU TALKING TO BEAN? WHAT'S GOING ON?
BLEEP BLEEP
AH, WE'RE ON APPROACH. IF YOU'LL EXCUSE ME, I HAVE SOME LAST-MINUTE... PREPARATIONS.
PREPARATIONS FOR WHAT?
TELL HER, LITTLE ONE.
I AM SORRY FOR THE DECEPTION, CAROL. IT WAS... NECESSARY.
I KNEW YOU'D COME IF I CALLED FOR YOUR HELP, AND I DO NEED IT. IF OUR PEOPLE ARE TO FULFILL OUR DESTINY, YOU TOO MUST JOIN US.
KID, WHAT ARE YOU TALKING ABOUT? THERE IS NO DESTINY. EVE IS A CUCKOO BIRD.
THEN A CUCKOO BIRD IS HALA'S LAST HOPE, AND YOU AND I MUST HELP A CUCKOO BIRD SAVE OUR PEOPLE.

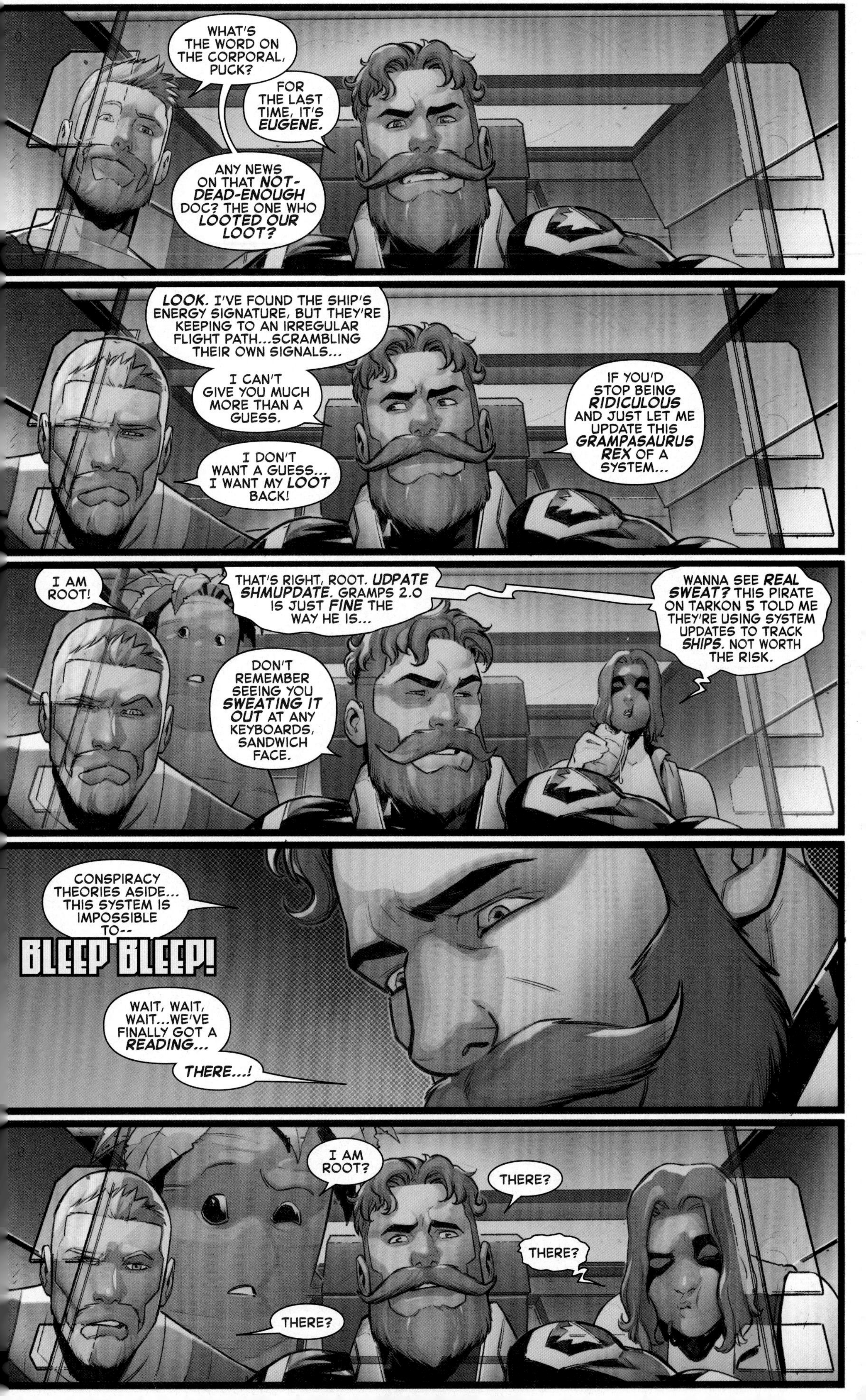
WHAT'S THE WORD ON THE CORPORAL, PUCK?
FOR THE LAST TIME, IT'S EUGENE.
ANY NEWS ON THAT NOT-DEAD-ENOUGH DOC? THE ONE WHO LOOTED OUR LOOT?
LOOK. I'VE FOUND THE SHIP'S ENERGY SIGNATURE, BUT THEY'RE KEEPING TO AN IRREGULAR FLIGHT PATH...SCRAMBLING THEIR OWN SIGNALS...
I CAN'T GIVE YOU MUCH MORE THAN A GUESS.
I DON'T WANT A GUESS... I WANT MY LOOT BACK!
IF YOU'D STOP BEING RIDICULOUS AND JUST LET ME UPDATE THIS GRAMPASAURUS REX OF A SYSTEM...
I AM ROOT!
THAT'S RIGHT, ROOT. UDPATE SHMUPDATE. GRAMPS 2.0 IS JUST FINE THE WAY HE IS...
DON'T REMEMBER SEEING YOU SWEATING IT OUT AT ANY KEYBOARDS, SANDWICH FACE.
WANNA SEE REAL SWEAT? THIS PIRATE ON TARKON 5 TOLD ME THEY'RE USING SYSTEM UPDATES TO TRACK SHIPS. NOT WORTH THE RISK.
CONSPIRACY THEORIES ASIDE... THIS SYSTEM IS IMPOSSIBLE TO--
BLEEP BLEEP!
WAIT, WAIT, WAIT...WE'VE FINALLY GOT A READING...
THERE...!
I AM ROOT?
THERE?
THERE?
THERE?

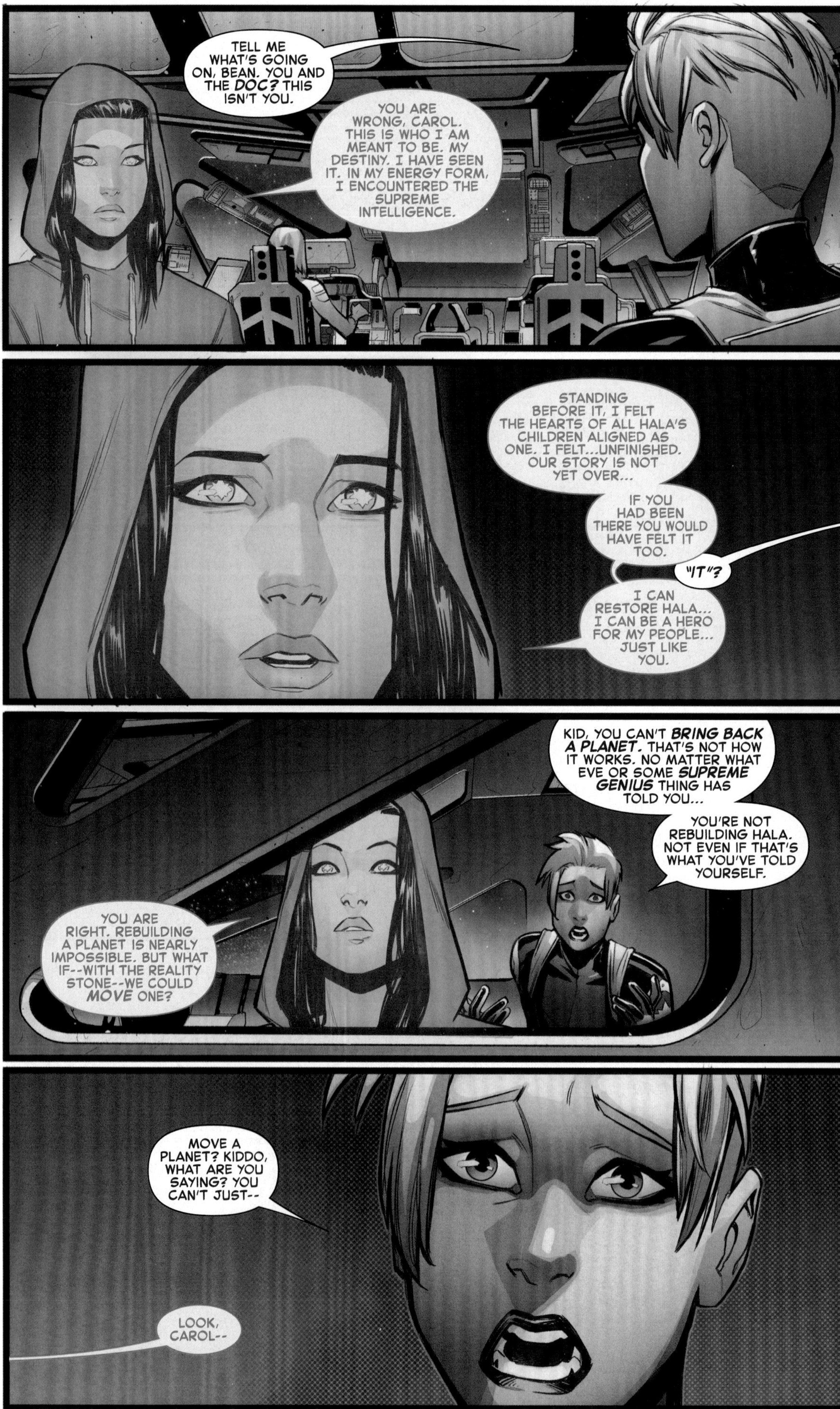
TELL ME WHAT'S GOING ON, BEAN. YOU AND THE DOC? THIS ISN'T YOU.
YOU ARE WRONG, CAROL. THIS IS WHO I AM MEANT TO BE. MY DESTINY. I HAVE SEEN IT. IN MY ENERGY FORM, I ENCOUNTERED THE SUPREME INTELLIGENCE.
STANDING BEFORE IT, I FELT THE HEARTS OF ALL HALA'S CHILDREN ALIGNED AS ONE. I FELT...UNFINISHED. OUR STORY IS NOT YET OVER...
IF YOU HAD BEEN THERE YOU WOULD HAVE FELT IT TOO.
"IT"?
I CAN RESTORE HALA... I CAN BE A HERO FOR MY PEOPLE... JUST LIKE YOU.
KID, YOU CAN'T BRING BACK A PLANET. THAT'S NOT HOW IT WORKS. NO MATTER WHAT EVE OR SOME SUPREME GENIUS THING HAS TOLD YOU...
YOU'RE NOT REBUILDING HALA. NOT EVEN IF THAT'S WHAT YOU'VE TOLD YOURSELF.
YOU ARE RIGHT. REBUILDING A PLANET IS NEARLY IMPOSSIBLE. BUT WHAT IF--WITH THE REALITY STONE--WE COULD MOVE ONE?
MOVE A PLANET? KIDDO, WHAT ARE YOU SAYING? YOU CAN'T JUST--
LOOK, CAROL--

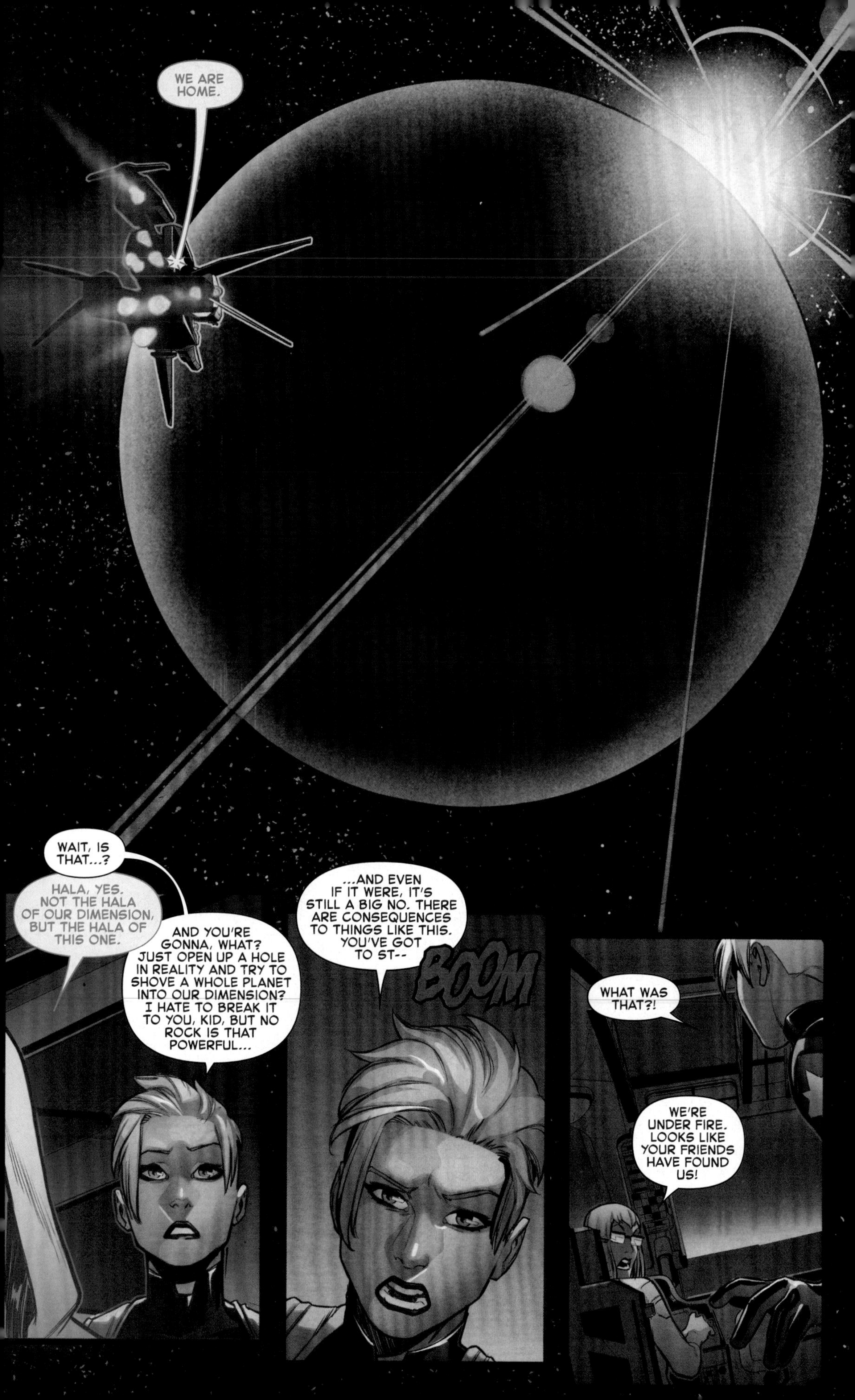
WE ARE HOME.
WAIT, IS THAT...?
HALA, YES. NOT THE HALA OF OUR DIMENSION, BUT THE HALA OF THIS ONE.
AND YOU'RE GONNA, WHAT? JUST OPEN UP A HOLE IN REALITY AND TRY TO SHOVE A WHOLE PLANET INTO OUR DIMENSION? I HATE TO BREAK IT TO YOU, KID, BUT NO ROCK IS THAT POWERFUL...
...AND EVEN IF IT WERE, IT'S STILL A BIG NO. THERE ARE CONSEQUENCES TO THINGS LIKE THIS. YOU'VE GOT TO ST--
BOOM
WHAT WAS THAT?!
WE'RE UNDER FIRE. LOOKS LIKE YOUR FRIENDS HAVE FOUND US!

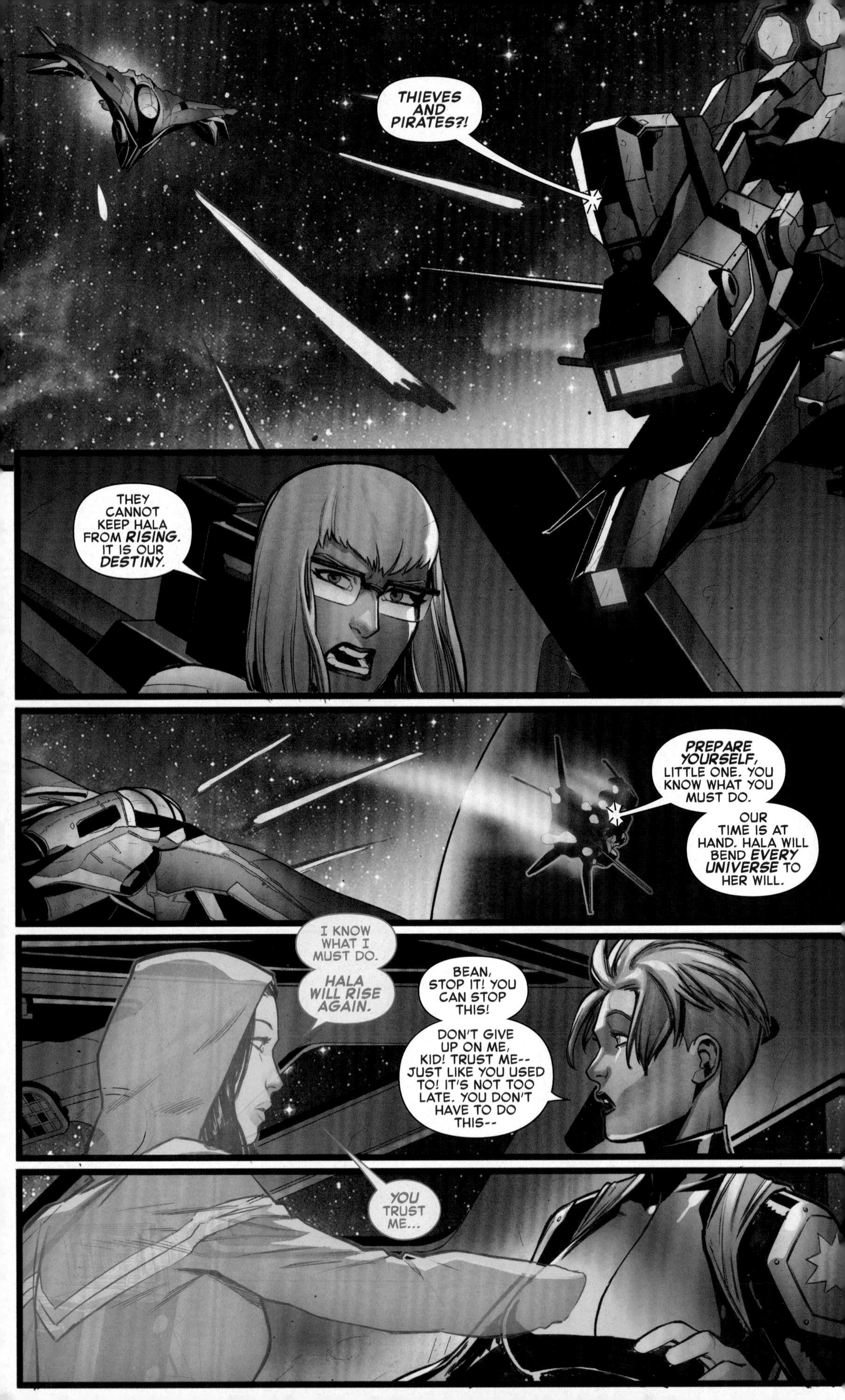
THIEVES AND PIRATES?!
THEY CANNOT KEEP HALA FROM RISING. IT IS OUR DESTINY.
PREPARE YOURSELF, LITTLE ONE. YOU KNOW WHAT YOU MUST DO.
OUR TIME IS AT HAND. HALA WILL BEND EVERY UNIVERSE TO HER WILL.
I KNOW WHAT I MUST DO.
HALA WILL RISE AGAIN.
BEAN, STOP IT! YOU CAN STOP THIS!
DON'T GIVE UP ON ME, KID! TRUST ME-- JUST LIKE YOU USED TO! IT'S NOT TOO LATE. YOU DON'T HAVE TO DO THIS--
YOU TRUST ME...

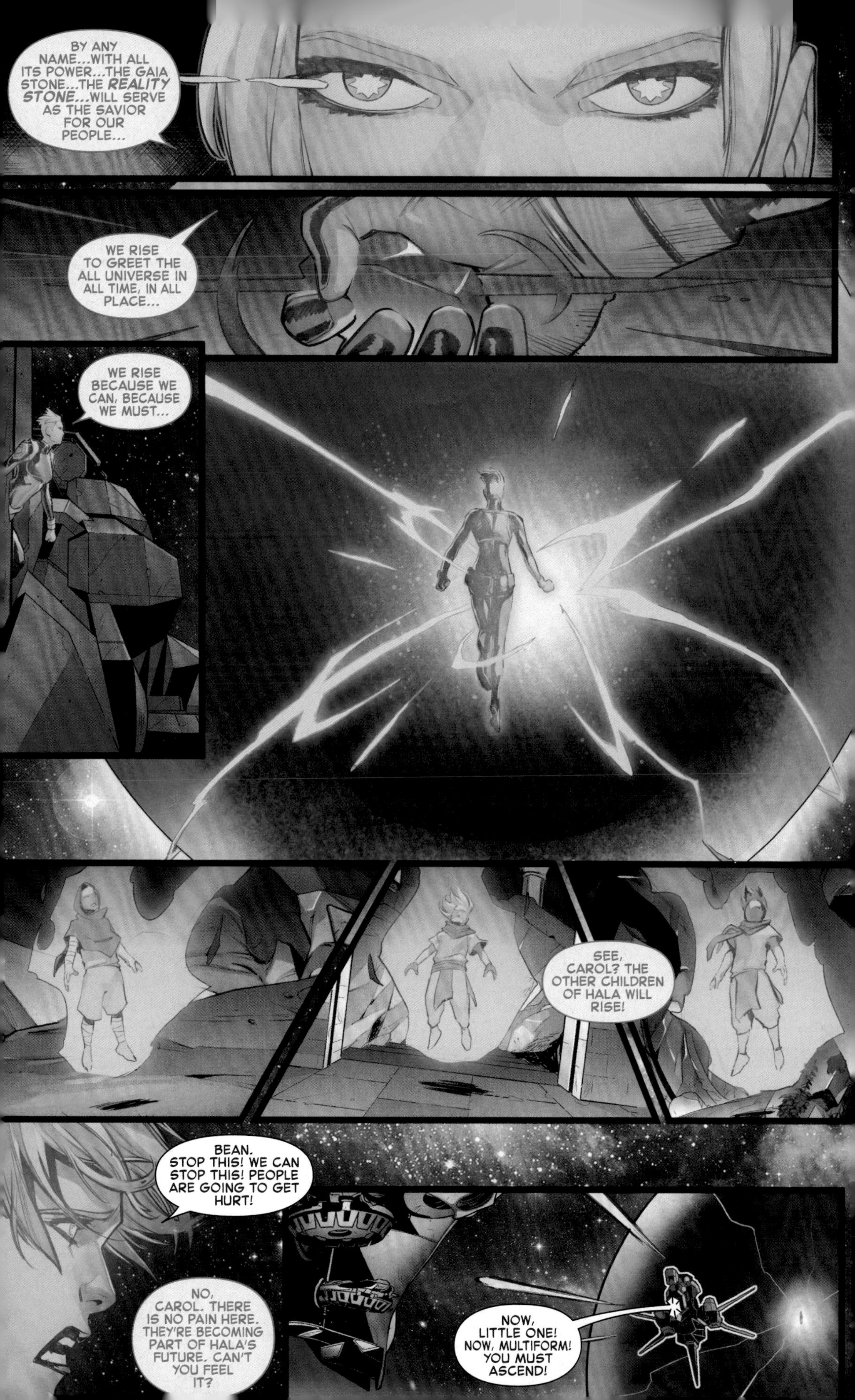
BY ANY NAME...WITH ALL ITS POWER...THE GAIA STONE...THE *REALITY STONE...*WILL SERVE AS THE SAVIOR FOR OUR PEOPLE...
WE RISE TO GREET THE ALL UNIVERSE IN ALL TIME, IN ALL PLACE...
WE RISE BECAUSE WE CAN, BECAUSE WE MUST...
SEE, CAROL? THE OTHER CHILDREN OF HALA WILL RISE!
BEAN. STOP THIS! WE CAN STOP THIS! PEOPLE ARE GOING TO GET HURT!
NO, CAROL. THERE IS NO PAIN HERE. THEY'RE BECOMING PART OF HALA'S FUTURE. CAN'T YOU FEEL IT?
NOW, LITTLE ONE! NOW, MULTIFORM! YOU MUST ASCEND!

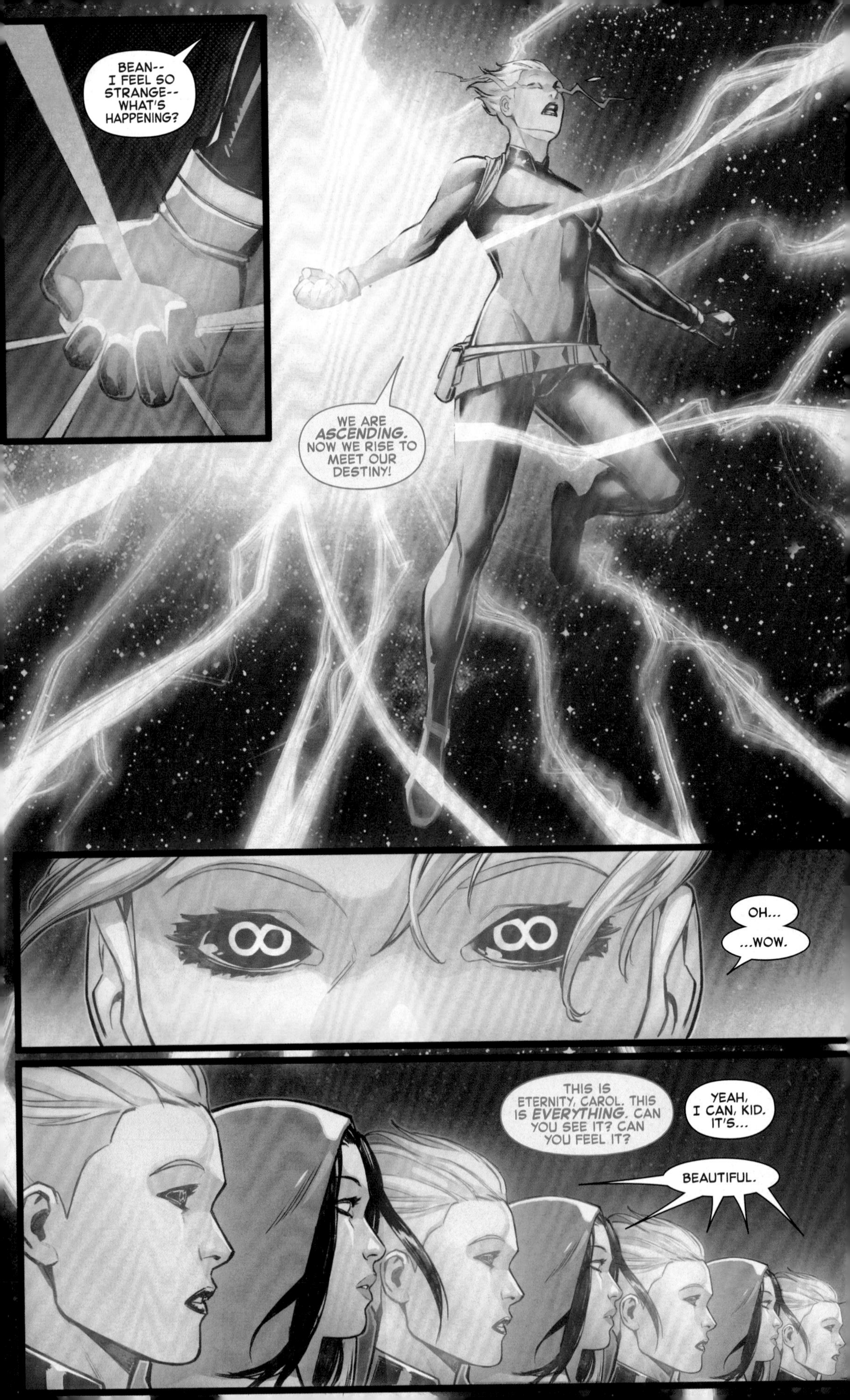
BEAN-- I FEEL SO STRANGE-- WHAT'S HAPPENING?
WE ARE *ASCENDING.* NOW WE RISE TO MEET OUR DESTINY!
OH...
...WOW.
THIS IS ETERNITY, CAROL. THIS IS *EVERYTHING.* CAN YOU SEE IT? CAN YOU FEEL IT?
YEAH, I CAN, KID. IT'S...
BEAUTIFUL.

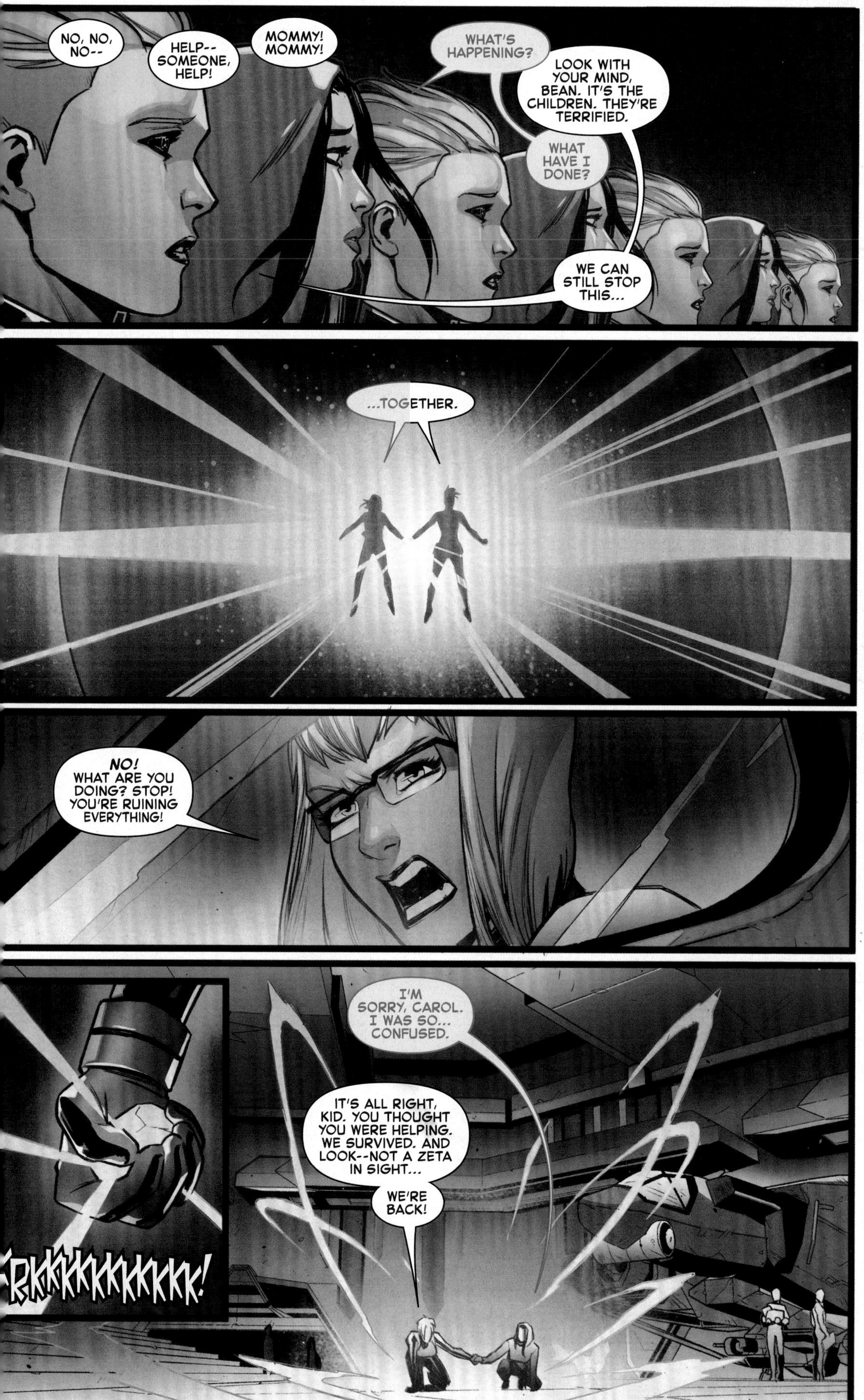

NO, NO, NO--
HELP-- SOMEONE, HELP!
MOMMY! MOMMY!
WHAT'S HAPPENING?
LOOK WITH YOUR MIND, BEAN. IT'S THE CHILDREN. THEY'RE TERRIFIED.
WHAT HAVE I DONE?
WE CAN STILL STOP THIS...
...TOGETHER.
NO! WHAT ARE YOU DOING? STOP! YOU'RE RUINING EVERYTHING!
RKKKKKKKKKKK!
I'M SORRY, CAROL. I WAS SO... CONFUSED.
IT'S ALL RIGHT, KID. YOU THOUGHT YOU WERE HELPING. WE SURVIVED. AND LOOK--NOT A ZETA IN SIGHT...
WE'RE BACK!

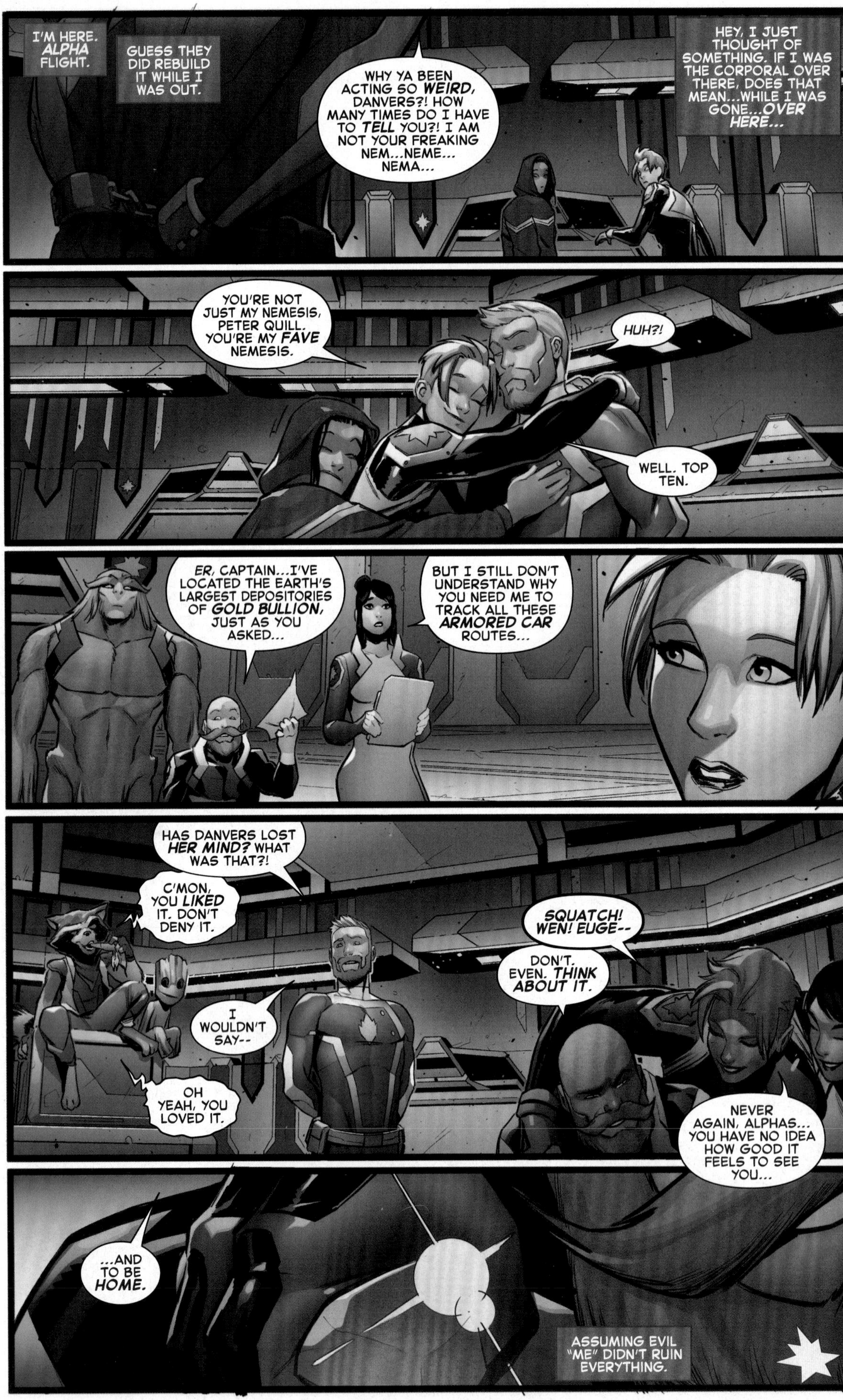

I'M HERE. ALPHA FLIGHT.
GUESS THEY DID REBUILD IT WHILE I WAS OUT.
WHY YA BEEN ACTING SO WEIRD, DANVERS?! HOW MANY TIMES DO I HAVE TO TELL YOU?! I AM NOT YOUR FREAKING NEM...NEME... NEMA...
HEY, I JUST THOUGHT OF SOMETHING. IF I WAS THE CORPORAL OVER THERE, DOES THAT MEAN...WHILE I WAS GONE...OVER HERE...
YOU'RE NOT JUST MY NEMESIS, PETER QUILL. YOU'RE MY FAVE NEMESIS.
HUH?!
WELL. TOP TEN.
ER, CAPTAIN...I'VE LOCATED THE EARTH'S LARGEST DEPOSITORIES OF GOLD BULLION, JUST AS YOU ASKED...
BUT I STILL DON'T UNDERSTAND WHY YOU NEED ME TO TRACK ALL THESE ARMORED CAR ROUTES...
HAS DANVERS LOST HER MIND? WHAT WAS THAT?!
C'MON, YOU LIKED IT. DON'T DENY IT.
I WOULDN'T SAY--
OH YEAH, YOU LOVED IT.
SQUATCH! WEN! EUGE--
DON'T. EVEN. THINK ABOUT IT.
NEVER AGAIN, ALPHAS... YOU HAVE NO IDEA HOW GOOD IT FEELS TO SEE YOU...
...AND TO BE HOME.
ASSUMING EVIL "ME" DIDN'T RUIN EVERYTHING.

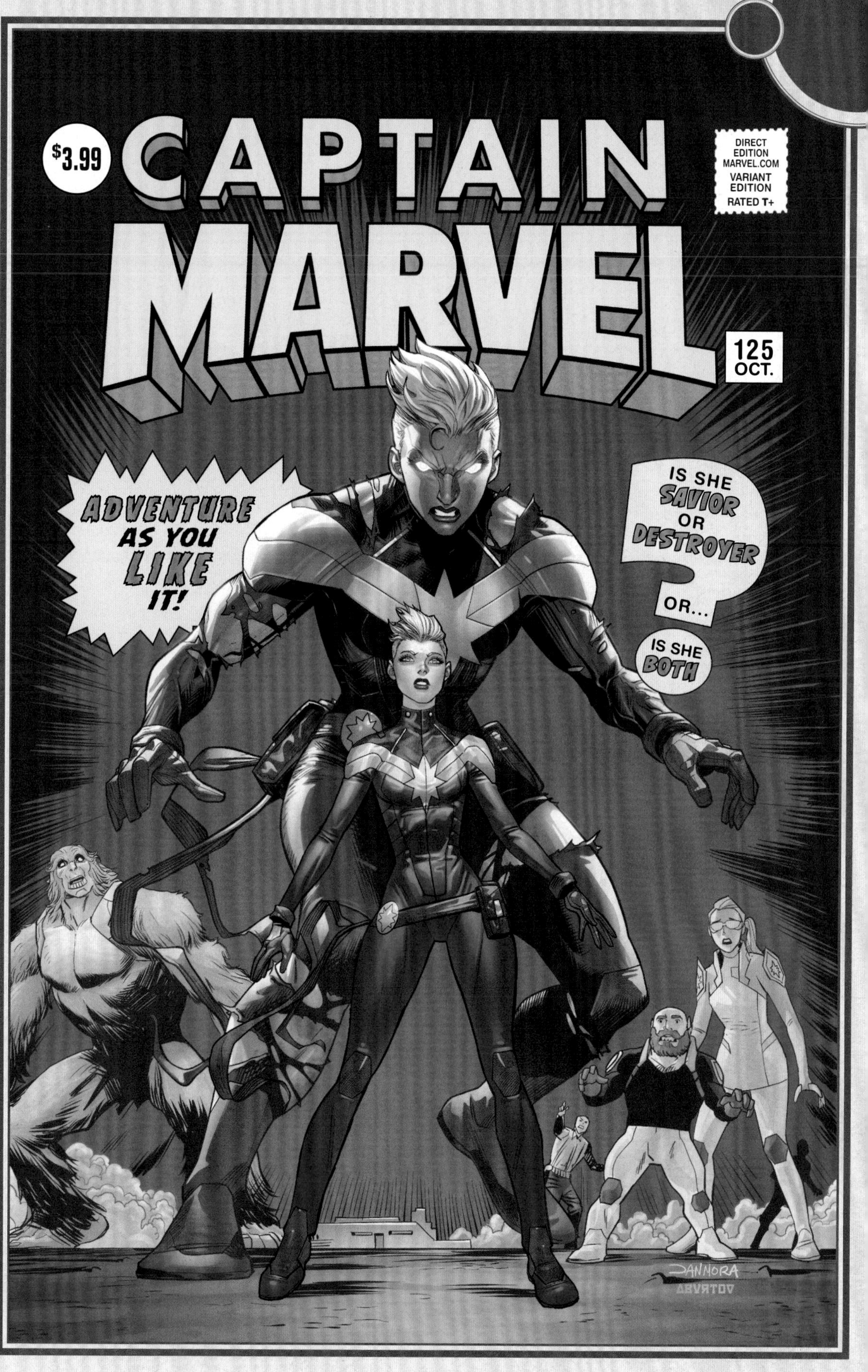
$3.99
CAPTAIN
MARVEL
DIRECT EDITION MARVEL.COM
VARIANT EDITION
RATED T+
125 OCT.
ADVENTURE AS YOU LIKE IT!
IS SHE SAVIOR OR DESTROYER?
OR...
IS SHE BOTH
DAN MORA
ABURTOV

#125 HOMAGE VARIANT BY
DAN MORA & JESUS ABURTOV

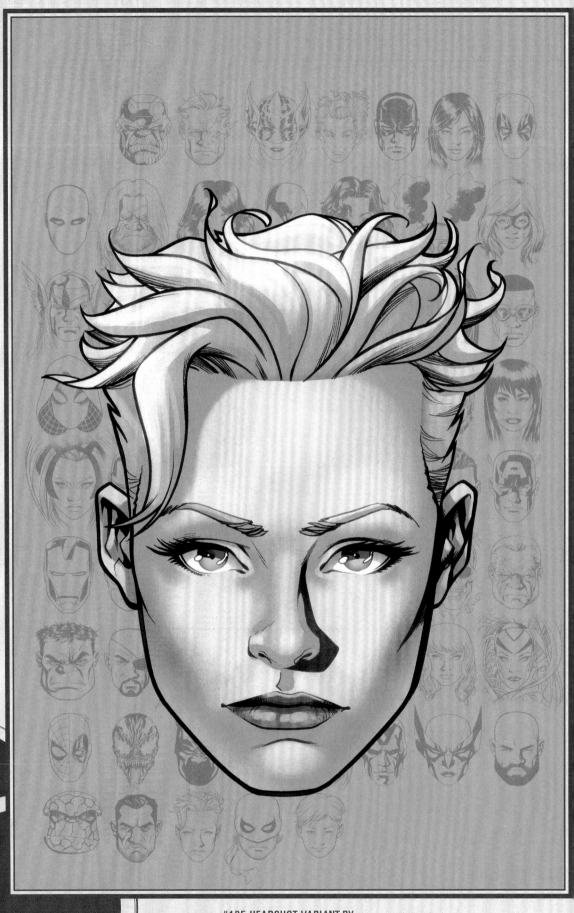

#125 HEADSHOT VARIANT BY
MIKE McKONE & RACHELLE ROSENBERG

CAPTAIN MARVEL

HOW TO DRAW CAPTAIN MARVEL
IN SIX EASY STEPS!

BY CHIP "PRIVATE MARVEL" ZDARSKY

Wow! A "sketch variant cover"! This is your big break! To prepare you to draw your very own CAPTAIN MARVEL (in theaters 2019??), here's a fun and informative step-by-step guide!

1

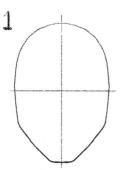

All right! First we start with the outline of the face! It kind of looks likes a top view of the *Millennium Falcon,* I guess.

2

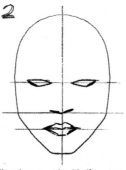

Place her eyes about halfway up the face, nose halfway of that, and mouth halfway of THAT! As a guide, the eyes should have enough space between them for another eye. I don't know—

3

—this doesn't look right to me. I'm mostly a writer, see. You should probably fix them on your drawing. I'm gonna plow on forward and regret it later. Anyway, let's add some mask lines!

4

Add ears, a chin strap, and some fine details to better define the mask! That's it! Oh, wait, one more thing—

5

—she has like a...I want to say...mohawk? Coming out of the top of her helmet? I don't—is that right?

6

Maybe if I add more hair it'll make sense and—gah! Not good. Maybe some more—NO! This is—look, maybe you can return this.

#125 HOW TO DRAW VARIANT BY
CHIP ZDARSKY

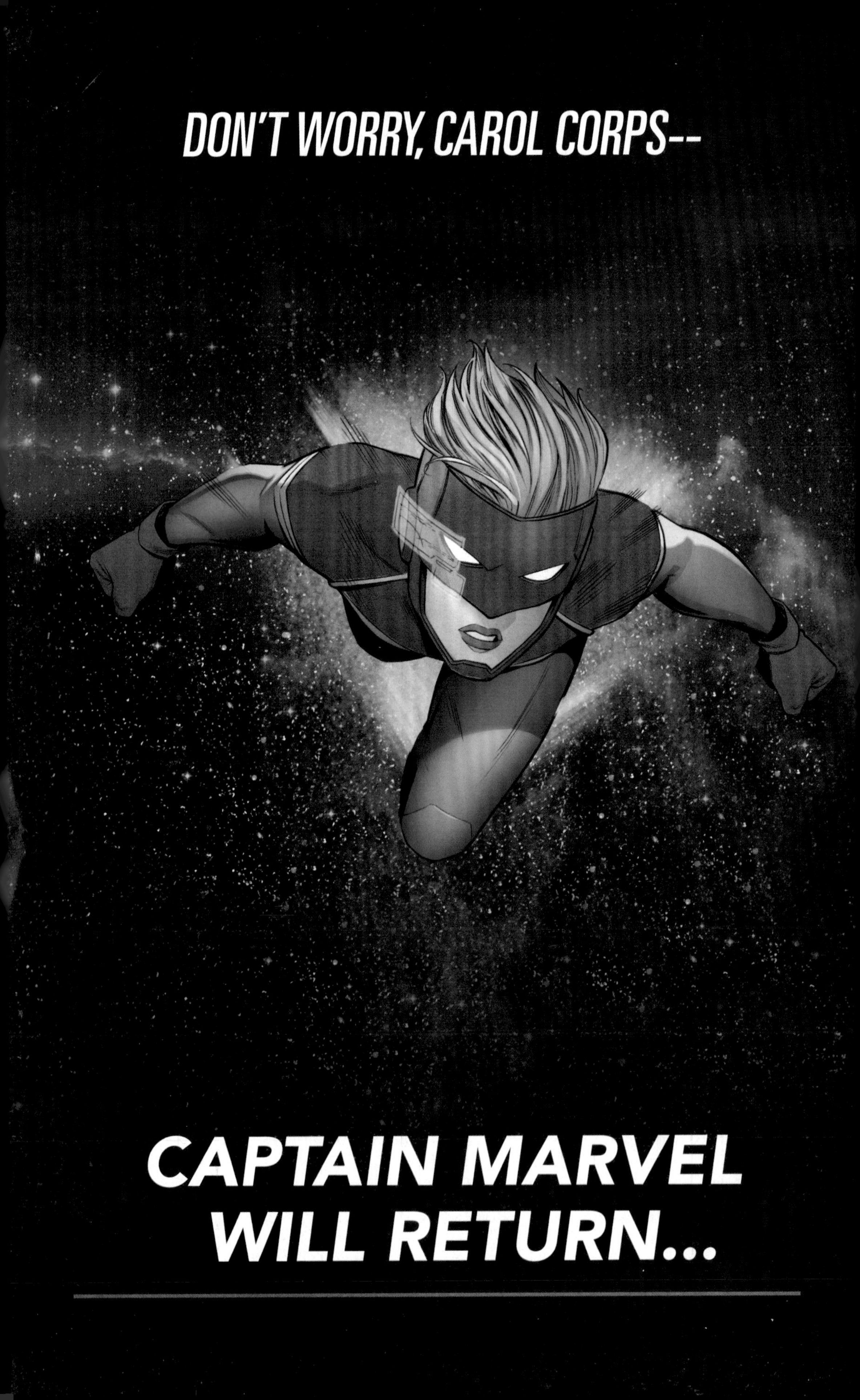
DON'T WORRY, CAROL CORPS--
CAPTAIN MARVEL WILL RETURN...